Leadership with a Conscience

Educational Leadership as a Moral Science

Robert Palestini

ROWMAN & LITTLEFIELD EDUCATION
A division of
ROWMAN & LITTLEFIELD PUBLISHERS, INC.
Lanham • New York • Toronto • Plymouth, UK

Published by Rowman & Littlefield Education
A division of Rowman & Littlefield Publishers, Inc.
A wholly owned subsidiary of The Rowman & Littlefield Publishing Group, Inc.
4501 Forbes Boulevard, Suite 200, Lanham, Maryland 20706
www.rowmaneducation.com

Estover Road, Plymouth PL6 7PY, United Kingdom

British Library Cataloguing in Publication Information Available

Library of Congress Cataloging-in-Publication Data

Palestini, Robert H.
Leadership with a conscience : educational leadership as a moral science / Robert Palestini.
p. cm.
ISBN 978-1-61048-393-3 (cloth : alk. paper)—ISBN 978-1-61048-394-0 (pbk. : alk. paper)—ISBN 978-1-61048-395-7 (electronic)
1. Educational leaders—Professional ethics. 2. Educational leadership—Moral and ethical aspects. 3. Leadership—Moral and ethical aspects. I. Title.
LB1779.P35 2012
371.2--dc22
2011031822

♾™ The paper used in this publication meets the minimum requirements of American National Standard for Information Sciences Permanence of Paper for Printed Library Materials, ANSI/NISO Z39.48-1992.

Printed in the United States of America

Contents

Preface

It is the destiny of man to learn that evil treads closely on the footsteps of
good.

—Sigmund Freud

As Americans worry about the character and conduct of supposed leaders in
business, education, entertainment, sports, and public affairs, they cry out for
models of effective leadership that might inform and inspire this and subse-
quent generations. There are literally hundreds of books, including a few that
I have written, that seek to identify the behaviors of successful leaders so as
to encourage educational leaders and aspiring leaders to adopt them as their
own. In this book, I take a different approach. I profile ten notoriously immoral and unethical leaders and suggest what behaviors leaders and aspiring
leaders need to *avoid* so as not to fall into the same trap as these leaders.

To a person, I found that the ten notorious leaders failed to operate out of
the moral frame of leadership behavior. They all failed to develop a moral
compass that they could used to guide their leadership behavior.

In contrast to these evil leaders, I have chosen ten successful leaders who
have consistently acted out of the moral frame and displayed a strong moral
code or philosophy. As a result, these leaders are recognized not only as
successful leaders but also as good and heroic leaders.

I argue that good and heroic leaders are able to place situational leadership theory into effective practice while great but not so heroic ones do not.
In analyzing their leadership styles, I use the Lee Bolman and Terrence Deal
model of situational leadership theory, which posits four frames of leadership
behavior: (1) structural, (2) human resource, (3) symbolic, and (4) political. I
supplement Bolman and Deal's model with a fifth frame, which I call the

moral frame. I further suggest that effective and impactful leaders combine and balance their use of these frames, rather than dwelling almost exclusively on one frame to the virtual exclusion of the others.

In addition to the Bolman and Deal model, I further analyze their leadership behavior through the lens of the Paul Hersey/Ken Blanchard leadership model, which stresses the readiness level of the leaders' followers in determining the appropriate leadership behavior to be applied. Hersey and Blanchard define *readiness level* as the follower's ability and willingness to accomplish a specific task; this is the major contingency that influences which leadership frame behavior should be applied. Follower readiness incorporates the follower's level of achievement motivation, ability, and willingness to assume responsibility for his or her own behavior in accomplishing specific tasks, as well as his or her education and experience relevant to that task.

So, in its simplest form, Hersey and Blanchard would posit that a person with a low readiness level should be dealt with by using structural frame leadership behavior (telling behavior), while a person with a very high readiness level should be dealt with using human resource and symbolic frame leadership behavior (delegating behavior).

Additionally, since we all aspire to be transformational leaders—leaders who inspire positive change in our organizations and our followers—we analyze the leaders' leadership behavior through the lens of transformational leadership theory. Transformational leaders use charisma to inspire their followers. They talk to the followers about how essential their performance is and how they expect the group's performance to exceed expectations. A transformational leader changes an organization by recognizing an opportunity and developing a vision, communicating that vision to organizational members, building trust in the vision, and achieving the vision by motivating organizational members to attain the vision.

Finally, I focus on moral frame leadership behavior. As I indicated, the moral frame is my own contribution to situational leadership theory. In my view, the moral frame *completes* situational leadership theory. Without it, leaders could just as easily use their leadership skills in the pursuit of evil rather than in promoting good. Leaders operating out of the moral frame are concerned about their obligations and responsibilities to their followers. Moral frame leaders use some type of moral compass to direct their behavior. They practice what has been described as servant leadership and are concerned with those individuals and groups that are marginalized in their organizations and in society. In short, they are concerned about equality, fairness, and social justice.

Basically, then, this is a book about leadership. The conventional wisdom is that leaders are born, not made. I disagree! My experience and, more important, scholarly research indicate that leadership skills can be learned.

Granted, some leaders will be superior to others because of genetics, but the basic leadership skills are learned behaviors and can be cultivated, enhanced, and honed.

The first chapter of this book speaks to the so-called science of leadership, while the second chapter deals with the "art" of administration and leadership. One needs to lead with both mind (science) and heart (art) to be truly effective. The next ten chapters are about the leadership behavior of twenty great leaders and are predicated on the belief that leadership skills can be learned—thus the subtitle, *Educational Leadership as a Moral Science*. In an attempt to make this book more interesting to the reader, I have paired a heroic leader with one of their contemporaries who was not a heroic leader; and I present them in the form of a legal case. For example, the first of these chapters is entitled "Lincoln v. Lenin." In the last chapter of the book, the leadership implications for educators and other leaders are explored.

The effective building blocks of quality leadership are the skills of communication, motivation, organizational development, management, and creativity. Mastering the theory and practice in these areas of study will produce high-quality leadership ability and, in turn, produce successful leaders; doing so with "heart," or integrity, will result in not only highly successful leadership, but what author Chris Lowney calls *heroic leadership*.

There is another broadly held assumption about effective leadership and administration that I would also dispute. Namely, that "nice guys (and gals) finish last." To be a successful administrator, the belief goes, one needs to be firm, direct, even autocratic. Once again, scholarly research, as well as my own experience, indicates that no one singular leadership style is consistently effective in all situations and at all times. Empirical and experiential studies indicate that effective leaders vary their styles depending on the situation.

This *situational* approach is the underlying theme of this book. In the concluding chapter, we assert that truly effective leaders use both their minds, in the form of structural and political leadership behavior, and their hearts, in the form of human resource, symbolic, and moral leadership behavior, and in doing so, nice guys and gals *do* oftentimes finish first.

Some forty years ago, when I was coaching high school basketball, I attended a coaching clinic where the main clinicians were Dean Smith, then coach of North Carolina University, and Bobby Knight, then coach of Indiana University. Both coaches were successful then, and almost four decades later, they remain respected and, in one case at least, revered.

In the morning session Bobby Knight explained how *fear* was the most effective motivator in sports. If you want your players to listen to and obey you and want to be successful as a coach, you need to instill fear in them, Knight declared. In the afternoon session, Dean Smith explained how *love* is the most effective motivator in sports. If you want to win and be successful, you must inspire love in your players.

You can understand my sense of confusion by the end of that clinic. Here were two of the most successful men in sports giving contradictory advice. As a young and impressionable coach, I was puzzled by these apparently mixed messages. Over the intervening years, I have often thought about that clinic and tried to make sense of what I had heard. After these many years, I have drawn two conclusions from this incident, both of which have had a significant impact on my philosophy of leadership and on this book.

The first conclusion has to do with the *situational* nature of leadership. Bobby Knight and Dean Smith impressed upon me the truism that there is no one singular leadership style that is effective at all times and in all situations; and the second, that despite reaping short-term success, the better style for ensuring continued success is one that inspires love, trust, and respect. Just as athletes become robotic and frightened of making mistakes when fear is the only motivator, so are employees who are too closely supervised by an autocratic manager. Initiative, creativity, and self-sufficiency are all stymied by the leader who instills fear in his or her subordinates. Thus, I arrived at my conclusion that effective school administration and leadership, and leadership in general, begins with love, trust, and respect, which are all moral frame leadership behaviors.

In addition to an emphasis on the nature of leadership, this book focuses on placing *theory* into practice. We should not underestimate the value and importance of theory. Without theory we have no valid way of analyzing and correcting failed practice. Without a theoretical base, we oftentimes lead by trial and error, or by the proverbial "seat of your pants." On the other hand, knowledge of theory without the ability to place it into reflective practice is of no value and will not lead to effective leadership. We suggest that leaders and aspiring leaders adopt one of the leadership theories described in this book and place it into reflective practice, modeled after the leadership behavior of the ten good and heroic leaders highlighted here.

This book uses the case study approach in order to facilitate placing theory into effective practice. Each chapter contains an extensive study of one of twenty effective leaders. We will analyze each case to demonstrate how these leaders were able or not able to place leadership theory into effective practice. I believe that the lessons learned will prove invaluable to leaders and aspiring leaders, whether they be a parent, teacher, school principal, or CEO.

This book also takes an organizational development approach to producing effective leadership. Picture yourself standing in the middle of a dense forest. Suppose you were asked to describe the characteristics of the forest: what types of trees are growing in the forest, how many acres of trees are there, where are the trees thriving, where are they not? Faced with this proposition, most people would not know where to start and would not be able "to see the forest for the trees."

Newly appointed executives and administrators often have this same feeling of confusion when faced with the prospect of having to assume a leadership role in a complex organization like a school, a school system, or a company. Where does one start? An effective place to start would be to systematically examine the vital components that make up an organization. Such a system of organizational diagnosis and prescription will lead to a comprehensive and integrated analysis of the organization's strengths and weaknesses and point the way toward possible improvement.

Using the leadership behaviors found among the successful leaders profiled here as a model, the final chapter of this book suggests such a sequential and systematic approach. In the appendix, there is a pair of diagnostic tools that I developed, called the *Heart Smart Survey I and II*, that assess the health of an organization. Heart Smart Survey I assesses whether one is leading with mind, while Heart Smart Survey II assesses whether the leader is leading with heart. Utilizing these analytical tools effectively can produce dramatic and useful results.

This leads me to what I presumptuously refer to as my Seven Principles of Effective Leadership.

Effective Leaders

- Need to be able to adapt their *leadership style* to the situation
- Must be keenly aware of the organizational *structure and culture* of the institution
- Must be able to engender a sense of *trust and respect* in their followers
- Need to continuously improve their organizations and, therefore, must be *agents for change*
- Need to be *well organized*, *creative*, and have a clearly articulated *vision*
- Must be able to *communicate* effectively
- Must know how to *motivate* their followers and to be able to *manage the conflicts* that arise

In my view, which is supported by a prodigious amount of empirical research, if an administrator can master the knowledge and skills encompassed in these seven principles, and do it with heart, he or she will be a highly successful and heroic leader.

Chapter One

Contemporary Leadership Theory

The effective functioning of social systems from the local PTA to the United States of America is assumed to be dependent on the quality of their leadership.

—Victor H. Vroom

Leadership is offered as a solution for most of the problems of organizations everywhere. Schools will work, we are told, if principals provide strong instructional leadership. Around the world, administrators and managers say that their organizations would thrive if only senior management provided strategy, vision, and real leadership. Though the call for leadership is universal, there is much less clarity about what the term means.

Historically, researchers in this field have searched for the one best leadership style that would be most effective. Current thought is that there is no one best style. Rather, a combination of styles, depending on the situation the leader finds himself or herself in, has been found to be more appropriate. To understand the evolution of leadership theory thought, we will take a historical approach and trace the progress of leadership theory, beginning with the trait perspective of leadership and moving to the more current contingency theories of leadership.

THE TRAIT THEORY

Trait theory suggests that we can evaluate leadership and propose ways of leading effectively by considering whether an individual possesses certain personality traits, social traits, and physical characteristics. Popular in the 1940s and 1950s, trait theory attempted to predict which individuals success-

1

fully became leaders and then whether they were effective. Leaders differ from nonleaders in their drive, desire to lead, honesty and integrity, self-confidence, cognitive ability, and knowledge of the business that they are in. Even the traits judged necessary for top-, middle-, and low-level management differed among leaders of different countries; for example, U.S. and British leaders valued resourcefulness, the Japanese intuition, and the Dutch imagination, but for lower and middle managers only (Kirkpatrick and Locke 1991, 49).

The trait approach has more historical than practical interest to managers and administrators, even though recent research has once again tied leadership effectiveness to leader traits. Some view the transformational perspective described later in this chapter as a natural evolution of the earlier trait perspective.

THE BEHAVIORAL PERSPECTIVE

The limitations in the ability of traits to predict effective leadership caused researchers during the 1950s to view a person's behavior rather than that individual's personal traits as a way of increasing leadership effectiveness. This view also paved the way for later situational theories.

The types of leadership behaviors investigated typically fell into two categories: production oriented and employee oriented. Production-oriented leadership, also called concern for production, initiating structure, or task-focused leadership, involves acting primarily to get the task done. An administrator who tells his or her department chair to do "everything you need to, to get the curriculum developed on time for the start of school no matter what the personal consequences" demonstrates production-oriented leadership. So does an administrator who uses an autocratic style or fails to involve workers in any aspect of decision making.

In contrast, employee-oriented leadership, also called concern for people or consideration, focuses on supporting the individual workers in their activities and involving the workers in decision making. A principal who demonstrates great concern for his or her teachers' satisfaction with their duties and commitment to their work has an employee-oriented leadership style (Stogdill and Coons 1957).

Studies in leadership at Ohio State University, which classified individuals' styles as initiating structure or consideration, examined the link between style and grievance rate, performance, and turnover. Initiating structure reflects the degree to which the leader structures his or her own role and subordinates' roles toward accomplishing the group's goal through scheduling work, assigning employees to tasks, and maintaining standards of performance. Consideration refers to the degree to which the leader emphasizes individuals' needs through two-way communication, respect for subordinates' ideas, mutual trust between leader and subordinates, and consideration of subordinates' feelings.

Although leaders can choose the style to fit the outcomes they desire, in fact, to achieve desirable outcomes on all three dimensions of performance, grievance rate, and turnover, the research suggested that managers should strive to demonstrate *both* initiating structure and consideration (Fleishman and Harris 1998, 43–56; Fleishman, Harris, and Buret 1955).

MANAGERIAL ROLES THEORY

A study of chief executive officers by Henry Mintzberg suggested a different way of looking at leadership. He observed that managerial work encompasses ten roles. Three focus on interpersonal contact: (1) figurehead, (2) leader, (3) liaison. Three involve mainly information processing: (4) monitor, (5) disseminator, (6) spokesman. And four are related to decision making: (7) entrepreneur, (8) disturbance handler, (9) resource allocator, and (10) negotiator. Note that almost all roles would include activities that could be construed as leadership—influencing others toward a particular goal.

In addition, most of these roles can apply to nonmanagerial positions as well as managerial ones. The role approach resembles the behavioral and trait perspectives because all three call for specific types of behavior independent of the situation; however, the role approach is more compatible with the situational approach and has been shown to be more valid than either the behavioral or trait perspective (Mintzberg 1979).

EARLY SITUATIONAL THEORIES

Contingency, or situational, models differ from the earlier trait and behavioral models in asserting that no single way of leading works in all situations. Rather, appropriate behavior depends on the circumstances at a given time. Effective managers diagnose the situation, identify the leadership style that will be most effective, and then determine whether they can implement the required style. Early situational research suggested that subordinate, supervisor, and task considerations affect the appropriate leadership style in a given situation. The precise aspects of each dimension that influence the most effective leadership style vary.

Theory X and Theory Y

One of the older situational theories, McGregor's Theory X/Theory Y formulation, calls for a leadership style based on individuals' assumptions about other individuals, together with characteristics of the individual, the task, the organization, and environment. Although managers may have many styles, Theories X and Y have received the greatest attention.

Theory X managers assume that people are lazy, extrinsically motivated, incapable of self-discipline or self-control, and want security and no responsibility in their jobs. Theory Y managers assume people do not inherently dislike work, are intrinsically motivated, exert self-control, and seek responsibility. A Theory X manager, because of his or her limited view of the world, has only one leadership style available, that is, autocratic. A Theory Y manager has a wide range of styles in his or her repertoire (McGregor 1961; Schein 1974, 3).

How can an administrator use McGregor's theory for ensuring leadership effectiveness? What prescription would McGregor offer for improving the situation? If an administrator had Theory X assumptions, he would suggest that the administrator change them and would facilitate this change by sending the administrator to a management development program. If a manager had Theory Y assumptions, McGregor would advise a diagnosis of the situation to ensure that the selected style matched the administrator's assumptions and action tendencies, as well as the internal and external influences on the situation.

Frederick Fiedler's Theory

While McGregor's theory provided a transition from behavioral to situational theories, Frederick Fiedler developed and tested the first leadership theory explicitly called a contingency or situational model. He argued that changing an individual's leadership style is quite difficult, but that organizations should put individuals in situations that fit with their style. Fiedler's theory suggests that managers can choose between two styles: task oriented and relationship oriented. Then the nature of leader-member relations, task structure, and position power of the leader influences whether a task-oriented or a relationship-oriented leadership style is more likely to be effective.

Leader-member relations refer to the extent to which the group trusts and respects the leader and will follow the leader's directions. Task structure describes the degree to which the task is clearly specified and defined or structured, as opposed to ambiguous or unstructured. Position power means the extent to which the leader has official power, that is, the potential or actual ability to influence others in a desired direction owing to the position he or she holds in the organization (Fiedler and Chemers 1984).

The style recommended as most effective for each combination of these three situational factors is based on the degree of control or influence the leader can exert in his or her leadership position, as shown in table 1.1. In general, high-control situations (I, II, and III) call for task-oriented leadership because they allow the leader to take charge. Low-control situations (VII and VIII) also call for task-oriented leadership because they require rather than allow the leader to take charge. Moderate-control situations (IV, V, VI, and VII) in contrast, call for relationship-oriented leadership because the situations challenge leaders to get the cooperation of their subordinates.

Despite extensive research to support the theory, critics have questioned the reliability of the measurement of leadership style and the range and appropriateness of the three situational components. This theory, however, is particularly applicable for those who believe that individuals are born with a certain management style, rather than the management style being learned or flexible (Fiedler and Garcia 1987).

Table 1.1.   Fiedler's Model of Effective Leadership

	Leader-Member Relations	Task Structure	Power Position	Example	Effective Style
I	Good	Structured	Strong	SWAT team	Task-oriented
II	Good	Structured	Weak	Basketball coach	Task-oriented
III	Good	Unstructured	Strong	Principal	Task-oriented
IV	Good	Unstructured	Weak	Board of Directors of Condo	Relations-oriented
V	Poor	Structured	Strong	Bomber crew	Relations-oriented
VI	Poor	Structured	Weak	Department chair	Relations-oriented
VII	Poor	Unstructured	Strong	ROTC	Either
VIII	Poor	Unstructured	Weak	Management teams	Task-oriented

Source: Adapted from F. E. Fiedler, *A Theory of Leadership Effectiveness* (New York: McGraw-Hill, 1967), 37.

CONTEMPORARY SITUATIONAL LEADERSHIP

Current research suggests that the effect of leader behaviors on performance is altered by such intervening variables as the effort of subordinates, their ability to perform their jobs, the clarity of their job responsibilities, the organization of the work, the cooperation and cohesiveness of the group, the sufficiency of resources and support provided to the group, and the coordination of work group activities with those of other subunits.

Thus, leaders must respond to these and broader cultural differences in choosing an appropriate style. A leader-environment-follower interaction theory of leadership notes that effective leaders first analyze deficiencies in the follower's ability, motivation, role perception, and work environment that inhibit performance and then act to eliminate these deficiencies (Biggart and Hamilton 1987, 429–41).

Path-Goal Theory

According to path-goal theory, the leader attempts to influence subordinates' perceptions of goals and the path to achieve them. Leaders can then choose among four styles of leadership: directive, supportive, participative, and achievement-oriented. In selecting a style, the leader acts to strengthen the expectancy, instrumentality, and valence of a situation, respectively, by providing better technology or training for the employees; reinforcing desired behaviors with pay, praise, or promotion; and ensuring that the employees value the rewards they receive (House 1971, 321–38; House and Mitchell 1974, 81–97).

Choosing a style requires a quality diagnosis of the situation to decide what leadership behaviors would be most effective in attaining the desired outcomes. The appropriate leadership style is influenced first by subordinates' characteristics, particularly the subordinates' abilities and the likelihood that the leader's behavior will cause subordinates' satisfaction now or in the future; and second by the environment, including the subordinates' tasks, the formal authority system, the primary work group, and organizational culture.

According to this theory, the appropriate style for an administrator depends on his or her subordinates' skills, knowledge, and abilities, as well as their attitudes toward the administrator. It also depends on the nature of the activities, the lines of authority in the organization, the integrity of their work group, and the task technology involved. The most desirable leadership style helps the individual achieve satisfaction, meet personal needs, and accomplish goals, while complementing the subordinates' abilities and the characteristics of the situation.

Application of the path-goal theory, then, requires first an assessment of the situation, particularly its participants and environment, and second, a determination of the most congruent leadership style. Even though the research about path-goal theory has yielded mixed results, it can provide a leader with help in selecting an effective leadership style.

The Vroom-Yetton Model

The Vroom-Yetton theory involves a procedure for determining the extent to which leaders should involve subordinates in the decision-making process. The manager can choose one of five approaches that range from individual problem solving with available information to joint problem solving to delegation of problem-solving responsibility. Table 1.2 summarizes the possibilities (Vroom and Jago 1988; Vroom and Yetton 1973).

Selection of the appropriate decision process involves assessing six factors: (1) the problem's quality requirement, (2) the location of information about the problem, (3) the structure of the problem, (4) the likely acceptance of the decision by those affected, (5) the commonality of organizational goals, and (6) the likely conflict regarding possible problem solutions. Figure 1.1 illustrates the original normative model, expressed as a decision tree.

To make a decision, the leader asks each question, A through H, corresponding to each box encountered, from left to right, unless questions may be skipped because the response to the previous question leads to a later one. For example, a "no" response to question A allows questions B and C to be skipped; a "yes" response to question B after a "yes" response to question A allows question C to be skipped. Reaching the end of one branch of the tree results in identification of a problem type (numbered 1 through 18) with an accompanying set of feasible decision processes.

When the set of feasible processes for group problems includes more than one process (e.g., a "no" response to each question results in problem type 1, for which every decision style is feasible), final selection of the single approach can use either a minimum number of hours (group processes AI, AII, CI, CII, and GII are preferred in that order) or maximum subordinate involvement (GII, CII, CI, AII, AI are preferred in that order) as secondary criteria. A manager who wishes to make the decision in the shortest time possible, and for whom all processes are appropriate, will choose AI (solving the problem himself or herself using available information) over any other process.

A manager who wishes to maximize subordinate involvement in decision making as a training and development tool, for example, will choose DI or GII (delegating the problem to the subordinate, or together with subordinates reaching a decision) if all processes are feasible and if time is not limited.

Table 1.2. Decision-Making Processes

For Individual Problems

AI: You solve the problem or make the decision yourself, using information available to you at that time.

AII: You obtain any necessary information from the subordinate, then decide on the solution to the problem yourself. You may or may not tell the subordinate what the problem is, in getting the information from him. The role played by your subordinate in making the decision is clearly one of providing specific information that you request, rather than generating or evaluating alternative solutions.

CI: You share the problem with the relevant subordinate, getting his ideas and suggestions. Then, you make the decision. This decision may or may not reflect your subordinate's influence.

GI: You share the problem with one of your subordinates, and together you analyze the problem and arrive at a mutually satisfactory solution in an atmosphere of free and open exchange of information and ideas. You both contribute to the resolution of the problem with the relative contribution of each being dependent on knowledge rather than formal authority.

DI: You delegate the problem to one of your subordinates, providing him with any relevant information that you possess, but giving responsibility for solving the problem independently. Any solution that the person reaches will receive your support.

For Group Problems

AI: You solve the problem or make the decision yourself, using information available to you at the time.

AII: You obtain any necessary information from subordinates, then decide on the solution to the problem yourself. You may or may not tell subordinates what the problem is, in getting the information from them. The role played by your subordinates in making the decision is clearly one of providing specific information that you request, rather than generating or evaluating solutions.

CI: You share the problem with the relevant subordinates individually, getting their ideas and suggestions without bringing them together as a group. Then you make the decision. This decision may or may not reflect your subordinates' influence.

CII: You share the problem with your subordinates in a group meeting. In this meeting you obtain their ideas and suggestions. Then, you make the decision, which may or may not reflect your subordinates' influence.

GII: You share the problem with your subordinates as a group. Together you generate and evaluate alternatives and attempt to reach agreement (consensus) on a solution. Your role is much like that of chairperson, coordinating the discussion, keeping it focused on the problem, and making sure that the crucial issues are discussed. You do not try to influence the group to adopt "your" solution and are willing to accept and implement any solution that has the support of the entire group.

A. Is there a quality requirement such that one situation is likely to be more correct than another?
B. Do I have sufficient information to make a high quality decision?
C. Is the problem structured?
D. Is acceptance of the decision by subordinates critical to effective implementation?
E. If I were to make the decision by myself, is it reasonably certain that it would be accepted by my subordinates?
F. Do my colleagues share the organizational goals to be attained in solving this problem?
G. Is conflict among subordinates likely in preferred solutions?
H. Do my colleagues have sufficient info to make a high quality decision?

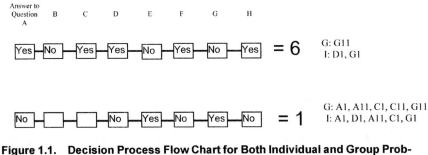

Figure 1.1.   Decision Process Flow Chart for Both Individual and Group Problems
Adapted from *Leadership and Decision-Making* by Victor H. Vroom and Philip W. Yetton

Similar choices can be made when analyzing individual problems. Research has shown that decisions made using processes from the feasible set result in more effective outcomes than those not included (Field 1982, 523–32).

Suppose, for example, the teacher evaluation instrument in your institution was in need of revision. Using the decision tree, we would ask the first question: Is there a quality requirement such that one solution is likely to be more rational than another? Our answer would have to be "yes." Do I have sufficient information to make a high quality decision? The answer is "no." Is the problem structured? Yes. Is acceptance of the decision by subordinates critical to effective implementation? Yes. If I were to make the decision myself, is it reasonably certain that it would be accepted by my subordinates? No. Do subordinates share the organizational goals to be attained in solving this problem? Yes. Is conflict among subordinates likely in preferred solutions? Yes. Do subordinates have sufficient information to make a high-quality decision? Yes.

Following this procedure, the decision tree indicates that GII would be the proper approach to revising the teacher evaluation form. GII indicates that the leader should share the problem with his or her faculty. Together they generate and evaluate alternatives and attempt to reach agreement on a solution. The leader's role is much like that of a chairperson coordinating the discussion, keeping it focused on the problem, and making sure that the critical issues are discussed. You do not try to influence the group to adopt "your" solution, and you are willing to accept and implement any solution that has the support of the entire faculty.

The recent reformulation of this model uses the same decision processes, AI, AII, CI, CII, GI, GII, DI, as the original model, as well as the criteria of decision quality, decision commitment, time, and subordinate development. It differs by expanding the range of possible responses to include probabilities, rather than yes or no answers to each diagnostic question, and it uses a computer to process the data. Although both formulations of this model provide a set of diagnostic questions for analyzing a problem, they tend to oversimplify the process. Their narrow focus on the extent of subordinate involvement in decision making also limits their usefulness.

The Hersey/Blanchard Model

In an attempt to integrate previous knowledge about leadership into a prescriptive model of leadership style, the Hershey/Blanchard theory cites the "readiness of followers," defined as their ability and willingness to accomplish a specific task, as the major contingency that influences appropriate leadership style (Hersey and Blanchard 1988). Follower readiness incorporates the follower's level of achievement motivation, ability, and willingness to assume responsibility for his or her own behavior in accomplishing specific tasks, and education and experience relevant to the task. The model combines task and relationship behavior to yield four possible styles, as shown in figure 1.2.

Leaders should use a telling style and provide specific instructions and closely supervise performance when followers are unable and unwilling or insecure. Leaders should use a selling style and explain decisions and provide opportunity for clarification when followers have moderate-to-low readiness. A participating style, where the leader shares ideas and helps facilitate decision making, should occur when followers have moderate-to-high readiness. Finally, leaders should use a delegating style and give responsibility for decisions and implementation to followers when followers are able, willing, and confident.

Although some researchers have questioned the conceptual clarity, validity, robustness, and utility of the model, as well as the instruments used to measure leadership style, others have supported the utility of the theory. For example, the Leadership Effectiveness and Description Scale (LEAD) and related instruments developed to measure leadership style are widely used in industrial training programs. This model can easily be adapted to educational administration as well as to other types of leadership positions and be used analytically to understand leadership deficiencies and combine it with the path-goal model to prescribe the appropriate style for a variety of situations.

LEADER BEHAVIOR

Readiness **Level III** **Participating Style**	Readiness **Level II** Selling Style
Readiness **Level IV** Delegating Style	Readiness **Level I** Telling Style

FOLLOWER READINESS

R IV	R III	R II	R I
Seasoned veteran and/or very secure	much experience and/or secure	some experience and/or confidence	inexperienced and/or insecure

Figure 1.2.   Model of Situational Leadership
Adapted from *Utilizing Human Resources*, 5th ed., by P. H. Hersey and K. H. Blanchard

Reframing Leadership

Lee Bolman and Terrence Deal have developed a unique situational leadership theory that analyzes leadership behavior through four frames of reference: structural, human resource, political, and symbolic. Each of the frames offers a different perspective on what leadership is and how it operates in organizations. Each can result in either effective or ineffective conceptions of leadership (Bolman and Deal 1991).

Structural Frame

Structural leaders develop a new model of the relationship of structure, strategy, and environment for their organizations. They focus on implementation. The right answer helps only if it can be implemented. These leaders emphasize rationality, analysis, logic, fact, and data. They are likely to believe strongly in the importance of clear structure and well-developed management systems. A good leader is someone who thinks clearly, makes good decisions, has good analytic skills, and can design structures and systems that get the job done.

Structural leaders sometimes fail because they miscalculate the difficulty of putting their designs in place. They often underestimate the resistance that it will generate, and they take few steps to build a base of support for their innovations. In short, they are often undone by human resource, political, and symbolic considerations. Structural leaders do continually experiment, evaluate, and adapt, but because they fail to consider the entire environment in which they are situated, they sometimes are ineffective.

Human Resource Frame

Human resource leaders believe in people and communicate that belief. They are passionate about "productivity through people." They demonstrate this faith in their words and actions and often build it into a philosophy or credo that is central to their vision of their organizations. They believe in the importance of coaching, participation, motivation, teamwork and good interpersonal relations. A good leader is a facilitator and participative manager who supports and empowers others. Human resource leaders are visible and accessible. Peters and Waterman popularized the notion of "management wandering around," the idea that managers need to get out of their offices and interact with workers and customers. Many educational administrators have adopted this aspect of management.

Effective human resource leaders empower, that is, they increase participation, provide support, share information, and move decision making as far down the organization as possible. Human resource leaders often like to refer to their employees as "partners" or "colleagues." They want to make it clear that employees have a stake in the organization's success and a right to be involved in making decisions. When they are ineffective, however, they are seen as naive or as weaklings and wimps.

Political Frame

Political leaders believe that managers and leaders live in a world of conflict and scarce resources. The central task of management is to mobilize the resources needed to advocate and fight for the unit's or the organization's goals and objectives. They emphasize the importance of building a power base: allies, networks, coalitions. A good leader is an advocate and negotiator and understands politics and is comfortable with conflict. Political leaders clarify what they want and what they can get. Political leaders are realists above all. They never let what they want cloud their judgment about what is possible. They assess the distribution of power and interests.

The political leader needs to think carefully about the players, their interests, and their power; in other words, he or she must map the political terrain. Political leaders ask questions such as whose support do I need? How do I go about getting it? Who are my opponents? How much power do they have? What can I do to reduce the opposition? Is the battle winnable? However, if ineffective, these leaders are perceived as being untrustworthy and manipulative.

Symbolic Frame

The symbolic frame provides still a fourth turn of the kaleidoscope of leadership. In this frame, the organization is seen as a stage, a theater in which every actor plays certain roles and attempts to communicate the right impressions to the right audiences. The main premise of this frame is that whenever reason and analysis fail to contain the dark forces of ambiguity, human beings erect symbols, myths, rituals, and ceremonies to bring order, meaning, and predictability out of chaos and confusion. They believe that the essential role of management is to provide inspiration. They rely on personal charisma and a flair for the dramatic to get people excited and committed to the organizational mission.

A good leader is a prophet and visionary, who uses symbols, tells stories, and frames experience in ways that give people hope and meaning. Transforming leaders are visionary leaders, and visionary leadership is invariably symbolic. Examination of symbolic leaders reveals that they follow a consistent set of practices and rules.

Transforming leaders use symbols to capture attention. When Diana Lam became principal of the Mackey Middle School in Boston, she knew that she faced a substantial challenge. Mackey had all the usual problems of urban public schools: decaying physical plant, lack of student discipline, racial tension, troubles with the teaching staff, low morale, and limited resources. The only good news was that the situation was so bad that almost any change would be an improvement.

In such a situation, symbolic leaders will try to do something visible, even dramatic, to let people know that changes are on the way. During the summer before she assumed her duties, Lam wrote a letter to every teacher to set up an individual meeting. She traveled to meet teachers wherever they wanted, driving two hours in one case. She asked teachers how they felt about the school and what changes they wanted.

She also felt that something needed to be done about the school building because nobody likes to work in a dumpy place. She decided that the front door and some of the worst classrooms had to be painted. She had few illusions about getting the bureaucracy of the Boston public school system to provide painters, so she persuaded some of her family members to help her do the painting. When school opened, students and staff members immediately saw that things were going to be different, if only symbolically. Perhaps even more important, staff members received a subtle challenge to make a contribution themselves.

Balancing the Frames

Each of the frames captures significant possibilities for leadership, but each is incomplete. In the early part of the century, leadership as a concept was rarely applied to management, and the implicit models of leadership were narrowly rational. In the 1960s and 1970s, human resource leadership became fashionable. The literature on organizational leadership stressed openness, sensitivity, and participation.

In recent years, symbolic leadership has moved to center stage, and the literature now offers advice on how to become a visionary leader with the power to transform organizational cultures. Organizations do need vision, but it is not their only need and not always their most important one. Leaders need to understand their own frame and its limits. Ideally, they will also learn to combine multiple frames into a more comprehensive and powerful style.

It is this Bolman/Deal leadership theory on which we will base our conclusions regarding the leadership behavior of the leaders profiled in this book. Before leaving our discussion of Bolman and Deal's approach, however, let us reinforce the point that balance needs to occur both *among* and *within* the frames. That is to say that in addition to utilizing all four frames, the effective leader needs to be careful not to behave to the extreme within any one frame. Striving for the Golden Mean is the goal.

TRANSFORMATIONAL LEADERSHIP

A charismatic or transformational leader uses charisma to inspire his or her followers and is an example of one who acts primarily in the symbolic frame of leadership outlined above. He or she talks to the followers about how essential their performance is, how confident he or she is in the followers, how exceptional the followers are, and how he or she expects the group's performance to exceed expectations.

Lee Iacocca and Jack Walsh in industry, and John Dewey and Notre Dame's former president, Reverend Theodore Hesburgh, are examples in education of this type of leader. Among the leaders that we profile in this study, the most successful of them were found to be transformational leaders. Such leaders use dominance, self-confidence, a need for influence, and conviction of moral righteousness to increase their charisma and consequently their leadership effectiveness (House 1977).

A transformational leader changes an organization by recognizing an opportunity and developing a vision, communicating that vision to organizational members, building trust in the vision, and achieving the vision by motivating organizational members. The leader helps subordinates recognize the need for revitalizing the organization by developing a felt need for change, overcoming resistance to change, and avoiding quick-fix solutions to problems.

Encouraging subordinates to act as devil's advocates with regard to the leader, building networks outside the organization, visiting other organizations, and changing management processes to reward progress against competition also help them recognize a need for revitalization. Individuals must disengage from and dis-identify with the past, as well as view change as a way of dealing with their disenchantments with the past or the status quo. The transformational leader creates a new vision and mobilizes commitment to it by planning or educating others. He or she builds trust through demonstrating personal expertise, self-confidence, and personnel integrity.

The charismatic leader can also change the composition of the team, alter management processes, and help organizational members reframe the way they perceive an organizational situation. The charismatic leader must empower others to help achieve the vision. Finally, the transformational leader must institutionalize the change by replacing old technical, political, cultural, and social networks with new ones. For example, the leader can identify key individuals and groups, develop a plan for obtaining their commitment, and institute a monitoring system for following the changes.

If an administrator wishes to make an innovative program acceptable to the faculty and the school community, for example, he or she should follow the above plan and identify influential individuals who would agree to champion the new program, develop a plan to gain support of others in the community through personnel contact or other means, and develop a monitoring system to assess the progress of the effort (Cogner and Kanungo 1987, 637–47; Willner 1984).

A transformational leader motivates subordinates to achieve beyond their original expectations by increasing their awareness about the importance of designated outcomes and ways of attaining them; by getting workers to go beyond their self-interest to that of the team, the school, the school system, and the larger society; and by changing or expanding the individual's needs. Subordinates report that they work harder for such leaders. In addition, such leaders are judged higher in leadership potential by their subordinates as compared to the more common transactional leader.

One should be cognizant, however, of the negative side of charismatic leadership, which may exist if the leader overemphasizes devotion to himself or herself, makes personal needs paramount, or uses highly effective communication skills to mislead or manipulate others. Such leaders may be so driven to achieve a vision that they ignore the costly implications of their goals.

The superintendent of schools that over-expands his or her jurisdiction in an effort to form an "empire," only to have the massive system turn into a bureaucratic nightmare, is an example of transformational leadership gone sour. A business that expands too rapidly to satisfy the ego of the CEO and as a result loses its quality control is another example. Nevertheless, recent research has verified the overall effectiveness of transformational leadership style.

Developing a Vision

A requisite for transformational leadership is a vision. Although there seems to be a sense of mystery on the part of some individuals regarding what a vision is and how to create one, the process for developing one is not at all complex. Using education as an example, the first step is to develop a list of broad goals. "All Children Achieving" is an example of such a goal. These goals should be developed in conjunction with representatives of all segments of the school community, otherwise there will be no sense of "ownership," the absence of which will preclude successful implementation.

The next step in the process is to merge and prioritize the goals and to summarize them in the form of a short and concise vision statement. The following is an example of a typical vision statement:

> Our vision for the Exeter School System is that all of our graduating students, regardless of ability, will say that "I have received an excellent education that has prepared me to be an informed citizen and leader in my community." Our students will have a world view, and as a result of their experience in the Exeter School System, will be committed to a process of lifelong learning and the making of a better world by living the ideals of fairness and justice through service to others.

The key concepts in the above vision are: all students achieving, excellence, leadership, multiculturalism, lifelong learning, values, and community service. It is these concepts that the transformational leader stresses in all forms of communication and in all interactions with the school community.

The final step in the process is the institutionalizing of the educational vision. This step ensures that the vision endures when the leadership changes. Operationalizing and placing the important concepts of the vision into the official policies and procedures of the school system is one way of helping to institutionalize the educational vision and incorporating it into the school culture. As we will see, virtually all of the effective leaders profiled in this book had a clear vision of what they wanted to achieve and convinced their followers to accept ownership of what would ultimately become their *shared* vision.

Implications for Leaders

The implications of leadership theory for educational and other administrators are rather clear. The successful leader needs to have a sound grasp of leadership theory and the skills to implement it. The principles of situational and transformational leadership theory are guides to effective administrative behavior. The leadership behavior applied to an inexperienced faculty member may be significantly different than that applied to a more experienced and tested one. Task behavior may be appropriate in dealing with a new teacher, while relationship behavior may be more appropriate when dealing with a seasoned teacher.

The four frames of leadership discussed by Bolman and Deal may be particularly helpful to school leaders and leaders in general. Consideration of the structural, human relations, political, and symbolic implications of leadership behavior can keep an administrator attuned to the various dimensions affecting appropriate leadership behavior.

With the need to deal with collective bargaining entities, school boards and a variety of other power issues, the political frame considerations may be particularly helpful in understanding the complexity of relationships that exist between administrators and these groups. Asking oneself the questions posed earlier under the political frame can be an effective guide to the appropriate leadership behavior in dealing with these groups.

SUMMARY

Recently, a plethora of research studies have been conducted on leadership and leadership styles. The overwhelming evidence indicates that there is no one singular leadership style that is most appropriate in all situations. Rather, an administrator's leadership style should be adapted to the situation so that at various times task behavior or relationship behavior might be appropriate. At other times and in other situations, various degrees of both task and relationship behavior may be most effective.

The emergence of transformational leadership has seen leadership theory come full circle. Transformational leadership theory combines aspects of the early trait theory perspective with the more current situational or contingency models. The personal charisma of the leader, along with his or her ability to formulate an organizational vision and to communicate it to others determines the transformational leader's effectiveness.

Since the effective leader is expected to adapt his or her leadership style to an ever-changing environment, administration becomes an even more complex and challenging task. However, a thorough knowledge of leadership theory can make some sense of the apparent chaos that the administrator faces on almost a daily basis.

Among scholars there is an assertion that *theory informs practice and practice informs theory*. This notion posits that to be an effective leader, one must base his or her practice on some form of leadership theory. If the leader consciously based practice on leadership theory, this would be an example of theory informing practice. On the other hand, when a leader utilizes theory-inspired behavior that is continually ineffective, perhaps the theory must be modified to account for this deficiency. In this case, practice would be informing or changing theory.

In this book, we will examine the leadership behavior of ten notoriously evil leaders and ten heroic ones to ascertain whether their behavior conforms to the principles of the Bolman/Deal situational leadership theory, and if not, does their practice need to be modified or does the theory need to be modified to reflect effective practice. We will also examine how these leaders' leadership practices can be applied to our own leadership behavior to make it more effective. However, before we do so, we will explore the *art* of leadership or what I call leading with heart.

Chapter Two

Leading with Heart

Do unto others what you would have them do unto you.

—The Golden Rule

How a leader utilizes the concepts contained in the preceding chapter depends largely on his or her philosophy of life regarding how human beings behave in the workplace. The two extremes of the continuum might be described as those leaders who believe that human beings are basically lazy and will do the very least that they need to do to "get by" in the workplace and those who believe that people are basically industrious and, if given the choice, will opt for doing a quality job. I believe that today's most effective leaders hold the latter view.

I agree with Max De Pree, owner and CEO of the highly successful Herman Miller Furniture Company. Writing in his book *Leadership Is an Art*, he says that a leader's function is to "liberate people to do what is required of them in the most effective and humane way possible" (De Pree 1989). Instead of catching people doing something wrong, our goal as enlightened leaders is to catch them doing something right. I would suggest, therefore, that in addition to a rational approach to leadership, a truly enlightened leader leads with heart.

Too often, leaders underestimate the skills and qualities of their followers. I remember Bill Faries, the chief custodian at a high school at which I was assistant principal in the mid 1970s. Bill's mother, with whom he had been extraordinarily close, had passed away after a long illness. The school was a religiously affiliated one and the school community went "all out" in its remembrance of Bill's mother. We held a religious service in which almost 3,000 members of the school community participated. Bill, of course, was very grateful. As a token of his gratitude he gave the school a six-by-eight-foot knitted quilt that he had personally sewn. From that point on I did not know if Bill was a custodian who was a quilt weaver, or a quilt weaver who was a custodian.

The point is that it took the death of his mother for me and others to realize how truly talented our custodian was. So our effectiveness as leaders begins with an understanding of the diversity of people's gifts, talents, and skills. When we think about the variety of gifts that people bring to organizations and institutions, we see that leading with heart lies in cultivating, liberating, and enabling those gifts.

LEADERSHIP DEFINED

The first responsibility of a leader is to define reality through a vision. The last is to say thank you. In between, the leader must become the servant of the servants. Being a leader means having the opportunity to make a meaningful difference in the lives of those who allow leaders to lead. This summarizes what I call leading with heart. In a nutshell, true leaders don't inflict pain; they bear pain.

Whether one is a successful leader can be determined by looking at the followers. Are they reaching their potential? Are they learning? Are they able to change without bitterness? Are they able to achieve the institution's goals and objectives? Can they manage conflict among themselves? Where the answer to these questions is an emphatic "yes," that is a place where a truly effective leader resides.

I prefer to think about leadership in terms of what the gospel writer Luke calls the "one who serves." The leader owes something to the institution he or she leads. The leader is seen in this context as steward rather than owner or proprietor. Leading with heart requires the leader to think about his or her stewardship in terms of legacy, values, direction, and effectiveness.

Legacy

Too many of today's leaders are interested only in immediate results that bolster their career goals. Long-range goals are left to their successors. I believe that this approach fosters autocratic leadership, which oftentimes produces short-term results but militates against creativity and its long-term benefits. In effect, this approach is the antithesis of leading with heart.

On the contrary, leaders should build a long-lasting legacy of accomplishment that is institutionalized for posterity. They owe their institutions and their followers a healthy existence and the relationships and reputation that enable continuity of that healthy existence. Leaders are also responsible for future leadership. They need to identify, develop, and nurture future leaders to carry on the legacy.

Values

Along with being responsible for providing future leaders, leaders owe the individuals in their institutions certain other legacies. Leaders need to be concerned with the institutional value system that determines the principles and standards that guide the practices of those in the organization. Leaders need to model their value systems so that the individuals in the organization can learn to transmit these values to their colleagues and to future employees. In a civilized institution, we see good manners, respect for people, and an appreciation of the way in which we serve one another. A humane, sensitive, and thoughtful leader will transmit his or her value system through his or her daily behavior. This, I believe, is what Peter Senge refers to as a "learning organization" (Senge 1990).

Direction

Leaders are obliged to provide and maintain direction by developing a vision. We made the point earlier that effective leaders must leave their organizations with a legacy. Part of this legacy should be a sense of progress or momentum. An educational administrator, for instance, should imbue his or her institution with a sense of continuous progress; a sense of constant improvement. Improvement and momentum come from a clear vision of what the institution ought to be, from a well-planned strategy to achieve that vision, and from carefully developed and articulated directions and plans that allow everyone to participate and be personally accountable for achieving those plans.

Effectiveness

Leaders are also responsible for effectiveness by being enablers. They need to enable others to reach their potential both personally and institutionally. I believe that the most effective ways of enabling one's colleagues is through participative decision making. It begins with believing in the potential of people and believing in their diversity of gifts. Leaders must realize that to maximize their own power and effectiveness, they need to empower others. Leaders are responsible for setting and attaining the goals in their organizations. Empowering or enabling others to help achieve those goals enhances the leader's chances of attaining the goals, ultimately enhancing the leader's effectiveness. Paradoxically, giving up power really amounts to gaining power.

EMPLOYEE OWNERS

We often hear managers suggest that a new program does not have a chance of succeeding unless the employees take "ownership" of the program. Most of us agree to the common sense of such an assertion. But how does a leader promote employee ownership? Let me suggest four steps as a beginning. I am certain that you can think of several more.

1. *Respect people.* As we have indicated earlier, this starts with appreciating the diverse gifts that individuals bring to your institution. The key is to dwell on the strengths of your coworkers, rather than on their weaknesses. Try to turn their weaknesses into strengths. This does not mean that disciplinary action or even dismissal will never become necessary. What it does mean, however, is that we should focus on the formative aspect of the employee evaluation process before we engage in the summative part.

2. *Let belief guide policy and practice.* We spoke earlier of developing a culture of civility in your institution. If there is an environment of mutual respect and trust, I believe that the organization will flourish. Leaders need to let their belief or value system guide their behavior. Style is merely a consequence of what we believe and what is in our hearts.

3. *Recognize the need for covenants.* Contractual agreements cover such things as salary, fringe benefits, and working conditions. They are part of organizational life and there is a legitimate need for them. But in today's organizations, especially educational institutions, where the best people working for these institutions are like volunteers, we need covenantal relationships. Our best workers may choose their employers. They usually choose the institution where they work based on reasons less tangible than salaries and fringe benefits. They do not need contracts, they need covenants. Covenantal relationships enable educational institutions to be civil, hospitable, and understanding of individuals' differences and unique charisms. They allow administrators to recognize that treating everyone equally is not necessarily treating everyone equitably and fairly.

4. *Understand that culture counts more than structure.* An educational institution that I have been associated with recently went through a particularly traumatic time when the credibility of the administration was questioned by the faculty and staff. Various organizational consultants were interviewed to facilitate a "healing" process. Most of the consultants spoke of making the necessary structural changes to create a culture of trust. We finally hired a consultant whose attitude was that

organizational structure has nothing to do with trust. Interpersonal relations based on mutual respect and an atmosphere of good will is what creates a culture of trust. Would you rather work as part of a school with an outstanding reputation or work as part of a group of outstanding individuals? Many times these two characteristics go together, but if one had to make a choice, I believe that most people would opt to work with outstanding individuals.

IT STARTS WITH TRUST, RESPECT, AND SENSITIVITY (HEART)

These are exciting times in education. Revolutionary steps are being taken to restructure schools and rethink the teaching-learning process. The concepts of empowerment, total quality management, the use of technology, and strategic planning are becoming the norm. However, while these activities have the potential to influence education in significantly positive ways, they must be based upon a strong foundation to achieve their full potential.

Achieving educational effectiveness is an incremental, sequential improvement process. This improvement process begins by building a sense of security within each individual so that he or she can be flexible in adapting to changes within education. Addressing only skills or techniques, such as communication, motivation, negotiation, or empowerment, are ineffective when individuals in an organization do not trust its systems, themselves, or each other. An institution's resources are wasted when invested only in training programs that assist administrators in mastering quick-fix techniques that at best attempt to manipulate, and at worst reinforce mistrust.

The challenge is to transform relationships based on insecurity, adversarialism, and politics into those based on mutual trust. Trust is the beginning of effectiveness and forms the foundation of a principle-centered learning environment that places emphasis upon strengths and devises innovative methods to minimize weaknesses. The transformation process requires an internal locus of control that emphasizes individual responsibility and accountability for change and for promoting effectiveness.

TEAMWORK

For many of us, there exists a dichotomy between how we see ourselves as persons and how we see ourselves as workers. Perhaps the following words of a Zen Buddhist will be helpful:

> The master in the art of living makes little distinction between his work and his
> play, his labor and his leisure, his mind and his body, his education and his
> recreation, his love and his religion. He hardly knows which is which. He
> simply pursues his vision of excellence in whatever he does, leaving others to
> decide whether he is working or playing. To him he is always doing both.

Work can be and should be productive, rewarding, enriching, fulfilling, and joyful. Work is one of our greatest privileges, and it is up to leaders to make certain that work is everything that it can and should be.

One way to think of work is to think of how a philosopher would lead an organization, rather than how a businessman or woman would lead an organization. Plato's *Republic* speaks of the "philosopher-king," where the king would rule with the philosopher's ideals and values.

Paramount among the ideals that leaders need to recognize in leading an organization is the notion of teamwork and the valuing of each individual's contribution to the final product. The synergy produced by an effective team is greater than the sum of its parts.

The foundation of the team is the recognition that each member needs every other member and no individual can be successful without the cooperation of others. As a young boy I was a very enthusiastic baseball fan. My favorite player was the Hall of Fame pitcher Robin Roberts of the Philadelphia Phillies. During the early 1950s his fast ball dominated the National League. My uncle, who took me to my first ballgame, explained that opposing batters were so intimidated by Roberts's fastball that they were automatic "outs" even before they got to the plate. My uncle claimed that Robin Roberts was unstoppable. Even as a young boy I intuitively knew that no one was unstoppable by himself. I said to my uncle that I knew how to stop Robin Roberts. "Make me his catcher."

Employees as Volunteers

Our institutions will not amount to anything without the people who make them what they are. And the individuals most influential in making institutions what they are, are essentially volunteers. Our very best employees can work anywhere they please. So, in a sense, they volunteer to work where they do. As leaders, we would do far better if we looked upon and treated our employees as volunteers. We made the point earlier that we should treat our employees as if we had a covenantal relationship rather than a contractual relationship with them.

Alexander Solzhenitsyn, speaking to the 1978 graduating class of Harvard College, said this about legalistic relationships: "A society based on the letter of the law and never reaching any higher, fails to take advantage of the full range of human possibilities. The letter of the law is too cold and formal to have a beneficial influence on society. Whenever the tissue of life is woven of legalistic relationships, this creates an atmosphere of spiritual mediocrity that paralyzes men's noblest impulses." And later: "After a certain level of the problem has been reached, legalistic thinking induces paralysis; it prevents one from seeing the scale and the meaning of events" (Solzhenitsyn 1978, 17–19).

Covenantal relationships, on the other hand, induce freedom, not paralysis. As the noted psychiatrist William Glasser explains, "Coercion only produces mediocrity; love or a sense of belonging produces excellence" (Glasser 1984). Our goal as leaders is to encourage a covenantal relationship of love, warmth, and personal chemistry among our employee volunteers. Shared ideals, shared goals, shared respect, a sense of integrity, a sense of quality, a sense of advocacy, a sense of caring; these are the basis of an organization's covenant with its employees.

THE VALUE OF HEROES

Leading with heart requires that an organization has its share of heroes, both present and past. We have often heard individuals in various organizations say that so and so is an "institution" around here. Heroes such as these do more to establish the organizational culture of an institution than any manual or policies and procedures handbook ever could.

The senior faculty member who is recognized and respected for his or her knowledge as well as his or her humane treatment of students is a valuable asset to an educational institution. He or she is a symbol of what the institution stands for. It is the presence of these heroes that sustains the reputation of the institution and allows those in the workforce to feel good about themselves and about where they work. The deeds and accomplishments of these heroes need to be promulgated and need to become part of the folklore of the institution.

The deeds of these heroes are usually perpetuated by the "tribal storytellers" in an organization (Bolman and Deal 1991). These are the individuals who know the history of the organization and relate it through stories of its former and current heroes. An effective leader encourages the tribal storytellers, knowing that they are serving an invaluable role in an organization.

They work at the process of institutional renewal. They allow the institution to continuously improve. They preserve and revitalize the values of the institution. They mitigate the tendency of institutions, especially educational institutions, to become bureaucratic. These concerns are concerns of everyone in the institution, but they are the special province of the tribal storyteller. Every institution has heroes and storytellers. It is the leader's job to see to it that things like manuals and handbooks don't replace them.

EMPLOYEE OWNERS

If an educational institution is to be successful, everyone in it needs to feel that he or she "owns the place." "This is not the school district's school; it is not the school board's school; it is my school." Taking ownership is a sign of one's love for an institution. In his book, *Servant Leadership*, Robert Greenleaf says, "Love is an undefinable term, and its manifestations are both subtle and infinite. It has only one absolute condition: unlimited liability!" (De Pree 1989, 12). Although it may run counter to our traditional notion of American capitalism, employees should be encouraged to act as if they own the place. It is a sign of love.

THE SIGNS OF HEARTLESSNESS

Up to now we have dwelled on the characteristics of a healthy organization. In contrast, here are some of the signs that an organization is suffering from a lack of heart:

- when there is a tendency to merely "go through the motions"
- when a dark tension exists among key individuals
- when a cynical attitude prevails among employees
- when finding time to celebrate accomplishments becomes impossible
- when stories and storytellers cease
- when there is the view that one person's gain needs to be at another's expense
- when mutual trust and respect erode
- when leaders accumulate power rather than distribute it
- when attainment of short-term goals becomes detrimental to the acquisition of long-term goals
- when individuals abide by the letter of the law, but not its spirit
- when people treat students or customers as impositions
- when the accidents become more important than the substance
- when a loss of grace, style, and civility occurs
- when leaders use coercion to motivate employees
- when administrators dwell on individuals' weaknesses rather than strengths
- when individual turf is protected to the detriment of institutional goals
- when diversity and individual charisms are not respected
- when communication is only one-way
- when employees feel exploited and manipulated

- when arrogance spawns top-down decision making
- when leaders prefer to be served rather than to serve

LEADERSHIP AS A MORAL SCIENCE

Here we address how educational administrators and other leaders should be educated and trained for such a position. Traditionally, there has been only one answer: practicing and future administrators should study educational administration in order to learn the scientific basis for decision making and to understand the scientific research that underlies proper administration.

Universities train future administrators with texts that stress the scientific research done on administrative behavior, review various studies of teacher and student performance, and provide a few techniques for accomplishing educational goals. Such approaches instill a reverence for the scientific method, but an unfortunate disregard for any humanistic and critical development of the art of administration (Foster 1986). These approaches teach us how to lead with our minds, but not necessarily with our hearts.

We are suggesting a different approach. Although there is certainly an important place for scientific research and empirically supported administrative behavior, we suggest that educational administrators also be *critical humanists* and also lead with their hearts. Humanists appreciate the usual and unusual events of our lives and engage in an effort to develop, challenge, and liberate human souls. They are critical because they are educators and are therefore not satisfied with the status quo; rather, they hope to change individuals and institutions for the better and to improve social conditions for all. We will argue that an *administrative* science be reconstructed as a *moral* science.

An administrative science can be empirical, but it also must incorporate hermeneutic (the science of interpreting and understanding others) and critical dimensions. Social science has increasingly recognized that it must be informed by moral questions. The paradigm of natural science does not always apply when dealing with human issues. As a moral science, the science of administration is concerned with the resolution of moral dilemmas. A critical and a literary model of administration helps to provide us with the necessary context and understanding wherein such dilemmas can be wisely resolved, and we can truly actualize our potentials as administrators and leaders.

One's proclivity to be a critical humanist oftentimes depends on one's philosophy on how human beings behave in the workplace. Worth repeating here are the two extremes of the continuum, which might be described as those leaders who believe that human beings are basically lazy and will do the very least that they need to do to "get by" in the workplace and those who believe that people are basically industrious and, if given the choice, would opt for doing the "right thing." I believe that today's most effective leaders hold the latter view.

THE CRITICAL TRADITION

A post-positivist leader combines the *humanist* tradition with *critical* theory. Dissatisfaction with current administrative approaches for examining social life stems from administrations' inability to deal with questions of value and morality and its inability to fulfill its promise.

For example, Griffiths criticizes orthodox theories because they "ignore the presence of unions and fail to account for the scarcity of women and minorities in top administrative positions" (Griffiths and Ribbins 1995). Erickson asks why "educational research [has] had so few real implications for educational policy" (Erickson and Ellett 2002). And he answers that an empiricist research program modeled on the natural sciences fails to address issues of understanding and interpretation. This failure precludes researchers from reaching a genuine understanding of the human condition. It is time, he argues, to treat educational research as a moral science. The science of administration can also be a moral one, a critically moral one (Erickson 1984, 525–46).

The term "moral" is being used here in its cultural, professional, spiritual, and ethical sense, not in a religious sense. The moral side of administration has to do with the *dilemmas* that face us in education and other professions. All educators face three areas of dilemmas: control, curriculum, and societal. Control dilemmas involve the resolution of classroom management and control issues, particularly the issue of who is in charge and to what degree.

Control dilemmas center around four questions: (1) Do you treat the child as a student, focusing narrowly on cognitive goals, or as a whole person, focusing more broadly on intellectual, aesthetic, social, and physical dimensions? (2) Who controls classroom time? In some classrooms, children are given latitude in scheduling their activities; in others, class activities follow a strict and mandatory schedule. (3) Who controls operations or what larger context of what it means to be human and how we resolve the inevitable conflicts that go on in the classroom? (4) Who controls the standards and defines success and failure?

Similar dilemmas occur in the curricular domain and relate to whether the curriculum is considered as received, public knowledge, or whether it is considered private, individualized knowledge, of the type achieved through discoveries and experiments. These curricular difficulties also depend on whether one conceives of the child as customer or as an individual. The customer receives professional services generated from a body of knowledge, whereas the individual receives personal services generated from his or her particular needs and context.

A final set of dilemmas has to do with what children bring to school and how they are to be treated once there. One concerns the distribution of teacher resources. Should one focus more resources on the less talented, in order to bring them up to standards, or on the more talented, in order for them to reach their full potential? The same question arises in regard to the distribution of justice. Should classroom rules be applied uniformly without regard to the differing circumstances of each child, or should family background, economic factors, and other sociological influences be considered? Should a teacher stress a common culture or ethnic differences and subculture consciousness?

Much of teaching involves resolving such dilemmas by making a variety of decisions throughout the school day. Such decisions can be made, however, in a *reflective* or an *unreflective* manner. An unreflective manner means simply teaching as one was taught, without giving consideration to available alternatives. A reflective approach involves an examination of the widest array of alternatives. Thus, reflective teaching suggests that dilemmas need not be simply resolved but can be transformed so that a higher level of teaching expertise is reached.

This same logic can be applied to administration. Administration involves the resolution of various dilemmas, that is, the making of moral decisions. One set of dilemmas involves control. How much participation can teachers have in the administration of the school? How much participation can parents and students have? Who evaluates and for what purpose? Is the role of administration collegial or authority centered? The area of the curriculum brings up similar questions. Is the school oriented to basic skills, advanced skills, social skills, or all three? Should the curricula be teacher made or national, state, or system mandated? Should student evaluation be based on teacher assessment or standardized tests? What is authentic assessment?

Finally, an additional set of dilemmas pertains to the idea of schooling in society. Should the schools be oriented to ameliorate the apparent deficits that some students bring with them, or should they see different cultures and groups as strengths? Should schools be seen as agents of change, oriented to the creation of a more just society, or as socializers that adapt the young to the current social structure?

Oftentimes, these questions are answered unreflectively and simply resolved on an "as needed" basis. This approach often resolves the dilemma but does not foster a real *transformation* in one's self, role, or institution. If administration and leadership encompasses transformation, and we would argue that it should, then an additional lens to structural functionalism must be found through which these questions can be viewed. We suggest that the additional lens be in the form of critical humanism and the Ignatian vision. In this context, then, administrative leadership can be viewed as a moral science.

THE IGNATIAN VISION

In addition to the critical humanist lens, another lens through which we can view leadership behavior is the Ignatian vision. More than 450 years ago, Ignatius of Loyola, a young priest born to a Spanish aristocratic family, founded the Society of Jesus, the Jesuits, and wrote his seminal book, *The Spiritual Exercises* (Ravier 1987).

In this book, he suggested a "way of life" and a "way of looking at things" that has been propagated by his religious community and his other followers for almost five centuries. His principles have been utilized in a variety of ways. They have been used as an aid in developing one's own spiritual life; they have been used to formulate a way of learning that has become the curriculum and instructional method employed in the sixty high schools and the twenty-eight Jesuit colleges and universities in the United States; and they have been used to develop a personal administrative style. Together, these principles comprise the *Ignatian vision.*

There are five Ignatian principles that we will explore here as a foundation for developing an administrative philosophy and leadership style: (1) Ignatius's concept of the *magis*, or the "more"; (2) the implications of his notion of *cura personalis*, or "care of the person"; (3) the process of *inquiry* or *discernment*; (4) the development of *men and women for others*; and (5) service to the *underserved* and marginalized, or his concept of *social justice*.

At the core of the Ignatian vision is the concept of the *magis*, or the "more." Ignatius spent the greater part of his life seeking perfection in all areas of his personal, spiritual, and professional life. He was never satisfied with the status quo. He was constantly seeking to improve his own spiritual life, as well as his secular life as leader of a growing religious community. He was an advocate of "continuous improvement" long before it became a corporate slogan, long before people like Edwards Deming used it to develop his Total Quality Management approach to management, and long before Japan used it to revolutionize its economy after World War II.

The idea of constantly seeking "the more" implies change. The magis is a movement away from the status quo; and moving away from the status quo defines change. The Ignatian vision requires individuals and institutions to embrace the process of change as a vehicle for personal and institutional improvement. For his followers, frontiers and boundaries are not obstacles or ends, but new challenges to be faced, new opportunities to be welcomed.

Thus, change needs to become a way of life. Ignatius further implores his followers to "be the change that you expect in others." In other words, we are called to model desired behavior—to live out our values, to be of ever fuller service to our communities and to aspire to the more universal good. Ignatius had no patience with mediocrity. He constantly strove for the greater good.

The magis principle, then, can be described as the main norm in the selection of information and the interpretation of it. Every real alternative for choice must be conducive to the advancement toward perfection. When some aspect of a particular alternative is *more* conducive to reaching perfection than other alternatives, we have reason to choose that alternative. Earlier, we spoke of the "dilemmas" that educators face during every working day. The magis principle is a "way of seeing" that can help us in selecting the better alternative.

At first hearing, the magis principle may sound rigid and frightening. It is absolute, and Ignatius is unyielding in applying it, but not rigid. On the one hand he sees it as the expression of our love of humanity, which inexorably seeks to fill all of us with a desire to not be content with what is less good for us. On the other hand, he sees that humanity not only has its particular gifts, but also has its limitations and different stages of growth. If a choice is more humane in the abstract than it would be in the concrete, that choice would not be seen as adhering to the magis principle. For example, tracking students according to ability can be seen as humane in the abstract, but in the concrete it can be dehumanizing. Ignatius would advise us to focus on the concrete in resolving this *dilemma.*

In every case, then, accepting and living by the magis principle is an expression of our love of humanity. So, whatever the object for choice, the measure of our love of neighbor will be the fundamental satisfaction we will find in choosing and acting by the magis principle. Whatever one chooses by this principle, no matter how undesirable in some other respect, will always be what one would most want as a moral and ethical member of the human race.

Closely related to the principle of the magis is the Ignatian principle of *inquiry* and *discernment*. In his writings, he urges us to challenge the status quo through the methods of inquiry and discernment. This is very similar to one of the tenants of critical theory. In fact the Ignatian vision and critical theory share a number of norms.

To Ignatius, the need to enter into inquiry and discernment is to determine God's will. However, this process is of value for the purely *secular* purpose of deciding on which "horn of a dilemma" one should grasp. To aid us in utilizing inquiry and discernment as useful tools in challenging the status quo and determining the right choice to be made, Ignatius suggests that the ideal disposition for inquiry and discernment is humility. The disposition of humility is especially helpful when, despite one's best efforts, the evidence that one alternative is more conducive to the betterment of society is not compelling.

When the discerner cannot find evidence to show that one alternative is more conducive to the common good, Ignatius calls for a judgment in favor of what more assimilates the discerner's life to the life of poverty and humiliation. Thus, when the *greatest* good cannot readily be determined, the *greater* good is more easily discerned in a position of humility. These are very demanding standards, but they are consistent with the magis principle and the tenets of critical humanism.

In addition to the magis principle norm, taking account of what has just been said and of what was said earlier about the norm of humility as a disposition for seeking the greater good, the relationship of the greater good norm to the greatest good norm can be clarified. The latter is absolute, overriding, and always primary.

The greater good norm is secondary; it can never, in any choice, have equal weight with the first magis principle; it can never justify a choice of actual poverty and humiliation over riches and honors if the latter are seen to be more for the service of humanity in a particular situation for choice, with all its concrete circumstances, including one's responsibilities to others and his or her own stage of psychological and spiritual development. In other words, if being financially successful allows one to better serve the poor and underserved, that would be preferred to actual poverty.

Ignatius presents us with several other supplemental norms for facing our "dilemmas." In choices that directly affect the individual person and the underserved or marginalized, especially the poor, Ignatius urges us to give preference to those in need. This brings us to his next guiding principle, *cura personalis*, or care of the person.

Another of Ignatius's important and enduring principles is his notion that, despite the primacy of the common good, the need to care for the individual person should never be lost. From the very beginning, the *cura personalis* principle has been included in the mission statement of virtually every high school and college founded by the Jesuits. It also impacts the method of instruction suggested for all Jesuit schools in the *Ratio Studiorum*, or the "course of study" in these institutions.

All Jesuit educational institutions are to foster what we now refer to as a "constructivist" classroom, where the student is an active participant in the learning process. This contrasts with the "transmission" method of instruction, where the teacher is paramount, and the student is a passive participant in the process. In the Ignatian vision, the care of the person is a requirement not only on a personal needs basis, but also on a "whole person" basis, which would, of course, include classroom education.

This principle also has implications for how we conduct ourselves as educational administrators. Ignatius calls us to value the gifts and charisms of our colleagues and to address any deficiencies that they might have and turn them into strengths. For example, during the employee evaluation process, Ignatius would urge us to focus of the formative or developmental stage of the evaluation far more than on the summative or employment decision stage. This would be one small way of applying *cura personalis* theory to practice.

The fourth principle that we wish to consider is the Ignatian concept of service. Once again, this principle has been propagated from the very outset. The express goal of virtually every Jesuit institution is "to develop men and women for others." Jesuit institutions are called on to create a culture of service as one way of ensuring that the students, faculty, and staffs of these institutions reflect the educational, civic, and spiritual values of the Ignatian vision.

Institutions following the Ignatian tradition of service to others have done so through community service programs, and more recently, service learning. Service to the community provides students with a means of helping others, a way to put their value system into action, and a tangible way to assist local communities. Although these were valuable benefits, there was no formal integration of the service experience into the curriculum and no formal intro-spection concerning the impact of service on the individual.

During the last twenty years there has been a movement toward creating a more intentional academic relationship. Service has evolved from a modest student activity into an exciting pedagogical opportunity. In the past, service was viewed as a co-curricular activity; today it plays an integral role in the learning process. For example, at Saint Joseph's University in Philadelphia, accounting majors help senior citizens complete their income tax returns.

Since many institutions are situated in an urban setting, service gives them a chance to share resources with surrounding communities and allows for reciprocal relationships to form between the university and local residents. Immersion into different cultures—economic, racial, educational, social, and religious—is the vehicle by which students make connections. Working side-by-side with people of varying backgrounds significantly impacts the students, forcing them outside of their comfort zones and into the gritty reality of how others live. Through reflection, these students have the opportunity to integrate these powerful experiences into their lives, opening their eyes and hearts to the larger questions of social justice.

Peter-Hans Kolvenbach, the superior general of the Jesuit order, in his address on justice in American Jesuit universities, used the words of Pope John Paul II to challenge Jesuit educators to "educate the whole person of solidarity for the real world," not only through concepts learned in the classroom, but also by contact with real people (Tripole 1994).

Upon assuming the position of superior general in 1973 and echoing the words of Ignatius, Pedro Arrupe declared, "Our prime educational objective must be to form men and women for others; men and women who will live not for themselves but for others." In the spirit of these words, the service learning movement has legitimized the educational benefit of all experiential activity.

The term "service learning" means different things to different people, and debates on service learning have been around for decades, running the gamut from unstructured "programmatic opportunities" to structured "educational philosophies."

At Ignatian institutions, service learning is a bridge that connects faculty, staff, and students with community partners and their needs. It connects academic and student life views about the educational value of experiential learning. It also connects students' textbooks to human reality, and their minds and hearts with values and action. The programs are built on key components of service learning, including integration into the curriculum, a reciprocal relationship between the community agency and student, and structured time for reflection, which is very much related to the Ignatian principle of *discernment* discussed earlier.

Participation in service by high school and college students, whether as a co-curricular or a course-based experience, correlates to where they are in their developmental process. Service work allows students to explore their skills and limitations, to find what excites and energizes them, to put their values into action, and to use their talents to benefit others, to discover who they are and who they want to become. By encouraging students to reflect on their service, these institutions assist in this self-discovery. The reflection can take many forms: an informal chat, a facilitated group discussion, written dialogue, journal entries, reaction papers, or in-class presentations on articles.

By integrating the service experience through critical reflection the student develops knowledge of the communities in which he or she lives, and knowledge about the world that surrounds them. It is only after the unfolding of this service-based knowledge that the students are able to synthesize what they have learned into their lives. Through this reflection the faculty members also have an opportunity to learn from and about their students. Teachers witness the change and growth of the students firsthand. In short, "service to others" changes lives.

The implications of "service to others" for administration are clear. Not only can educational administrators enhance their effectiveness by including the idea of service to others in their curricula, but also by modeling it in their personal and professional lives. The concept of administrators becoming the "servant of the servants" is what we have in mind here. Servant leaders do not inflict pain, they bear pain, and they treat their employees as "volunteers," a concept explored earlier.

The Ignatian concept of "service" leads into his notion of solidarity with the underserved (poor) and marginalized and his principle of *social justice*. We begin with an attempt to achieve some measure of clarity on the nature and role of social justice in the Ignatian vision. According to some, Ignatius defined justice in both a narrow and wide sense (Toner 1991). In the *narrow* sense, it is "justice among men and women" that is involved. In this case, it is a matter of "clear obligations" among "members of the human family." The application of this kind of justice would include not only the rendering of material goods, but also immaterial goods such as "reputation, dignity, the possibility of exercising freedom" (Tripole 1994).

Many of his followers also believe Ignatius defined justice in a *wider* sense, "where situations are encountered which are humanly intolerable and demand a remedy" (Tripole 1994). Here the situations may be a product of "explicitly unjust acts" caused by "clearly identified people" who cannot be obliged to correct the injustices, yet the dignity of the human person requires that justice be restored; or they may be caused by nonidentifiable people.

It is precisely within the structural forces of inequality in society where injustice of this second type is found, where injustice is "institutionalized," that is, built into economic, social, and political structures both national and international, and where people are suffering from poverty and hunger, from the unjust distribution of wealth, resources, and power. The critical theorists, of whom we spoke earlier, would likely prefer this wider definition of social justice.

It is almost certain that Ignatius did not only concern himself with injustices that were purely economic. He often cites injustices about "threats to human life and it quality," "racial and political discrimination," and loss of respect for the "rights of individuals or groups" (Chapple 1993). When one adds to these the "vast range of injustices" enumerated in his writings, one sees that the Ignatian vision understands its mission of justice to include "the widest possible view of justice," involving every area where there is an attack on human rights.

We can conclude, therefore, that although Ignatius was to some degree concerned about commutative justice (right relationships between private persons and groups) and distributive justice (the obligations of the state to render to the individual what is his or her due), he is most concerned about what is generally called today social justice, or "justice of the common good." Such justice is comprehensive and includes the above strict legal rights and duties, but is more concerned about the natural rights and duties of individuals, families, communities, and the community of nations toward one another as members of the common family of human beings.

Every form of justice is included in and presupposed by social justice, but with social justice, it is the social nature of the person that is emphasized, as well as the social significance of all earthly goods, the purpose of which is to aid all members of the human community to attain their dignity as human beings. Many of Ignatius's followers believe that this dignity is being undermined in our world today, and their main efforts are aimed toward restoring that dignity.

In the pursuit of social justice, Ignatius calls on his followers to be "in solidarity with the poor." The next logical question might then be, who are the poor? The poor are usually thought to be those who are economically deprived and politically oppressed. Thus, we can conclude that the promotion of justice means to work to overcome the oppressions or injustices that make the poor poor.

The fallacy here, however, is that the poor are not necessarily oppressed or suffering injustice, and so Ignatius argues that our obligation toward the poor must be understood to be linking "inhuman levels of poverty and injustice" and not be understood to be concerned with the "lot of those possessing only modest resources," even though those of modest means are often poor and oppressed. So, we conclude that the poor include those "wrongfully" impoverished or dispossessed (Institute of Jesuit Sources 1995).

An extended definition of the poor, one that Ignatius would espouse, would include any of these types of people:

- First are those who are economically deprived and socially marginalized and oppressed, especially, but not limited to, those with whom one has immediate contact and is in a position to positively affect.
- The second group includes the "poor in spirit." That is, those who lack a value system or an ethical and moral sense.
- The third group includes those who are emotionally poor; those who have psychological and emotional shortcomings and are in need of comfort.

In defining the poor in the broadest way, Ignatius exhorts us to undertake social change in our role as leader; to do what we can do to bring an end to inequality, oppression, and injustice. Once again we can see the close connection between the Ignatian principles of social justice and the main tenets of critical theory.

IMPLICATIONS FOR ADMINISTRATION

Each of the principles of the Ignatian vision noted above has a variety of implications for leaders. The *magis* principle has implications for administrators in that it calls for us to continually be seeking perfection in all that we do. In effect, this means that we must seek to continually improve. And, since improvement implies change, we need to be champions of needed change in our institutions. This means that we have to model a tolerance for change and embrace not only our own change initiatives, but also those in other parts of the organization. In effect, the Ignatian vision prompts us not to be merely leaders but transformational leaders. The principle of *cura personalis* has additional implications. To practice the Ignatian vision, one must treat people with dignity under all circumstances. *Cura personalis* also requires us to extend ourselves in offering individual attention and attending to the needs of all those in whom we come in contact. Being sensitive to the individual's unique needs is particularly required. Many times in our efforts to treat people equally, we fail to treat them fairly and equitably. Certain individuals have greater needs than others, and many times these needs require exceptions to be made on their behalf.

For example, if an adult student does not hand in an assignment on time, but the tardiness is due to the fact that he or she is going through some personal or family trauma at the moment, the principle of *cura personalis* calls on us to make an exception in this case. It is likely that some would consider such an exception to be unfair to those who made the effort to complete the assignment in a timely manner or, that we cannot possibly be sensitive to the special needs of all of our students and colleagues. However, as long as the exception is made for everyone in the same circumstances, Ignatius would not perceive this exception as being unfair. In fact, the exception would be expected if one is practicing the principle of "care of the person."

The Ignatian process of *discernment* requires educational administrators to be reflective practitioners. It calls on us to be introspective regarding our administrative and leadership behavior. We are asked to reflect on the ramifications of our decisions, especially in light of their cumulative effect on the equitable distribution of power and on the marginalized individuals and groups in our communities. In effect, the principle of discernment galvanizes the other principles embodied in the Ignatian vision. During the discernment process, we are asked to reflect upon how our planned behavior will manifest the *magis* principle, *cura personalis*, and service to the community, especially the underserved, marginalized, and oppressed.

The development of men and women for others requires leaders to have their own sense of service toward those with whom they interact, and also that they develop this spirit of service in others. The concept of "servant leadership" requires us to encourage others toward a life and career of service and to assume the position of being the "servant of the servants." Ignatius thinks about leadership in terms of what the gospel writer Luke calls the "one who serves." The leader owes something to the institution he or she leads. The leader is seen in this context as steward rather than owner or proprietor.

The implications of Ignatius' notion of social justice are myriad for a leader. Being concerned about the marginalized among our constituencies is required. We are called to be sensitive to those individuals and groups that do not share equitably in the distribution of power and influence. Distinctions according to race, class, and gender should be corrected. Participative decision making and collaborative behavior is encouraged among administrators imbued with the Ignatian tradition.

Equitable representation of all segments of the school community should be provided whenever feasible. Leadership behavior such as this will assure that the dominant culture is not perpetuated to the detriment of the minority culture, rendering the minorities powerless. We will find in the succeeding chapters that the most heroic of the leaders profiled incorporate many of the Ignatian concepts into their leadership behavior.

Thus, in my view, the Ignatian vision and the moral frame *completes* situational leadership theory. Left on its own, situational leadership theory is secular and amoral. Utilizing situational leadership theory alone is as likely to produce a leader like Adolf Hitler as it is to produce a leader like Abraham Lincoln. But by using the additional lens of the Ignatian vision to view our situational leadership behavior will ensure that we have more Lincolns and fewer Hitlers in our world.

SUMMARY

We began this book by suggesting that leaders are made, not born. We posited that if one could master the skills involved in effective leadership, one could become a successful administrator. In this chapter, however, we make the assertion that learning the skills involved in effective leadership is only part of the story. Leadership is as much an art, a belief, a condition of the heart, as it is mastering a set of skills and understanding leadership theory. A truly successful and heroic leader, therefore, is one who leads with both the *mind* and the *heart*.

When we look at the leadership behavior of the leaders included in the study, we should observe not only if their leadership practices conform to the Bolman/Deal situational leadership theory, but also if they are leading with *heart*. I believe that we will find that those leaders that are most comfortable consistently operating out of the moral frame of leadership are most likely to be leading with heart. At any rate, the most effective leaders will be those who lead with both mind (structural, political frames) and heart (human resource and symbolic frames) and view their leadership behavior through the lens of the Ignatian vision or some similar moral philosophy.

Chapter Three

Lincoln v. Lenin

I. ABRAHAM LINCOLN

When he shall die, Take him and cut him out in little stars, And he will make the face of heaven so fine, that all the world shall be in love with night.

—William Shakespeare

Background

Abraham Lincoln was born in 1909 in Kentucky and served as the sixteenth president of the United States from March 1861 until his assassination in April 1865. Among other things, the Lincoln legend includes the familiar one-room Kentucky log cabin where he was born, the nicknames "Honest Abe" and "the Rail-Splitter," the inspiring oratory of the Gettysburg Address, and the lofty rhetoric of the Emancipation Proclamation.

In 1832, Lincoln was elected to the Illinois House for the first of four terms. In 1847 he began a term in the U.S. House of Representatives, but it was not until the enacting of the Kansas-Nebraska Act, sponsored by Senator Stephen Douglas, that Lincoln's national reputation became firmly established. In 1858 he ran for the Senate against Douglas. The seven debates that ensued set the stage for his presidential future.

Although Lincoln won the debates and established a national reputation, Douglas prevailed. But Lincoln won the presidential nomination in 1860, and running on an antislavery platform, defeated Douglas, Buchanan, and others to become president. With his election, seven of the fifteen slave states seceded from the Union.

In 1861, when Confederate guns fired on Fort Sumter, the Civil War began. General George McClellan, the leader of the Union army, was not proactive enough for Lincoln's tastes and was eventually replaced by Ulysses S. Grant, a brilliant and ruthless military man who eventually led the North to victory.

In 1863, in the midst of the Civil War, Lincoln issued his Emancipation Proclamation declaring slavery unlawful in the rebel states. The Union forces won a great victory at Gettysburg, and General Sherman was nearing the end of his annihilating "March to the Sea," when, finally, on April 9, 1865, General Robert E. Lee surrendered to General Grant on the steps of Appomattox Court House.

Five nights later, a bullet fired by the proslavery actor John Wilkes Booth during a performance at Ford's Theatre in Washington, D.C., killed Lincoln. In most historians' minds, Lincoln is considered to be one of the very best U.S. presidents (Aronson 1997; Felzenberg 2008; McGovern 2009; Taranto and Leo 2004).

The Structural Frame

Structural frame leaders seek to develop a new model of the relationship of structure, strategy, and environment for their organizations. Strategic planning, extensive preparation and effecting change are priorities for them. The effective use of the structural frame of leadership was one of Abraham Lincoln's many strengths. In typical structural frame leadership form, Lincoln established the goals of his presidency very early on in his administration. He was absolutely determined to preserve the Union. He was supremely committed to this goal and he vowed to accomplish it no matter how long or costly the task. At his inauguration in March 1961, he swore a sacred oath— "registered in Heaven," he said—"to preserve, protect, and defend the Constitution" (McGovern 2009, 5). He delivered his message clearly and logically in a very structural frame way.

Lincoln saw the contradiction of having a union of states that promoted democracy and allowing those same united states to willfully secede whenever they did not agree with the majority's view. Thus, he was absolutely and fundamentally against allowing states to secede and practiced structural frame leadership behavior, like going to war to prevent them from doing so.

One of Lincoln's traits that we have all come to admire about him is his amazing capacity to live and work with a strong sense of discipline, which is very much in the structural frame. When asked what made for a successful lawyer, he replied, "Work, work, work is the main thing" (McGovern 2009, 10). He carried this work ethic to the White House, rising each day at six in the morning and staying up late, cramming as much work into a day as he could.

Unlike most politicians, who leave war strategy to their generals, Lincoln took a hands-on approach to running the war, reading volumes on military strategy, tactics, and maneuvers to make up for his lack of military training. Much like George Washington, his attention to detail resulted in a new, expanded definition of the president as commander-in-chief. He was an extremely intelligent man and recognized that fact at an early age. Despite his lack of formal education, he was seldom, if ever, intimidated in the courtroom, a political debate, in battlefield strategy, or in the Oval Office.

Lincoln had many traits of a structural leader, including his great intelligence. He was serious and eager to learn. He had the analytical mind of a lawyer and was a voracious reader. He was drawn to the works of Shakespeare and Robert Burns. Ultimately, he thought that he could use his mind and forensic skills to advance himself to a position where he could also advance society.

Using his structural leadership skills of organization, preparation, and vision, Lincoln was able to make the metamorphosis from country lawyer to candidate to statesman. No other American president had ever faced the challenges of disunion, rebellion, and civil war. Making prolific use of structural frame leadership behavior, Lincoln met the challenges with firm resolve. For example, in his inaugural address, he declared, "The man does not live who is more devoted to peace than I am; none who would do more to preserve it. But it may be necessary to put the foot down firmly" (McGovern 2009, 54).

And put his "foot down firmly" he did. In March 1863 in the midst of the Civil War, Congress passed the Habeas Corpus Indemnity Act, which gave Lincoln much leeway in dealing with suspected war criminals and allowed him the power to suspend habeas corpus throughout the United States. Lincoln's unprecedented suspension of habeas corpus was criticized, but he believed that the rebellion justified and vindicated his use of such strong structural frame leadership behavior.

Once again using structural frame thinking, Lincoln recognized that the Emancipation Proclamation had to be followed by a law or constitutional amendment that would legitimize the prohibition of slavery. So he lobbied hard and was successful in having the Thirteenth and Fourteenth Amendments passed.

By the middle of the Civil War, Lincoln began to take a far more active role in managing military affairs. He engaged in structural frame behavior by reading books on military theory, consulting with his advisors, and carefully studying maps and battle plans. These efforts enabled Lincoln to begin to formulate a basic war strategy in his own mind. He had fully assumed the role of the military's commander-in-chief, and he was steadily transforming himself to the position of a war president.

Lincoln used still more structural leadership behavior in conducting the Civil War when he finally, after much procrastination, replaced General McClellan as general-in-chief of the Union army, even though had recently won a narrow victory at Antietam but did not follow through in pursuit of General Robert E. Lee's retreating army. So after one year of command, McClellan was discharged. Since McClellan was not using his army, Lincoln sarcastically noted, "he would like to borrow it" for a while (McGovern 2009, 85).

In yet another display of structural frame leadership behavior, Lincoln moved to total war by 1863. This was no longer just a match between two armies. Anyone, or anything, that aided and abetted the Rebels was now considered fair game. This approach ultimately led to Sherman's famous March to the Sea that devastated great swaths of land from Atlanta to Savannah. Until he found a commander whom he could trust, namely Ulysses S. Grant, Lincoln would remain the primary strategist of the Civil War.

Underlying Lincoln's strategy was the basic conviction that, given the North's advantage in numbers of men, weapons, railways, and industrial resources, the Union army should remain aggressive and would eventually prevail.

In typical structural frame fashion, once the war was finally over Lincoln stated firmly that the war-ending peace negotiations were to be left to him. "The President holds them in his own hands, and will submit them to no military conferences and conventions," he said (McGovern 2009, 139).

The Human Resource Frame

Human resource leaders believe in people and communicate that belief. They are passionate about *productivity through people*. Another of Lincoln's strengths was his ability to apply the human touch in his interaction with others. Lincoln's own words give an indication of his position on the importance of human resource leadership behavior. Government's role, he said, was to "elevate the conditions of men—to lift artificial weights from all shoulders—to clear the paths of laudable pursuit for all, to afford all, an unfettered start, and a fair chance in the race of life" (McGovern 2009, 5).

Lincoln's remarkable quality of tolerance and human concern has been a constant source of admiration for generations of Americans. His compassion touched every area of his life. He loved his children so much that he could not bear to discipline them. He often represented financially needy clients in court without charge and repeatedly spoke out against the nativist movements (the Know-Nothings and the American Party) for their racial, ethnic, and religious prejudices and stereotyping. And he was convinced that the best way to deal with his adversaries was to apply friendly persuasion rather than some form of coercion.

Lincoln used human resource behavior especially when relating to soldiers, whom he regarded as the real heroes in American society. He loved meeting them, particularly those who had been held prisoner or had endured hardship. He pardoned, reprieved, or granted leniency to hundreds of soldiers who were charged with being derelict in their duties, because he believed in giving a man a second chance. He wrote touching letters to the mothers of fallen soldiers, with words that obviously came from his heart. And he felt no sense of revenge toward the Rebel soldiers and commanded his generals to "let 'em up easy" (McGovern 2009, 8).

Ever the humanist, Lincoln scoffed at those who defended slavery on the grounds that blacks were better off as slaves in America than heathens in Africa or performing menial tasks in the North. He was also quick to point out the hypocrisy of the slave-owners and politicians who supported this view. "We never hear of a man who wishes to take the good of it, by being a slave *himself*," he declared (McGovern 2009, 68).

Lincoln felt that the majority of Southerners had been duped into thinking that the only way of protecting their way of life from destruction by Lincoln was by secession and war. Therefore, after the war, Lincoln extended the olive branch to his Southern brethren and wanted reconstruction to take place without rancor and with a great deal of good will and forgiveness. Even before the war ended, Lincoln issued a Proclamation of Amnesty and Reconstruction aimed at Southern areas already occupied by federal forces. He hoped that the generous terms of the proclamation would entice war-weary Southern soldiers from the unoccupied areas to lay down their arms and surrender.

The Symbolic Frame

In the symbolic frame, the organization is seen as a stage, a theater in which every actor plays certain roles and the symbolic leader attempts to communicate the right impressions to the right audiences. One could argue that the symbolic frame was perhaps Lincoln's strongest. Lincoln took symbolic leadership behavior very seriously. As a communicator, Lincoln took advantage of the latest technical advances. For example, he used the telegraph office to keep abreast of news from the front and to send orders to his generals in the field. He also made abundant use of the railways, not only to move armies and supplies, but also to transport him to the battlefields. He understood the importance of his personal presence both in his executive responsibilities and on the frontlines as a motivation and inspiration to his officers and their soldiers.

Knowing that after the Civil War it would be crucial for former enemies to become friends, he symbolically got this point across by appointing to his cabinet what he called "the team of rivals." He named three of his major rivals to his cabinet, confident in his ability to curb their ambitions and inspire them to function as a team. "Keep your enemies close," he advised (Felzenberg 2008, 120).

The part of the his image that Lincoln worked particularly hard on was his humility. In running for the Illinois state legislature, he said: "I am in favor of the internal improvement system and a high protective tariff. These are my sentiments and political principles. If elected I shall be thankful; if not it will be all the same." He is also famous for saying, "You may fool all the people some of the time; you can even fool some of the people all the time; but you can't fool all the people all the time" (McGovern 2009, 30).

Most of Lincoln's symbolic behavior came in the form of his inspiring speeches, many of which reflected his position on slavery and the moral evil that he thought it was. In 1854, Lincoln gave his first great speech that clearly set forth his arguments against the Kansas-Nebraska Act and his personal views on slavery. He said that the institution of slavery was morally wrong and a "monstrous injustice," because it denied the "humanity of the Negro." "Bleeding Kansas," as Lincoln referred to it, became a battleground for proslavery and antislavery forces, clashing over whether Kansas would be admitted into the Union as a Free or Slave state. Thus, Lincoln repudiated the Kansas-Nebraska Act as "conceived in violence, passed in violence, and executed in violence" (McGovern 2009, 38).

"Slavery is founded in the selfishness of man's nature—opposition to it in his love of justice," he so eloquently said in another of his famous speeches in Peoria in 1854. Slavery, he declared, violated the promise of the Declaration of Independence and its principle that "all men are created equal" (McGovern 2009, 67).

In his second great speech, Lincoln further reinforced his position on slavery with his 1858 acceptance speech at the statehouse in Springfield, Illinois. Using familiar biblical language and again decrying the enactment of the Kansas-Nebraska Act, which invalidated the Missouri Compromise, he said:

> We are now in the fifth year since the policy was initiated with the avowed object and confident promises of putting an end to slavery. Under the operation of the policy, that agitation has not only not ceased, but has been constantly augmented. . . . A house divided against itself cannot stand. I believe this government cannot endure permanently half slave and half free (McGovern 2009, 42).

His words were prophetic when two years later, the Civil War broke out.

In another display of symbolic behavior, the Lincoln-Douglas debates, the center piece of the Illinois Senatorial campaign, became one of the most famous political events in the history of American politics. Newspapers around the country closely followed the contest between "the Little Giant" and "Honest Abe."

Lincoln's third great speech was delivered at New York's Cooper Union in 1860 and supported his position that the founding fathers had meant for slavery to gradually fade away. He pointed out that twenty-nine of the signers of the Constitution had favored congressional regulation of slavery in the territories. Thus, those who spoke of secession were misguided. Republicans should stay the course, he urged. "Let us have faith that right makes might, and in that faith, let us to the end, dare to do our duty as we understand it" (McGovern 2009, 445).

Lincoln's Inaugural Address was another instance of his frequent use of symbolism. "The rights of the minority would always be protected by the majority, which was held safely in restraint by constitutional checks and balances," he declared. "That is how the national government endured. For the minority to break from the Union—to secede—simply because it found itself in the minority was," Lincoln said, "the essence of anarchy" (McGovern 2009, 54).

The Emancipation Proclamation was at once a symbolic, structural, human resource, and political gesture. Lincoln's order freed 4 million slaves with one stroke of his pen. Of those, over 150,000 joined the Union forces and gave African Americans the incentive to rebel against their Southern masters. Politically, he made sure it did not apply to border slave states like Delaware, Maryland, Kentucky, and Missouri, that did not secede from the Union. He also made certain that he signed the Emancipation Proclamation, which had been written almost a year earlier, after a Union victory at Antietam.

Of course there is the famous use of symbolic leadership behavior in defense of Ulysses S. Grant upon being informed of his drinking problems. Lincoln said, "Find out what he's drinking and order it for my other generals" (McGovern 2009, 87).

In November 1863, Lincoln traveled by train to Gettysburg, Pennsylvania, for the dedication of a new national Soldiers Cemetery on the site of the battlefield. Lincoln's two-minute speech (272 words) remains his most famous. The Gettysburg Address added a second reason to fight the Civil War. The battle was no longer simply over the survival of the Union. Now, abolishing slavery and guaranteeing the ideals of freedom for *all* Americans as called for in the Declaration of Independence became a rallying cry. The Gettysburg Address, along with at least five other great speeches, made Lincoln the most masterful speech writer of any president in our national history.

In his typically symbolic way, after being nominated for a second term, he humbly said: "I have not permitted myself, gentlemen, to conclude that I am the best man in the country; but I am reminded, in this connection, of an old Dutch farmer, who remarked to a companion once that it was not best to swap horses when crossing streams" (McGovern 2009, 104).

Upon being criticized by the Democrats and the press, Lincoln once again used symbolic behavior in his astute observation that, "If the end brings me out all right, what is said against me won't amount to anything. If the end brings me out wrong, ten angels swearing I was right would make no difference" (Felzenberg 2008, 120).

The Political Frame

Leaders operating out of the political frame clarify what they want and what they can get. Political leaders are realists above all. They never let what they want cloud their judgment about what is possible. They assess the distribution of power and interests. Lincoln would not be listed among the most effective presidents in American history if he were not facile in his use of the political frame of leadership. Unlike the radical abolitionists, Lincoln believed that if the slave system could be confined to the Southern states, it would eventually go asunder. And when the free territories became free states, the national political balance would shift inexorably toward freedom. Thus, in order to avoid war, he was very willing to practice political frame leadership behavior and wait out the inevitable even if it took a considerable amount of time. Of course the Southern states were not about to allow social Darwinism to determine their destiny and their inflexibility and their attempts to extend slavery to the territories led to the Civil War.

Lincoln was a quintessential politician. He was a savvy politician who knew and had grown up in the Illinois world of hard-knock politics. In fact, it was a political decision that drew him back into public service after losing a senatorial election. He was "thunderstruck" and "astounded" as the Kansas-Nebraska Act was passed, allowing a state vote on slavery, in effect, nullifying the Missouri Compromise that outlawed slavery in the new territories and that Lincoln naively believed had "settled the slavery question forever" (McGovern 2009, 37).

With his presidential nomination assured, Lincoln immediately engaged in political frame behavior in appointing his presidential rival and Secretary of the Treasury, Salmon Chase to the Supreme Court. In doing so, Lincoln could count on Chase not to thwart the administration's policies the way deceased Chief Justice Roger Taney, who presided over the Dred Scott decision, did.

In agreeing to join and ultimately becoming the standard bearer of the newly established Republican Party in 1856, Lincoln used political leadership behavior and made some demands: The party must have an antislavery platform but must respect the Constitution's protection of slavery where it already existed. The party had to avoid "dangerous extremes," such as the radical abolitionists demanded, and rule from the center. To attract foreign-born voters, the party must officially advocate religious toleration, and to appease the Know-Nothings. It must oppose state funds to parochial schools as a violation of the Establishment Clause of the First Amendment.

Recognizing that his party consisted of differing interest groups, Lincoln tried to strike an unusual balance, selecting men who had been his chief rivals for the Republican nominations. Recently, Doris Kearns Goodwin wrote about Lincoln's cabinet in her book, *Team of Rivals*. In true political frame style, Lincoln believed in the concept of keeping your friends close and your enemies even closer.

Lincoln also tried unsuccessfully to utilize political frame behavior to delay the onset of the Civil War. He scheduled a series of informal peace talks, all of which he anticipated would be ineffective, but he believed that his willingness even to consider such talks would send a message to the public that he was willing to negotiate and compromise.

In campaigning for reelection against General George McClellan, Illinois, Indiana, New Jersey, Delaware, Rhode Island, Nevada, and Oregon did not allow votes from the field or the casting of absentee ballots. Soldiers from those states had to gain leave and return home to vote. Once again using political leadership behavior, Lincoln made sure that such leave was granted because he knew he had the support of the great majority of the soldiers.

In the process of passing the Thirteenth Amendment, which abolished slavery, Lincoln was particularly astute in employing political frame behavior in using his talents as a master politician to work tirelessly to gain the necessary congressional votes. Lincoln offered federal jobs to congressmen and their family members of both parties in exchange for their votes. At the instant it was passed, he engaged in a little symbolic behavior and had a hundred-gun salute commence that rattled the city of Washington. And he was proud of the fact that the very first state to ratify the amendment was his home state of Illinois.

The Moral Frame

The moral frame is my own contribution to situational leadership theory. In my view, the moral frame completes situational leadership theory. Without it, leaders could just as easily use their leadership skills for promoting evil as for promoting good. Leaders operating out of the moral frame are concerned about their obligations and responsibilities to their followers. Moral frame

leaders use some type of moral compass to direct their behavior. They practice what has been described as servant leadership and are concerned with those individuals and groups that are marginalized in their organizations and in society. In short, they are concerned about equality, fairness and social justice.

Although Lincoln never belonged to an established religion, he readily acknowledged a higher power. Indeed, it often seemed that the connection between Lincoln and the Almighty enabled him to face the great challenges that fate presented to him. He saw himself as an instrument of God's will. In his view, by becoming president, he had been charged with a sacred trust. He spoke of Divine Providence, and the idea of both retribution and forgiveness. He believed that God might punish the nation for the sin of slavery, both the North for allowing racial discrimination to continue to take place, and the South for the institution of slavery itself.

So, Lincoln had high standards of morality and ethics. He charged that the institution of slavery was morally wrong and a "monstrous injustice" because it denied the "humanity of the Negro." He also described it as "the eternal struggle between right and wrong—throughout the world" (McGovern 2009, 37).

As mentioned earlier, Lincoln's Emancipation Proclamation fundamentally and dramatically transformed the character of the Civil War. Now there was a moral dimension added to the Union cause, and this new ideal would transcend the original war effort to preserve the Union.

Situational Leadership Analysis

Situational models of leadership differ from earlier trait and behavioral models in asserting that no single way of leading works in all situations. Rather, appropriate behavior depends on the circumstances at a given time. Effective managers diagnose the situation, identify the leadership style or behavior that will be most effective, and then determine whether they can implement the required style.

Lincoln was a prototypical situational leader. For example, when he issued the Emancipation Proclamation, he convened a cabinet meeting, informed the attendees of his decision, and declared that he did not wish their "advice about the main matter," which, he said he had already "determined for himself" (Felzenberg 2008, 123). He then sought their input on exactly how it would best be promulgated and any legal issues that might have to be considered.

Further demonstrating his flexibility regarding the use of leadership behavior, Lincoln began his administration promising not to disturb slavery where it existed. Later on, he tried to persuade slaveholders to accept compensated emancipation. Finally, when nothing else proved effective, he banned slavery altogether.

Basically a humanist, Lincoln was situational enough to also be Machiavellian when the occasion called for it. It was a combination of qualities that made Lincoln's contribution to the antislavery movement so demonstrably effective. Lincoln was a relentless foe of slavery but bade his time to strike at the most opportune moment—the timing of the Emancipation Proclamation coincided with a major victory, for example. Whether consciously doing so or not, Lincoln was expert in placing the principles of situational leadership theory into effective practice.

Leadership Implications and Conclusion

In Abraham Lincoln we see the essence of situational leadership. He used symbolic behavior to inspire a people and an army and used structural behavior to sustain and support them. He mobilized and energized the nation by appealing to the best and highest of ideals (moral frame behavior); that is, he convinced the nation that "a more perfect Union"—a Union of justice and freedom—was worth the fight. As a human resource frame leader, he wished for the "kindly spirit" of America, "a Union of hearts and minds as well as of States" (McGovern 2009, 147).

Lincoln holds perhaps the highest place in American history. General William Tecumseh Sherman said, "Of all the men I ever met, he seemed to possess more of the elements of greatness, combined with goodness, than any other" (McGovern 2009, 249). He is the president against whom all others will forever be measured. We hope all leaders can be more like he was. By reflecting on the many lessons in situational leadership that Lincoln modeled, perhaps we can come to manifest his leadership ideals in our own leadership behavior.

II. VLADIMIR LENIN

We must put down the resistance with such brutality that they will not forget it for several decades. The greater the number of representatives of the reactionary clergy and reactionary bourgeoisie we succeed in executing the better.

—Vladimir Lenin

Background

Vladimir Lenin was born in 1870 in Simbirsk, Russia, and was the Russian revolutionary who founded the Bolshevik political party. He was a statesman who led the so-called October Revolution and presided over Russia's transformation from a country ruled for centuries by czars to the Union of Soviet Socialist Republics (USSR).

Since his father was born of Russian royalty, Lenin grew up in relatively privileged circumstances. But the execution of his older brother Alexander in 1887 after Alexander and others had plotted to kill the czar radicalized Lenin. What further rankled Lenin was that his sister, who had nothing to do with the plot, was exiled.

Lenin graduated from secondary school with high honors and enrolled at Kazan University, but he was expelled after participating in a communist demonstration. He retired to the family estate but was permitted to continue his studies away from the university. He obtained a law degree in 1891.

In 1893 Lenin moved to St. Petersburg, Russia. By this time he was already a dedicated and committed Marxist. In 1897 he was arrested and spent some time in prison. He then was sentenced to three years of exile in the remote area of Siberia. While in Siberia, he met fellow Marxist, Nadezhda Kostantinovna Krupskaya, whom he married in 1898. During this time he wrote a major book on the Russian economy, *The Development of Capitalism in Russia.*

In 1902 Lenin further enunciated his ideologies in his seminal book, *What's to Be Done?* As a result of his writings, Russian Marxism eventually split into two factions. The one led by Lenin labeled itself the majority faction (Bolsheviks), while the other called itself the minority faction (Mensheviks) The Bolsheviks and the Mensheviks disagreed not only over how to organize the movement but also over many other political and ideological questions.

During World War I Lenin lived in Switzerland. He also wrote another important book, *Imperialism: The Highest Stage of Capitalism*, in 1916. The influence of this book led to the overthrow of the Russian czar in the winter of 1917, marking the beginning of the Russian Revolution.

As a result of the October Revolution Lenin found himself not only the leader of his party but also the chairman of the Council of People's Commissars of the newly proclaimed Russian Socialist Federation Soviet Republic, which was the genesis of the USSR.

From 1918 to 1921 a fierce civil war raged in which the Bolsheviks finally defeated the Mensheviks against seemingly overwhelming odds. During the civil war Lenin tightened his reins on the party and virtually eliminated all rival political parties. At the conclusion of the civil war, the economy was in ruins and much of the general population was bitterly opposed to the

Bolsheviks. At this point Lenin reversed many of his past economic policies and instituted a reform called the New Economic Policy (NEP). It was only a temporary retreat, however, from the ultimate goal of establishing radical socialism. Instead, the stressing the importance of ideology, the party's focus would be on rebuilding the economy and on the education of the peasant population for a life of radical socialism in the future.

But on May 26, 1922, Lenin suffered a series of strokes. He was so seriously ill that he could no longer govern. He moved to a country home at Gorki, Russia, near Moscow, where he died on January 21, 1924, at age fifty-three. Almost a million mourners passed by his casket during the several days that his body lay in state (Service 2000).

Situational Leadership Analysis

Situational models of leadership differ from earlier trait and behavioral models in asserting that no single way of leading works in all situations. Rather, appropriate behavior depends on the circumstances at a given time. Effective managers diagnose the situation, identify the leadership style or behavior that will be most effective, and then determine whether they can implement the required style.

Although we will find that Vladimir Lenin was less flexible that many of the leaders profiled in this book, he had definite situational leadership tendencies. On most occasions he altered his leadership behavior depending on the situation. He was willing, for example, to modify his policies in light of popular demands. In the *April Theses*, he had called for land nationalization. But after a poll of the peasants indicated a rejection of such nationalization, Lenin dropped the idea.

Another change in policy occurred when he learned that employers in Petrograd were beginning to encourage participative decision making in their factories. Just as he had previously objected to allowing peasant communes to control the villages, so he had never liked the idea of workers having too much power in their factories without direction from the Party. But this was a revolutionary situation, and workers had to be encouraged to join the cause. Thus their creativity and initiative had to be fostered, so he allowed employee empowerment to continue.

In another indication of his situational nature, although no one would accuse Lenin of not being a Marxist hard-liner, the reality is that Lenin treated the Marxist ideal ambivalently whenever pragmatism was a better way to reach a party goal. Although he thought seriously about social and economic theory and liked to remain within its basic ideologies, his adherence was not absolute by any means. In the mid-1920s, the priority for him was the global release of revolutionary energy. Ideas about the formal, protracted stages of social development were pushed to his subconscious. Better to conduct a successful revolution, however inefficiently, than to create a sophisticated but impractical theory.

The Structural Frame

Structural frame leaders seek to develop a new model of the relationship of structure, strategy, and environment for their organizations. Strategic planning, extensive preparation, and effecting change are priorities for them. This was one of Lenin's strongest frames. In Lenin's era, there was a great emphasis in Russia on the part of parents in encouraging their sons to obtain a quality education. Lenin's parents were no exception to this rule, and Lenin became not only an outstanding student but also a well-recognized scholar. His obsession to thoroughly research problems, plan and strategize, and adhere strictly to timelines—all structural frame traits—remained with him for his entire life.

In true structural leadership form, he became a party boss who was almost a one-man court of appeal. Lenin alone was to be respected as the great and glorious leader by all members of the Bolshevik party, and his patriarchal style strengthened his dominance. He also had a way of handling the party officials with finesse, managing to sound radical even when he was making compromises.

Being the structural leader that he was, he adhered closely to his ideological plan, and as a result, Lenin made history. In the *April Theses* of 1917, he drafted a strategy for the party to seize power. In March 1918, he headed off a German invasion of Russia by negotiating a separate treaty signed at Brest-Litovsk. In 1921, he introduced the New Economic Policy and saved the Soviet Bloc from being overthrown by a popular rebellion. If Lenin had not initiated these strategies, the USSR would have gone asunder before it had any real chance of succeeding.

But Lenin was sometimes a structural leader to a fault. He had no concern for morality and ethics. To him, the goal justified the means. He justified dictatorship and terror and encouraged the need for firm leadership that often condoned violence and murder. He convinced his party that his Marxism was pure and that it embodied the only correct interpretation.

In strategy, organization, and planning, however, Lenin had a lasting impact on how to operationalize radical socialism for his country and the world. He was so obsessed with his cause that in his adult years he gave up his leisure-time interests in chess, classical music, and ice-skating to concentrate on his revolutionary tasks.

Many of Lenin's party colleagues wanted the right to have at least some independent thought, but in true radical structural frame fashion, Lenin was in favor of leadership, leadership, and more leadership. Everything else was to be subordinate to this end.

Lenin, therefore, lived life on his own terms. His bookishness, his demands on other peoples' time, his dedication to regular physical exercise, and his willingness to give advice on virtually every topic were all structural frame traits. These characteristics were treated as evidence of his great genius.

Another obsessive-compulsive tendency was Lenin's insistence on absolute silence when he was working. He and his staff moved around on tiptoe so as not to interrupt his train of thought. A slave to detail, everything had to be in its place, from his pencils to his political and economic policy files.

During the wartime years, Lenin used structural behavior to develop strategies to compress the schedule of the revolution. Conventional Marxism held that there would be two stages to the revolution. First a bourgeois-democratic revolution would occur to bring down the monarchy and to consolidate power between democracy and capitalism. Then, the socialistic revolution would take place, putting the working class into power. Lenin hastened the process by abandoning the consolidation step and proceeding directly to socialism, which, in effect, he accomplished with the Bolshevik Revolution of 1917.

Once, on a train ride back to Russia, Lenin showed his structural frame compulsions by sketching his proposed strategy for the revolution in the form of his *April Theses*, which consisted of ten theses on how to operationalize and institutionalize the revolution. After he convinced the party members of his strategy, he next went about developing a propaganda campaign to convince the workers and peasants.

Lenin's vision of world communism evolved in a very structural frame way. His view was that capitalism would be overthrown by a violent revolution that would be consummated by the "dictatorship of the proletariat." The dictatorship would initially be and would steadily institutionalize the practices and ideals of socialism. Under communism, the ultimate goal of a fair and compassionate society would be realized. "From each according to his abilities, to each according to his needs," Lenin declared (Service 2000, 296).

Sometimes, however, Lenin was slow to apply structural leadership behavior when it was needed. For instance, no great skill was required of Lenin to create his New Economic Policy (NEP) when Russia had experienced a devastating famine, but Lenin put off the decision until it was too late. It was a no-brainer that farmers should be allowed to more freely decide what they wanted to grow and to exchange their goods more readily.

The NEP was an obvious way to restore the easy exchange of products between village and town. This policy was also a remedy for famine, disease, industrial ruin, and popular rebellion. Even though he was late in implementing it, along with the Brest-Litovsk Treaty, the NEP was Lenin's most significant accomplishment—except for the Bolshevik Revolution, of course.

The Human Resource Frame

Human resource leaders believe in people and communicate that belief. They are passionate about productivity through people. Despite giving lip service to this leadership frame, instances of Lenin's use of human resource leadership behavior are few and far between. Ironically, even though the ultimate goal of communism is giving power to the workers, the reality was that the power was concentrated in the hands of Lenin and a few influential party members. So, in effect, even though communism as an ideology is humanistic, Lenin's interpretation of it was not so.

Lenin could never be characterized as gregarious or sensitive, but when his brother Alexander was in prison and later executed, he became very depressed and maudlin, showing that he did have a human side. As a rule, however, Lenin did not let human affairs or affairs of the heart get in the way of public affairs, and this was to remain the case even during his involvement with Inessa Armand before World War I.

Still, the death of his comrade and soul mate Inessa Armand left Lenin noticeably overcome with grief. At her funeral, he had to be supported by a couple of the mourners so that he did not collapse. No one present could forget his pitiful countenance. The testimony of many of his friends and associates who were by his side on that day indicated that he was a mere shadow of his former self emotionally after her death.

There were other rare instances in which Lenin did demonstrate a human touch. For example, when Nikolai Valentinov, a new young Bolshevik recruit arrived penniless from Geneva, Lenin helped him obtain a part-time job as a barrow pusher. Valentinov once had a delivery that he could not fulfill by himself. Lenin leaned a shoulder to the barrow to help, and Valentinov never forgot the favor. But Lenin's family had instilled in him the idea that pride in oneself was anathema, and that good deeds had to be done without recognition or fuss. This reserve stayed with him throughout his life and precluded any significant use of the human resource frame.

Not unlike what we have seen regarding Adolf Hitler, Lenin's saving grace regarding human resource behavior was his genuine love of children. His greatest pleasure came not from his political achievements but from the presence of children. It was clear that Lenin and his wife would have loved to have children of their own, and the visits of their young relatives and friends brought them great joy. They took responsibility for the Armand children after his friend Inessa's death, and there is much evidence to indicate that Lenin and his wife made provisions for their future welfare and treated them well. Nevertheless, in his professional life, there is a paucity of evidence that Lenin practiced a great deal of human resource leadership behavior.

The Symbolic Frame

In the symbolic frame, the organization is seen as a stage, a theater in which every actor plays certain roles, and the symbolic leader attempts to communicate the right impressions to the right audiences. As with many of his dictator counterparts, Vladimir Lenin was adept at the effective use of the symbolic frame. Lenin's austere personality and inadequacies as a public speaker were more than compensated for by his considerable ability as an intellectual and author. He was a member of the literati, a man of the printed word, a ardent reader and an excellent writer. His many books and publications were the primary vehicle through which he expressed symbolic leadership behavior.

Lenin's most revered book as a young man was *Uncle Tom's Cabin*. Its focus on human rights and racial equality appealed to him. Thus Harriet Beecher Stowe was among his early influences, even predating that of Karl Marx, and promulgating his ideals symbolically through the written word became his mantra.

Another of Lenin's early influences was Nikolai Chernyshevski, a revolutionary agrarian socialist. He demanded a democratic political system based upon universal suffrage elections. He advocated a classless society and depicted the imperial monarchies as mostly barbaric, hypocritical, and outdated. Lenin adopted these ideals and often promulgated them through symbolic leadership behavior.

Lenin was attracted to Chernyshevski emotionally as well as rationally, affected by the heroic example of a man who endured imprisonment in Siberia for the sake of his political ideals. Lenin even carried a photo of Chernyshevski in his wallet. Thus, when Lenin was arrested and served time in jail, he looked upon the experience as symbolically honoring his hero.

By the early 1900s, Marxism had become Lenin's preoccupation. It so dominated his life that he began to translate *The Communist Manifesto* into Russian. As students, he and his companions wanted to change the world for the benefit of the lower social classes. However, Lenin and his followers rejected concepts such as conscience, compassion, and charity. He perceived the mercantile middle class as parasites on society and he expressed these views symbolically in his book *The State and Revolution*.

Lenin's book, *The Development of Capitalism in Russia*, demonstrated that Russia was already a capitalist country and as such, should not be ruled by a monarchy. He claimed that a capitalist country needed political democ-

racy and a guarantee of human rights. Ultimately, he argued, after the monarchy had been overthrown for democracy and capitalism, democracy and
capitalism would then be overthrown by Marxist socialism.

In another display of symbolic behavior, his book *What Is to Be Done?*
thrust him further into the limelight. It ultimately led to the October Revolution of 1917 and became a political classic. In it he called for a disciplined
and centralized party that would persuade the working class, but not the
peasants, to lead the revolution against the czars.

Quick to exploit an opportunity to identify himself with a dramatic and
symbolic event, on January 9, 1905, known as Bloody Sunday, when demon-
strators in a peaceful anti-czarist march in St. Petersburg were fired upon by
the army, Lenin used the incident to signify the beginning of the symbolic
downfall of the throne of the once great czars.

After being forced to spend ten years abroad in exile in Finland, Lenin
made his triumphant and symbolic return to Russia to take charge of the
Bolshevik Revolution. As his train arrived at the station, Lenin made certain
that when he stepped down from the train platform he would have a throng of
the disciples and the press waiting for him. In his opening speech he declared
in typically dramatic fashion that he was leading not just a Russian revolution but a "world socialist revolution" (Service 2000, 261).

As mentioned earlier, Lenin was not a brilliant orator, but his countenance conveyed the impression of passion and willpower and that he was a
man of the people, one with the workers. In typical symbolic frame mode, he
cultivated and promoted that image.

Again in symbolic terms, in the October Revolution of 1917, Lenin declared, "Comrades! The workers' and peasants' revolution, which the
Bolsheviks have all this time been talking about the need for, has been
accomplished" (Service 2000, 313). Films were made of the event, novels
written, songs sung, and even ballets performed. The familiar image of Lenin
with his fist raised, mouth tensed, and bearded chin was seen everywhere.

Despite writing about the incompatibility of democracy and dictatorship,
he could not wait to impose absolute authority and would let nothing get in
his way. Coercion was used instead of persuasion. He sanctioned violence,
including outright terrorism. The quote with which we began this chapter
was a symbolic indication of Lenin's true beliefs: "We must put down the
resistance with such brutality that they will not forget it for several decades.
The greater the number of representatives of the reactionary clergy and reactionary bourgeoisie we succeed in executing the better" (Service 2000, 321).

Even in death, his flair for the dramatic was evident. The Lenin Mausole-
um was to be favorably compared to that of the ancient pharaohs. However,
the Soviets did the Egyptians one better. A giant statue and picture of Lenin
were to be visible to all visitors to Red Square. Simultaneously, Lenin's
writings acquired the status of the Bible. An Institute of the Brain was estab-

lished in his honor; thirty thousand slices of his cerebral tissue were collected so that research might be done on the secrets of his great genius. Of course, all of this changed with the dissolution of the Soviet Union, but not until then.

The Political Frame

Leaders operating out of the political frame clarify what they want and what they can get. Political leaders are realists above all. They never let what they want cloud their judgment about what is possible. They assess the distribution of power and interests. Along with the symbolic and structural frames, the political frame was among Lenin's strongest. We saw earlier that Lenin could be somewhat inflexible in the application of his leadership behavior. However, we also saw that even though he remained steadfast to certain understandings, he was a man who saw the advantage of temporary and partial compromise. He modified his policies when his power was threatened. Thus Lenin was a political animal and was not beyond exploiting people and events to his own advantage. By his own admission, he was a devotee of Machiavelli.

For example, even though the working class was his primary focus, Lenin altered his plan and utilized political frame leadership behavior to also attract the peasants by campaigning for the restoration of some of the land they had lost under the 1861 Emancipation Edict. He was keenly aware of the fact that 85 percent of the Russian population were peasants.

Lenin was adept in the use of political behavior in making friends and influencing people. When he decided that a friendly relationship with Alexander Bogdanov, a brilliant young Marxist writer, was necessary if he was to have access to the money and personal support he would need in order to resurrect his party career, he befriended him, even though Bogdanov could have been an ideological threat to him.

As with most leaders operating out of the political frame, he enjoyed and relished power and yearned to keep his party in the ascendancy. But he wanted power with a purpose and that purpose was worldwide communism. For example, in 1917 while his party received money from Germany, he did not regard himself as a sympathizer with the German cause of world domination any more than the Germans felt that they had bought into communism. Each side was exhibiting political leadership behavior, confident that it had outmaneuvered the other.

In another display of political frame behavior, once World War I was over Lenin took the opportunity to invade the western boarder of Russia. The Red Army gained a number of victories and Lenin was able to form independent

Soviets in Estonia, Lithuania, Belorussia, Latvia, and the Ukraine. Of course, the alleged independence was only a facade. In time, those countries became Soviet satellites, solidly under Moscow's control.

Lenin said to his aides, "Let us, the Great Russians, display caution, patience, etc., and gradually we'll get back into our hands all these Ukrainians, Latvians . . ." (Service 2000, 403). In true political frame fashion, he pretended that the Ukrainian Soviet Republic was truly independent of Russia. Of course, in reality the Ukrainian government would remain strictly under the control of the Soviet Union.

In Lenin's view, extreme circumstances called for desperate measures. And desperate measures usually involved political leadership behavior. Toward the end of his life, no longer having an ally in Joseph Stalin, Lenin turned to the very person against whom he had formed the alliance with Stalin, namely Leon Trotsky. Since Trotsky supported the state foreign trade monopoly that Stalin opposed, Lenin and Trotsky again became bed fellows.

Once Trotsky threw his support to him, Lenin returned the favor and spoke on Trotsky's behalf.

> Comrade Stalin, having become General Secretary, has concentrated unlimited power in his hands, and I am not convinced that he will always manage to use this power with sufficient care. On the other hand, comrade Trotsky, as is shown by his struggle against the Central Committee in connection with the People's Commissariat of the Means of Communication, is characterized not only by outstanding talents. To be sure, he is personally the most capable person in the present Central Committee.

However, despite this display of political leadership behavior, Lenin was unable to prevent Joseph Stalin from succeeding him as leader of the Soviet Union (Service 2000).

The Moral Fame

The moral frame is my own contribution to situational leadership theory. In my view, the moral frame completes situational leadership theory. Without it, leaders could just as easily use their leadership skills for promoting evil as for promoting good. Leaders operating out of the moral frame are concerned about their obligations and responsibilities to their followers. Moral frame leaders use some type of moral compass to direct their behavior. They practice what has been described as servant leadership and are concerned with those individuals and groups that are marginalized in their organizations and in society. In short, they are concerned about equality, fairness, and social justice.

Vladimir Lenin is typical of a leader who fails to operate out of the moral frame of leadership. The human atrocities that occurred during and after his regime are a direct result of his abhorrence of God and religion and their accompanying moral and ethical codes. Much of the violence and denial of human rights that occurred during the atheistic communist regimes could have been prevented if the leaders were filtering their behavior through a moral or ethical lens. Even if their moral compass had been that of a secular humanist, many of the atrocities would not have taken place. Vladimir Lenin is an example of a great leader who was not a good leader—defining the word *good* in the moral/ethical sense. The opening quote in this chapter gives evidence of Lenin's disregard for moral philosophy. Suffice it to say, Lenin had little time for moral frame leadership behavior (Service 2000).

Conclusion

There is no question that Vladimir Lenin was one of the greatest leaders in history. He had a worldwide impact that still exists today, although the spread of communism appears to be on the decline. There is also no question that Lenin, whether consciously or not, practiced situational leadership theory. We saw how he selectively used leadership behavior from the various frames, with the possible exception of the moral frame. He operated out of the structural frame in carefully planning the Russian Revolution well before it took place. Although not one of his strongest frames, to say the least, he did show evidence of acting out of the human resource frame on occasion.

The symbolic and political frames were his forte. He practiced symbolic leadership in building his image as a revolutionary and agent of social and political change by his prolific publications, including the *April Theses*, *The Development of Capitalism in Russia*, *What Is to Be Done?* and *The State and Revolution*. In these and other writings, he established the need and outlined his plans for a worldwide communist revolution. We then saw how he used political frame leadership behavior to further his plans and finally implement and sustain the Bolshevik Revolution.

So, by most traditional standards, Lenin would be considered to be among the great leaders in world history. Both *Life* and *Time* magazines named him one of the one hundred most influential people of the second millennium. Although he is acknowledged to have been a great leader, the question arises as to whether he was a *good* leader, in the moral/ethical sense of the term. We pointed out earlier that there is a dearth of evidence of him operating out of the moral frame. As a result, like Adolf Hitler and Mao Zedong, Lenin does not meet the definition of a complete and heroic leader. He failed to filter his behavior through a moral lens and as a result a number of human atrocities occurred during his tenure. In examining Lenin's leadership behavior, the clear message for leaders and aspiring leaders is the need to engage oneself in all five leadership frames, including the moral frame, if one wishes to be a complete and maximally effective leader.

Chapter Four

Roosevelt v. Hitler

I. THEODORE ROOSEVELT

Look what we've got! That damn cowboy is president of the United States.

—Mark Hanna

Background

Theodore Roosevelt was born in 1858 in New York City and was the twenty-sixth president of the United States. If ever there was a president who embodied the characteristics of our national identity, especially in the early 1900s, it was Theodore Roosevelt.

Roosevelt was a frail and asthmatic child but never allowed his physical shortcomings to affect him. He was a brilliant scholar, graduating Phi Beta Kappa from Harvard and obtaining a doctorate in jurisprudence at Columbia Law School.

A larger-than-life leader, Roosevelt was only twenty-three when he was elected to the New York state assembly and twenty-six when appointed chairman of the New York State delegation to the Republican National convention in 1884. In that same year, however, tragedy struck, and his beloved wife, Alice, died only two days after giving birth. Retreating to his ranch in the Dakota Territory, he found comfort in working as a cowboy and taking on the duties of the deputy sheriff.

Roosevelt returned to the East Coast in 1889 and served as civil service commissioner under President Benjamin Harrison. From there he moved to New York City as a very hands-on police commissioner. In 1897 President McKinley appointed him assistant secretary of the navy, and as relations with Spain worsened, Roosevelt prepared for war by recruiting cowboys and former college athletes for the First United States Volunteer Cavalry Regiment, known in history as the Rough Riders. He subsequently etched his name in American military history by leading the Rough Riders on the victorious charge up San Juan Hill.

After the Spanish-American War, Roosevelt was elected governor of New York. Conservative Republicans, concerned about his gaining the presidential nomination, nominated him for what they hoped to be a dead-end job as McKinley's vice president. This strategy failed, however, when McKinley was assassinated and, at forty-three, Roosevelt became the youngest U.S. president in American history.

As president, Roosevelt became known for his trust-busting, but when a United Mine Workers strike promised to drag on indefinitely, he declared a national emergency and forced the mine owners to submit to mediation, becoming the first president to intervene in a labor dispute. He also established the first Department of Commerce and Labor, and expanded the military in keeping with his celebrated motto, "Speak softly and carry a big stick."

In his second term, he endorsed the Pure Food and Drug Act as well as the Elkins Act aimed at ending railroad corruption. He doubled the number of national parks and increased America's forest reserve by 150 million acres. In addition, he negotiated the purchase of Panama, which led the way for the construction of the Panama Canal. He also won the Nobel Peace Prize. Theodore Roosevelt is consistently rated by historians as one of the most effective U.S. presidents (Aronson 1997; Auchincloss 2001; Felzenberg 2008; Taranto and Leo 2004).

The Structural Frame

Structural frame leaders seek to develop a new model of the relationship of structure, strategy, and environment for their organizations. Strategic planning, extensive preparation and effecting change are priorities for them. We will find that Theodore Roosevelt was strong in all five leadership frames, including the structural frame. Theodore Roosevelt's political career began when President McKinley appointed him assistant secretary of the navy under John Long, an easygoing gentleman who was delighted to let his more aggressive and industrious assistant handle most of the job. Showing his structural leadership tendencies, Roosevelt immediately got to work to increase the number of U.S. warships and made the existing ones more efficient. He gloried in the fact that America's deteriorating relations with Spain over Cuba would present him with the opportunity to prove U.S. superiority at sea in both oceans by sinking the Spanish fleet.

During one of Long's frequent absences, Roosevelt took it upon himself to cable Commodore George Dewey to mobilize his fleet in case of war. Long was far from thrilled by Roosevelt's premature action, but it eventually facilitated Dewey's dramatic victory over the Spanish in Manila Bay.

Roosevelt's strong structural leanings helped enable him to accomplish a great deal as president. His major legislative accomplishments during his two terms of office can be summed up as these: The Elkins' Law prohibiting the railroads' practice of granting rebates to favored customers like John D. Rockefeller; the creation of the Department of Commerce and Labor with its Bureau of Corporations, which grew to regulate every business that crossed state lines; the Hepburn Bill, which gave government the power to regulate railroad rates; the Pure Food and Meat Inspection Laws, which remedied some of the abuses of the meatpacking industry, as exposed by Upton Sinclair's novel *The Jungle*; and the Employers' Liability and Safety Appliance Laws, which limited the working hours of children and other employees.

Roosevelt further displayed his structural frame tendencies during the 1902 United Mine Workers strike. The strike shut down the anthracite coals mines in West Virginia and Pennsylvania. Roosevelt announced that if an accord was not reached, federal troops would take over the mines and run them as a receivership. The operators reluctantly agreed to binding arbitration, but without a union member on the panel. This time Roosevelt used political leadership behavior along with structural behavior and stepped in and broke the impasse by suggesting a union man who was also a well-known sociologist.

Over time, Roosevelt's structural frame reputation preceded him. In his negotiations with Panama over the building of the canal, he wanted to take advantage of the spirit of cooperation of the Panamanian government, so he immediately granted them diplomatic recognition, but without congressional approval. Referring to his having recognized the new government of Panama without waiting for Congress to be in session, he stated in typical structural frame fashion: "I took the Canal Zone and let Congress debate" (Auchincloss 2001, 58).

Roosevelt utilized structural leadership behavior well before he became president. As undersecretary of the navy he improved the navy status from fifth in the world in size to second only to Great Britain. "I do believe there is enough chance of war with Japan to make it extremely wise to secure against it by building a navy as to forbid Japan's hope of success," he declared (Auchincloss 2001, 70).

In yet another display of structural behavior, Europe and Latin American learned that Roosevelt's interpretation of the Monroe Doctrine would not permit any European attempt to collect debts in the North America by force.

So when the government of Santo Domingo tumbled, Roosevelt assumed virtual control of the republic and made sure that they continued to pay their foreign debts.

After post-presidency ideological differences occurred between Roosevelt and Howard Taft, Roosevelt once again used structural frame behavior and decided to run on the Progressive ticket. He did so mostly because he feared that several reforms that he had been able to institute might be voided by his conservative successor.

Roosevelt's structural tendencies were always evident. After all, he had in turn been a forceful young reformer in the New York State Assembly; a frontier rancher; a Progressive U.S. Civil Service commissioner; a crusading police commissioner; an aggressive assistant secretary of the navy who assertively lobbied for war with Spain; a Rough Rider in the same war; governor of New York; and vice president of the United States even before becoming the Progressive twenty-sixth president of the United States.

The Human Resource Frame

Human resource leaders believe in people and communicate that belief. They are passionate about productivity through people. Although Theodore Roosevelt is depicted by some historians as being egocentric, there is much evidence that he was concerned with the welfare of others as much as he was about his own. First of all, he was a devoted father and never missed some sort of interaction with his offspring every evening, even on the busiest days. But beyond his love for his family was his real affection for humankind. For example, early in his first term Roosevelt invited Booker T. Washington to dine at the White House, which aroused front-page protests in newspapers throughout the South. "As things have turned out I am very glad that I asked him," he said, " for the clamor aroused by the act makes me feel as if the act was necessary" (Auchincloss 2001, 63).

Roosevelt had his deficiencies and could be impetuous and egotistical. He often portrayed his opponents as cowards or scoundrels. But he was honest, courageous, persistent, just, and visionary. He believed that the moral obligations that applied to individuals applied to government as well. These convictions prompted him to operate out of the human resource frame of leadership behavior quite often.

The Symbolic Frame

In the symbolic frame, the organization is seen as a stage, a theater in which every actor plays certain roles and the symbolic leader attempts to communicate the right impressions to the right audiences. One could argue that this was Theodore Roosevelt's strongest frame. Theodore Roosevelt is one of the few presidents whose life, because of his frequent use of symbolic behavior, is even more important historically than his political accomplishments. What survives and endures even more than his trust-busting, or his building of the Panama Canal, or his negotiation of the Russo-Japanese War peace treaty, which were all accomplished via structural frame and political leadership behavior, is the symbolic vision of the intrepid Rough Rider who charged up San Juan Hill, the fearless opponent of political vice and corruption, and the wielder of the "big stick" who sent his Great White Fleet around the globe to impress and intimidate our enemies with America's might.

Roosevelt acted in a symbolic leadership way when he promptly resigned his post as assistant secretary of the Navy and joined the fighting forces leading to his great victory commanding his "Rough Riders" in the Battle of San Juan Hill during the Spanish American War. He was nominated for the Medal of Honor for his efforts, but lack of political frame behavior in criticizing the readiness level of the army earned him enough enemies in the military to block his receiving the award. It was only in 2001 that Congress posthumously awarded him the Medal of Honor.

Roosevelt also used symbolic frame behavior in his very creative coining of terms. For example, during his trust-busting days he referred to the tycoons with whom he was dealing as the "malefactors of great wealth." When he declared his candidacy for president in 1912, he used the occasion to coin the phrase, "My hat is in the ring." And, during his second term, he coined his new socially progressive principles as his "Square Deal." His cousin "borrowed" the term and altered it slightly twenty-five years later with FDR's "New Deal" (Auchincloss 2001, 62).

Symbolic leadership behavior was once again used by Roosevelt during his second term when he sent his newly constructed "Great White Fleet" around the world in a show of force to the world powers that the United States was in a position to respect its treaties and back up its word. And again in 1906, he used symbolic behavior by donating his prize money to charity when he received the Nobel Peace Prize for helping to negotiate a peace treaty between Russia and Japan after their conflict.

Roosevelt utilized symbolic leadership behavior when he reluctantly chaired a conference on world peace where thirteen nations assembled in Spain in 1906 to discuss the dispute among England, France, and Germany over Morocco. The Kaiser had asked Roosevelt to chair the session, and he reluctantly did so in the interest of world peace. He did not want the United States too involved with European affairs in that he foresaw the coming of World War I. The eight years of peace that followed the treaty were at least something, and the world owed them at least in part to Theodore Roosevelt.

In another symbolic frame move, almost immediately after taking office as president Roosevelt ceremoniously appointed Gifford Pinchot, the great forest conservationist, to head up his conservation reform efforts. Pinchot, throughout Roosevelt's two terms, had a significant influence on anything even remotely related to conservation. He never obtained cabinet status, but he had constant access to the president, who always listened to him. Despite strong opposition, Roosevelt increased the national forests from 42 to 172 million acres and created 51 wildlife preserves.

In 1912 Roosevelt was shot in the chest by a would-be assassin while making a speech in Milwaukee. In a typical display of symbolic behavior, he said: "Friends, I shall ask you to be as quiet as possible. I don't know whether you fully understand that I have been shot; but it takes more than a bullet to kill a bull moose" (Auchincloss 2001, 122). It was another dramatic performance in a lifetime of dramatic performances. Later in the twentieth century another wounded president took a page out of Roosevelt's book and told his wife, Nancy, that he "forgot to duck."

Being the symbolic frame leader that he was, he firmly believed that one of his great misfortunes was not having a war during his presidency, during which he could act upon his principles and beliefs. His most depressing time was after the outbreak of WWI, which he viewed as a perfect historical occasion for his kind of heroic and symbolic leadership. He strenuously opposed Woodrow Wilson's cautionary approach every step of the way.

In his symbolic view of the world, it was Roosevelt who should have been the hero of the play. It was a role for the Rough Rider, for the man who built the Panama Canal, who had won the Nobel Peace Prize, policed the streets of New York, and risked his life in facing lions in the jungles of Africa, and not for the Princeton University scholar who had never fired a shot in his life.

In one last grasp for glory, Roosevelt volunteered to raise a company of fighting men similar to the Rough Riders and go to France to fight in WWI. Of course, President Wilson denied the request. In voicing his discouragement to the president's aid, Colonel House, Roosevelt said: "After all, I'm only asking to be allowed to die." House is supposed to have replied: "Oh? Did you make that quite clear to the President?" (Auchincloss 2001, 132).

The Political Frame

Leaders operating out of the political frame clarify what they want and what they can get. Political leaders are realists above all. They never let what they want cloud their judgment about what is possible. They assess the distribution of power and interests. Theodore Roosevelt was a master at engaging in political frame leadership behavior. He was a political realist who had the wisdom to know that only through astute compromise during the legislative process and at other times could he hope to see enacted even a fraction of the programs that he deemed essential to the welfare and progress of the nation.

At the 1884 Republican convention, for example, both Roosevelt and his lifelong friend, Henry Cabot Lodge, were against the nomination of the corrupt James G. Blaine as the party's presidential nominee, but despite his nomination, Roosevelt remained in the Republican Party. He adhered to Disraeli's famous political truism: "Damn your principle! Stick to your party" (Auchincloss 2001, 19). This came to be a wise political frame decision on Roosevelt's part when he was named the party's nominee for vice president in 1900.

Roosevelt had second thoughts about taking the dead-end job of vice president under William McKinley, but out of party loyalty he took it. As fate would have it, when McKinley was assassinated, Roosevelt became president. Mark Hanna, who was instrumental in convincing the party to offer him the vice presidency to "get him out of the way," wailed: "Look what we've got! That damned cowboy is president of the United States" (Auchincloss 2001, 38).

In a particularly radical use of political frame leadership behavior, Roosevelt encouraged a civil war in Panama. When his patience ran out over negotiating with Columbia regarding the rights to build the Panama Canal, Roosevelt supported an insurgency group of Panamanians who would eventually defeat Columbia. Roosevelt then purchased the Canal Zone from the new regime.

In the Russo-Japanese War of 1904, Roosevelt favored Japan but did not want them to gain too sweeping a victory for fear that their new found power would someday endanger the United States, which of course it did. He decided to use political frame behavior, using his considerable standing in the international community, while influencing the two sides to settle on a pact that did not favor either party, for which he received the Nobel Peace Prize.

Toward the end of Roosevelt's second term the opposition to his conservation policies, which had long festered, came to a head. A bill was introduced in Congress to deprive the president of his power to create national forests in various western states. Knowing it was sure to pass, Roosevelt indulged in blatantly political behavior and asked Pinchot to identify areas that he could reserve as forestland while he still had the power to do so. Pinchot found thirty-three such areas, and the president added sixteen million acres to forestland—much to the chagrin of the lumber lobby.

The Moral Frame

The moral frame is my own contribution to situational leadership theory. In my view, the moral frame completes situational leadership theory. Without it, leaders could just as easily use their leadership skills for promoting evil as for promoting good. Leaders operating out of the moral frame are concerned about their obligations and responsibilities to their followers. Moral frame

leaders use some type of moral compass to direct their behavior. They practice what has been described as servant leadership and are concerned with
those individuals and groups that are marginalized in their organizations and
in society. In short, they are concerned about equality, fairness and social
justice.

There are many instances in Theodore Roosevelt's life that indicate that
he possessed a strong sense of morality. For example, the NAACP declared
"that he (Roosevelt) was our friend proves the justice of our cause, for
Roosevelt never championed a cause that was not in essence right: (Felzenberg 2008, 28). Roosevelt envisioned his role as head of the federal government as that of a disinterested moral "umpire," mediating disputes between
two organized minorities, the Republicans and the Democrats, on behalf of
the majority.

In another display of moral frame behavior earlier in his life, in considering whether to marry Edith after his first wife died, he suffered greatly from
his sense of guilt in betraying the memory of Alice. This attitude was characteristic of Roosevelt, who tended to see life in terms of good and evil.

As a deeply moral man, Roosevelt was taken up in a lifelong and enthusiastic fight against lawbreakers; he was a policeman at heart, which was
obviously why he had done so well as a police commissioner in New York.
And as a trust-buster, he was not so much against big corporations, but their
ambivalence toward the law in order to gain a competitive advantage.

With Roosevelt the nature of almost every great decision was a moral
one. As pointed out above, he was not against big businesses per se, he was
just against the ones that practiced selfish greed under the leadership of men
like Jay Gould and J. P. Morgan. To Roosevelt there were good trusts and
bad trusts. "Of all forms of tyranny," he posited, "the least attractive and
most vulgar is the tyranny of mere wealth" (Auchincloss 2001, 50). He felt
so strongly that he instructed his attorney general, Philander Knox, to prose-
cute Northern Securities for restraint of trade without ever consulting his
cabinet, let alone Congress.

Because of his strong moral frame leanings, Roosevelt had never been
much drawn to the study of law. He had always been repelled by the legal
doctrine of caveat emptor (buyer beware), which flew in the face of what he
referred to as "a gentleman's agreement."

Roosevelt professed a deep faith in America's moral virtues that inspired
Americans to believe they have a sacred duty to impart their values to others
for the sake of humanity. "We cannot sit huddled within our own borders,"
he warned, "and avow ourselves merely an assemblage of well-to-do huck-
sters who care nothing for what happens beyond" (Taranto and Leo 2004,
127).

Situational Leadership Analysis

Situational models of leadership differ from earlier trait and behavioral models in asserting that no single way of leading works in all situations. Rather, appropriate behavior depends on the circumstances at a given time. Effective managers diagnose the situation, identify the leadership style or behavior that will be most effective, and then determine whether they can implement the required style.

As we have seen, Theodore Roosevelt was very much the situational leader and was active in all five leadership frames. We saw how he operated out of the structural frame in gaining the reputation of "speaking softly but carrying a big stick." His image as the Rough Rider and trustbuster was garnered from his effective use of symbolic leadership behavior.

Roosevelt's well-known concern for the "little guy" is evidence of his use of human resource behavior. His peace negotiations that led to the end of the Russo-Japanese War were but one indication of his facility in utilizing political frame leadership behavior. And, his social justice concerns lead us to believe that his unique version of a moral compass guided his leadership behavior.

Theodore Roosevelt's ranking as one of the most effective U.S. presidents in history is well earned. His leadership style reflected a balance both among and within the five leadership frames. He has left as part of his legacy a roadmap for leaders and aspiring leaders, which if followed, could be a pragmatic and useful guide in our journey to become the best leaders we can be.

Leadership Implications and Conclusion

Theodore Roosevelt used structural leadership behavior in liberally interpreting the constitutional authority of the Oval Office to address the imbalance of power between the executive and legislative branches that had tilted toward Congress since the end of the Civil War. He challenged party bosses who valued political privileges more than fair and just government. He extracted reforms from legislators whose only thought was to whom they would award patronage.

He used human resource behavior and fought for the common person by calling for the elimination of corporate campaign contributions because he knew they influenced elected officials to favor the wealthy few at the expense of the less influential many. His concern for humanity motivated him to investigate the notoriously unsanitary meatpacking industry, and with the enactment of the Pure Food and Drug Act, put public health before industry profits.

But he was not a radical reformer. He used political leadership behavior not to destroy big business, but to save it from its own excesses. So he imposed reasonable and incremental regulations on commerce. Neither was he a zealot who disdained the compromises essential to lawmaking. He wanted to get things done, and through the use of astute political frame behavior, he did.

Many leaders in his age and ours tend to be preoccupied with extending their own power. Self-aggrandizement is part of human nature, and Roosevelt had his share. He gave up the presidency at the end of his second term, but wanted it back four years later for personal as well as public reasons. Yet the very thought that he would seek high office for self-purposes rather than to serve others was deeply repugnant to him.

However much he craved the spotlight, however grand his personal ambitions, he could not satisfy himself unless his actions had a moral purpose. And that deeply personal and moral sense of public service made him the man many still admire—and a man whose effective situational leadership behavior would be worth emulating in our own personal and professional lives (Taranto and Leo 2004).

II. ADOLF HITLER

Today Germany, Tomorrow the World.

—A popular Nazi campaign slogan

Background

Adolf Hitler was born in 1889 in Austria. He left school at an early age to become an artist. In 1909, after his mother had died, he moved to Vienna to earn a better living and pursue his interest in art. Within a year, however, he was living in homeless shelters and eating at soup kitchens.

In 1913, Hitler, still not able to gain consistent employment, moved to Munich, Germany. At the outbreak of the World War I, in 1914, he volunteered for service in the German Army and fought bravely in the war and was promoted to corporal and decorated with both the Iron Cross Second Class and First Class.

After the war, he became involved in German politics and was able to hone his oratory skills and become a member of the German Workers Party. Given responsibility for publicity and propaganda, Hitler succeeded in attracting large audiences with his often fiery oratory. At one such meeting he presented a twenty-five-point program of ideas which were to be the basis of the party's campaign platform. The name of the party was then changed to the National Socialist German Workers Party (Nazi Party).

Hitler continued to expand his influence in the party and began to form a private group of thugs which he used to enforce Nazi Party protocols. This group subsequently became popularly known as Hitler's Brownshirts. During the summer of 1920, Hitler also chose the swastika as the Nazi Party emblem.

On November 8, 1923, Hitler led an attempt to take over the local Bavarian government in Munich in an action that became known as the Beer Hall Putsch. Hitler fled the scene and was later arrested and charged with treason. After his trial he was sentenced to five years in prison, during which he wrote the book *Mein Kampf* (My Struggle).

The Great Depression hit Germany especially hard. These desperate conditions were helpful to Hitler and his Nazi Party in gaining power, and by 1933 the Nazi Party became the largest in the Reichstag. At that point, Hitler demanded that he be made chancellor but was offered only the position of vice-chancellor in a coalition government, which he refused. Finally on January 30, 1933, President Hindenburg, under great pressure, decided to appoint Hitler chancellor. By the end of 1933, Hitler had a law passed that made the Nazi Party the only political party in Germany. When Hindenburg died in 1934, Hitler was named both president and chancellor.

During the years following Hitler's consolidation of power he set about the Nazification of Germany. Among other things, all youth associations were abolished and reformed as a single entity known simply as the Hitler Youth. As part of the Nazification movement, the Jewish population was increasingly persecuted and ostracized from society.

Hitler and the Nazi Party pursued a foreign policy based on the goal of providing *Lebensraum* (living space) for the German people. The first significant implementation of this policy was the German invasion of Poland in 1939 which caused the British and French to declare war on Germany, leading to the outbreak of World War II.

Eventually Germany and its major allies, Italy and Japan, were defeated and by 1945 Germany was in ruins. Hitler's vision of territorial conquest and racial subjugation caused the deaths of tens of millions of people, including the systematic genocide of an estimated six million Jews in what is known as the Holocaust.

On April 30, 1945, with the Allies breathing down his neck, Hitler committed suicide, shooting himself while also swallowing a cyanide capsule (Redlich 1998).

Situational Leadership Analysis

Situational models of leadership differ from earlier trait and behavioral models in asserting that no single way of leading works in all situations. Rather, appropriate behavior depends on the circumstances at a given time. Effective managers diagnose the situation, identify the leadership style or behavior that will be most effective, and then determine whether they can implement the required style. Despite his overreliance on some frames and underreliance on others, there is much evidence to conclude that Adolf Hitler practiced situational leadership. After his failed Beer House Putsch in 1923, when he attempted to overturn the German government by force, Hitler learned the value of situational leadership. He realized that he had to bring both the German bourgeoisie and conservatives to his side. He needed—at least for the time being—an alliance with them that would require him to be flexible in his leadership behavior.

The unsuccessful putsch caused a turning point in Hitler's life. He decided to change his tactics and achieve power in Germany not through armed revolution but by convincing the masses of the German people that in their hearts they knew he was right. He realized it was time to abandon structural frame leadership behavior and embrace the human resource, symbolic, and political frames.

Another notable instance of Hitler's use of situational leadership came in 1936. That year saw him shift his emphasis from domestic to foreign matters and preparations for war. The real Hitler was being revealed. What he could not achieve by persuasion and bullying, he would acquire through military means. The military buildup would no longer be hidden. Hitler began to openly express what he had always felt in his heart, that a war to accomplish his goals was necessary. But he knew that the timing had to be right. By 1936, he believed the situation was right.

One would never accuse Adolf Hitler of being a human resource leader. However, he was situational enough to know that he could not depend exclusively on structural and political behavior to be successful. Once again, when the situation called for it, he could adjust and practice human resource and symbolic leadership behavior and be a seductive prophet to the German people. Carl Jung called him "the loudspeaker that magnified the inaudible whispers of the German soul" (Redlich 1998, 302).

The Structural Frame

Structural frame leaders seek to develop a new model of the relationship of structure, strategy, and environment for their organizations. Strategic planning, extensive preparation, and effecting change are priorities for them. It is fair to say that Hitler spent a good deal of his time operating out of the structural frame of leadership. Hitler, we are told, was a man with a rudimentary intellect devoid of scruples, an individual with no respect for God or humankind. He owed his success to two outstanding qualities: his rhetorical skills and his theatrical delivery. Despite these obvious symbolic frame strengths, however, he utilized a good deal of structural frame leadership behavior

Hitler often spoke of the primacy of mind over matter, the will over the flesh—a typical structural behavior approach. In *Mein Kampf*, he wrote about a visit to the local government offices where he was devastated by the amount of laziness, apathy, and corruption—all characteristics that he abhorred.

In contrast to what he witnessed in the government, Hitler continually displayed the characteristics of a structural frame leader. His associates agreed that he possessed an exceptionally good memory. He was able to store and retrieve a large body of knowledge, citing figures of gun calibers and ship tonnage with great accuracy.

Hitler distained formal education, but in true structural frame fashion, he was an avid reader and devoured books, pamphlets, and other reading material. And he was a great fan of the great German composer Richard Wagner—especially appreciating his military compositions. However, he had a very limited knowledge of the famous German philosophers like Schopenhauer and Nietzsche.

Being knowledgeable about military matters was of the utmost importance to Hitler. According to the generals who worked under him, as well as military historians, Hitler's knowledge of military science was impressive. In addition, Hitler was by and large perceived to have good judgment. During the long years of successful operations, Hitler made few mistakes

In an extreme use of structural behavior, any questionable lack of judgment was rationalized away. In the Borman papers, for example, Hitler offered the following explanations: (1) The putsch had not been successful because he had no choice but to act; (2) the destruction of the Czech state was not a mistake; instead he had acted too late; (3) he did not pursue the British at Dunkirk because he did not want to humiliate the British, who he hoped would join him in his fight against the Bolsheviks; (4) the attack on Russia was not a mistake because the conquest of Russian soil and mineral reserves was of the utmost importance to his ultimate goal of world domination; he blamed Stalingrad on the lack of fighting spirit in his generals; and (5) he admitted misjudgment on his declaration of war on the United States, but he lauded Japan for attacking the United States at his urging and making it divide its forces on two fronts (Redlich 1998, 296).

Hitler's goals and ideals of racial superiority led him to believe that the Germans should establish European hegemony and ultimately rule the world. This ultimate goal, and the plans to achieve it, was outlined very clearly in *Mein Kampf*. Thus he went about his pursuit of these goals in a very structural frame way. He had an elaborate and well-thought-out plan.

Hitler's economic achievements in his first years as führer, such as the abolition of unemployment, the military buildup, and the elimination of the last vestiges of the Treaty of Versailles, were just preliminary steps on the way to his real goal. His real goal was to rule the world, and because the Germans did not possess the resources necessary for their survival, they would have to obtain those resources from other nations, and if other nations were not willing to give up their resources, the Germans would acquire them through force.

Hitler pursued his goals in a very structural way—methodically, and with forethought. For example, to obtain purity of race, he had a law passed stipulating compulsory sterilization by surgical procedure for genetically ill persons. On another front, to Hitler, education and schooling meant first and foremost indoctrination in the spirit of National Socialism. He put training in physical education first and character formation second, because they were prerequisites for military training, and general education a distant third.

Although Hitler was very conservative regarding his preference for an agrarian society over an industrialized one; in sharp contrast, he advocated technical change, particularly in automotive transportation—he was responsible for the Autobahn and the Volkswagen—but also in modern city planning, protection of the environment, and even modernization of household equipment to improve the lot of the German housewife. He used structural leadership behavior to make these dreams a reality.

As part of his long-term plan to dominate the world, one of Hitler's major short-term goals was to forge an alliance among Germany, Italy, and Great Britain against Russia. A secondary goal was to undermine the relationship between Great Britain and France. Of course he was never able to fully achieve either the ultimate goal or many of the intermediate goals, but having such a systematic plan is endemic to a structural frame leader.

As is often the case when a leader practices structural frame behavior to the extreme, Hitler considered himself to be irreplaceable. "I am convinced," he declared, "of the power of my brain and decisiveness. I have the greatest experience in all questions of armament; I will not shy away from anything and will destroy anybody who is against me" (Redlich 1998, 303).

The Human Resource Frame

Human resource leaders believe in people and communicate that belief. They are passionate about productivity through people. Needless to say, this will be a very brief section because Hitler's leadership behavior was notoriously bereft of the human touch. According to Percy Schramm, an early acquaintance of Hitler's, he did have a human side, but it was often subverted by a darker side. According to Schramm, Hitler was "the friend of women, children and animals—this was one face of Hitler neither acted nor feigned, but entirely genuine. There was, however, a second face which he did not show to his table companions, though it was no less genuine" (Machtan 2001, 69).

Albert Speer, Hitler's notorious armament chief, had become an important member of the inner circle by the beginning of World War II. Speer's statement that if Hitler had been capable of having a friend, he would have been his friend is probably accurate (Redlich 1998, 188). However, there were many more instances of Hitler lacking the capacity to express human resource behavior than there were of the reverse.

Hitler's relationship with his general staff was always one of aloofness, especially when the assassination attempts increased. Apart from his relationships with his companion, Eva Braun, young people, and animals, he did not display much by way of human resource frame behavior.

Although officers as well as enlisted men described Hitler in very complimentary terms during his World War I days, he was also considered to be aloof, brooding, and restless. He read abridged editions of philosophical works and wandered around at night shooting rats, of all things.

By most accounts, Hitler was a self-aggrandizing narcissist. However, narcissism is a characteristic trait of nearly all outstanding political leaders. Hitler just took his narcissism to the extreme, which left him almost incapable of operating out of the human resource frame when it would have been appropriate to do so.

The Symbolic Frame

In the symbolic frame, the organization is seen as a stage, a theater in which every actor plays certain roles, and the symbolic leader attempts to communicate the right impressions to the right audiences. One could argue that in addition to the political frame, Hitler's skill in effectively utilizing the symbolic frame was one of his great strengths. One of the reasons that Hitler was so effective in his use of the symbolic frame was that he possessed the ability to become completely absorbed in his role of the moment and to believe in the truth of what he happened to be saying at the time. This helped him to convince others of his sincerity and successfully conceal his obsession with acquiring power and influence. Hitler cultivated a myth around himself and employed it to his own ends.

Hitler used symbolic leadership behavior in supporting his efforts toward implementing the doctrine of social Darwinism in Germany and beyond. "National Socialism," he said, "is nothing but applied biology." In *Mein Kampf*, he wrote, "It is a half measure to let incurably sick people steadily contaminate the remaining healthy ones. This is in keeping with the humanitarianism which, to avoid hurting one individual, lets a hundred others perish. The demand that defective people be prevented from propagating equally defective offspring is a demand of the clearest reason and, systematically executed, it represents the most human act of mankind" (Redlich 1998, 113). Although logically convoluted, this argument convinced many Germans of the validity of social Darwinism because of Hitler's way with symbolic leadership behavior.

Hitler also used symbolic leadership behavior to garner allegiance among the young people of Germany by establishing propagandizing youth clubs. His alternative to the educational system in Germany was the Hitler Youth, along with the League of German Girls. By 1939, an amazing seven million young people were members of these clubs.

The familiar Nazi symbols of the swastika and the salute with the cry "Heil Hitler" were but two examples of Hitler's use of the symbolic frame. Hitler copied much of the organization of the militia from the leisure organization Dopo Lovore, and the fascist greeting with the outstretched arm from Mussolini. Italians called Hitler "*Il Imitatore*" (the Imitator). The title of the leader, *Duce I Capo di Governimiento*, was translated by the Germans as *Führer* and *Reichskanzler*. Hitler admitted that there would never have been Brownshirts without there first being Blackshirts (Redlich 1998, 137).

In another display of symbolic behavior, Hitler insisted that the armistice with France be staged in the forest of Compiegne, and in the same dining car in which the Treaty of Versailles was signed in 1919.

Two additional incidents demonstrated Hitler's flair for the dramatic. In 1942, Hitler expressed to Heinrich Himmler one of his favorite comparisons, equating Jews to bacilli: "It is one of the greatest revolutions of the world. The Jew will be recognized. The same fight that Koch and Pasteur had to fight will be waged by us. Innumerable illnesses have been caused by this bacillus: the Jew," he asserted (Redlich 1998, 185). In a similar display of symbolic behavior, after an assassination attempt in 1944, Hitler took Mussolini to the wrecked room and dramatically remarked, "After today's miraculous escape, I am more convinced than ever that I am destined to bring our great task to a happy ending" (Redlich 1998, 185).

Even in defeat, Hitler managed to utilize symbolic behavior. "If fate has decreed that we should be crushed by a superior force, then let us go down with our head held high and secure in the knowledge that the honor remains without blemish," he said. He was referring to the proud stand of the Greek leader Leonidas and the three hundred Spartans who fought to the death to hold off a superior force until the Spartan army could be reinforced (Redlich 1998, 190).

Hitler's understanding of the masses and his exceptional ability to relate to them is well documented. The responses of large groups of people, in mass meetings and at the national congresses, contributed more than any other factor to his identity as a charismatic leader. At the end, Hitler lost his strength because, being sequestered, he could no longer touch the masses.

Nevertheless, Hitler was successful largely because, like the true situational leader that he was, he correctly gauged the readiness level of the German people for his message.

Two German authors, Alexander Mitscherlich and Peter Hofstatter, both believed that the Germans had an openness for such symbolic behavior. They opined that a charismatic leader need not actually be a strong leader as long as his followers believe he is strong—perception becomes reality. And, as we have seen, Hitler was expert at projecting an omniscient and confident image through the masterful application of symbolic leadership behavior (Redlich 1998).

The Political Frame

Leaders operating out of the political frame clarify what they want and what they can get. Political leaders are realists above all. They never let what they want cloud their judgment about what is possible. They assess the distribution of power and interest. As stated above, along with the symbolic frame, the political frame was Hitler's strongest. His perceptions were keen when it involved human weakness, deception, and bluffing, resulting in a basically cynical and mistrustful view of human beings. These traits made Hitler expert in the effective use of political frame leadership behavior.

In *Mein Kampf*, Hitler describes himself as fundamentally a political frame leader of the worst kind. He was a self-proclaimed Machiavellian who was concerned solely with his personal accumulation of power and was prepared to destroy his adopted country to retain it. He was not motivated by any formal ideology but was driven to acquire power for power's sake.

Hitler recognized early on in Vienna that life is not ruled by the principles of humanity but by victory and defeat. His belief was that the stronger and abler will always win. So, in 1926, he fought and won office against the radical opposition by using political frame behavior and agreeing to vote in favor of a restitution of properties to the former German princes that had been taken from them in 1918, a cause dear to the older German conservatives. Again in 1932, he knew that in order to come to power, he had to appeal to the anticommunism of the German conservatives. So he warned Hindenburg that "the Bolshevization of the masses proceeds rapidly" (Lukacs 1997, 87). He knew this was not true, but he also knew that this kind of argument would impress Hindenburg and the conservatives.

Hitler even used sports to his political advantage. His only physical workouts were expander exercises that enabled him to endure giving the familiar Nazi greeting with an outstretched arm during the endless parades. His interest in spectator sports was once again politically motivated, the most famous example being his use of the 1936 Olympics for propaganda purposes to show the world his benign leadership of a civilized country and to demonstrate Aryan superiority.

Hitler used a combination of political frame leadership behavior and symbolic behavior in pointing out that the National Socialist revolution was the most bloodless and disciplined revolution of all time. Unlike the bloody French Revolution and the American Revolution, Hitler was proud to declare that "no windows had been broken" during the German revolution (Redlich 1998, 125).

In the late 1930s when the Western democracies and Russia protested Hitler's aggressive behavior but took no punitive action, the politically minded Hitler correctly interpreted it as a sign of weakness. He had an astute sense for identifying weakness in his enemies, and in the absence of any resistance his use of political frame behavior proliferated.

Sometimes, however, his use of political frame behavior backfired. In a 1939 sarcastic speech about Franklin D. Roosevelt, Hitler neither considered nor cared that his speech might offend Roosevelt and the American people, or that it might make it easier for the American president, in spite of stubborn U.S. isolationism, to reinforce ties between the United States and Great Britain. In a similar incident, Hitler miscalculated in thinking that Great Britain and France would not honor their treaty with Poland, when in 1939 Germany invaded Poland and France and England immediately declared war on Germany.

In 1939, when the German-Polish conflict was acute, the ten-year Soviet-German nonaggression pact was signed. Hitler, the archenemy of the Bolshevists and Jews and the antifascist Stalin, made for strange bedfellows. Of course, the pact was for political purposes only (i.e., to keep Russia from interfering in Poland), and Hitler had no intention of adhering to it. According to him, "It was a pact with Satan in order to drive out the devil" (Redlich 1998, 147). Hitler used more political frame behavior when, shortly before the outbreak of World War II, he signed major treaties with Japan and later Italy. The Tripartite Pact of 1940 carved the Eastern Hemisphere into spheres of influence controlled by Germany, Italy, and Japan. Ultimately, however, his use of political frame behavior became increasingly ineffective and helped lead to Germany's final humiliation and defeat.

The Moral Frame

The moral frame is my own contribution to situational leadership theory. In my view, the moral frame completes situational leadership theory. Without it, leaders could just as easily use their leadership skills for promoting evil as for promoting good. Leaders operating out of the moral frame are concerned about their obligations and responsibilities to their followers. Moral frame

leaders use some type of moral compass to direct their behavior. They practice what has been described as servant leadership and are concerned with those individuals and groups that are marginalized in their organizations and in society. In short, they are concerned about equality, fairness, and social justice.

Adolf Hitler was the antithesis of a leader acting out of the moral frame. Both during his life and after his death, Hitler was considered by many to be the devil incarnate. At the very least, he was an evil man. Because he was almost totally devoid of any well-intentioned human resource behavior, he became amoral at best and immoral at worst. This is what can happen when an otherwise great leader fails to operate out of the moral frame. Instead, Hitler drifted into a policy of amoral radical social Darwinism. He became what German psychiatrist Oswald Bumke described as a "hysterical sociopath" (Redlich 1998, 333).

Conclusion

As we have seen, Hitler was a highly intelligent man with a large store of knowledge—much of it half-knowledge, especially in critical areas. The centerpiece of his philosophy was social Darwinism and anti-Semitism. He was a fanatic but was an effective leader for much of his life. His defense mechanisms, especially his projections, could fill a psychiatry textbook. He was fixated on the paranoid belief of a Jewish world conspiracy against Germany.

When his military and political programs failed, he became rigid and extremely vindictive. His destructiveness far exceeded his constructive programs, which made him both one of the world's greatest leaders and one of its greatest criminals. No one who knew Hitler before 1919 would have predicted an extraordinary career but then a fundamental change occurred. He discovered that he could speak dramatically and convincingly.

But it would be naive to assume that Hitler had such an impact solely because he was an effective orator. He changed Germany and the world because he had a message and carried out a program that Germany at that time wanted to hear. As with great leaders before and after him, he was able to accurately gauge the readiness level of his followers to receive his message. He promised that he would make up for Germany's defeat and humiliation by making it the most powerful nation in Europe. He vowed to create a proud, patriotic Germany, to restore the German army to its former glory, and to create full employment and economic prosperity. He came dangerously close to fulfilling his promises.

There is no question but that Hitler was an effective leader. His effective use of the structural, symbolic, and political leadership frames was exemplary. However, his deficiencies in the use of the human resource and moral frames rendered him a leader in the pursuit of evil rather than good and ultimately led to his demise. He is a tragic example of what can happen when an otherwise outstanding leader does not operate out of the moral frame and has no moral compass to direct his or her leadership behavior (Redlich 1998).

Chapter Five

Edison v. Ponzi

I. THOMAS EDISON

> If a man can write a better book, preach a better sermon, or make a better mousetrap than his neighbor, though he build his house in the woods, the world will make a beaten path to his door.
>
> —Ralph Waldo Emerson

Background

Thomas Edison was born in 1847 in Milan, Ohio. He did not have much formal education, being home-schooled by his mother, who was previously a teacher. Edison had been partially deaf since he was a youngster but became a telegraph operator as a result of saving little Jimmie Mackenzie from being hit by a derailed train. Jimmie's father, stationmaster J. U. Mackenzie, was so grateful that he hired Edison as his apprentice and taught him to be a telegraph operator. Edison's deafness was a blessing in disguise, as it helped him by blocking out the noise and prevented him from being disturbed by the other telegraph machines in the room.

This early training enabled Edison to experience a long string of inventive and entrepreneurial successes. These talents eventually led him to found General Electric and thirteen other companies. He earned his first patent in 1869 with the invention of the first electric voting machine.

In 1871, Edison married Mary Stilwell, whom he had met as an employee at one of his shops. They had three children, but Mary died at an early age in 1884. In 1886, Edison married twenty-year-old Mina Miller. They had three children and remained married until Edison's death.

The invention that made Edison famous was the phonograph machine, which he invented in 1877. His first phonograph was recorded on tinfoil around a grooved cylinder. It had poor sound quality and could only be replayed a few times. Nevertheless, the phonograph was so novel and affordable that it captivated the nation.

His most significant innovation, however, was the establishment of the first research and development laboratory. It was the first industrial complex built to ensure the continuous production of technological innovations and improvements. At this laboratory located in Menlo Park, New Jersey, Edison invented the first commercially practical incandescent light bulb.

Edison's incandescent light bulb consisted of a high-resistance light bulb in a total vacuum with a tungsten filament that would burn for hundreds of hours. Also around this same time, Edison invented and developed the carbon microphone, which was used in all telephones, along with the Bell receiver, until the 1880s. The carbon microphone was also used in radio broadcasting and public address systems through the 1920s.

Edison patented an electric distribution system in 1880, which was essential if his invention of the light bulb was to be maximally profitable. He established his Pearl Street station in New York, which in 1882 provided direct electric current to its first fifty-nine customers in lower Manhattan.

Another invention that Edison patented was the fluoroscope, or X-ray machine. Wilhelm Röntgen's screens were capable of producing only very faint images. The fundamental design of Edison's fluoroscope is still in use today. Coincidentally, Edison nearly lost his eyesight while developing the fluoroscope.

Besides his home in West Orange, New Jersey, Edison bought property in Fort Myers, Florida, and built a winter retreat and laboratory there in the 1880s. His next-door neighbor was his good friend Henry Ford. They had a symbiotic relationship, with Edison providing technological advice for Ford's automobiles, and Ford providing manufacturing advice to Edison. They remained friends until Edison's death.

Active in business right up to his passing, Edison died on October 18, 1931, in his home in West Orange at the age of eighty-four (Baldwin 1995).

Situational Leadership Analysis

Situational models of leadership differ from earlier trait and behavioral models in asserting that no single way of leading works in all situations. Rather, appropriate behavior depends on the circumstances at a given time. Effective managers diagnose the situation, identify the leadership style or behavior that will be most effective, and then determine whether they can implement the required style.

Although we will find that Thomas Edison was basically a structural leader who was constantly developing new models of the relationship of structure, strategy, and environment for his company, there is much evidence that he saw the value in practicing situational leadership and varying his leadership behavior depending on the circumstances. In addition to structural leadership behavior, he displayed human resource, symbolic, and political frame behavior when the need arose.

Early in his career, Edison separated his invention activities from his manufacturing efforts because of their different focus (i.e., situations). He was always trying to find a different and better way to be a more creative and effective inventor. Then, he continually sought the most efficient method to connect his ideas with their implementations, in conformity with his will and the production process.

In this manner, Edison was defining, delineating, and examining the dynamics of what we now refer to as R & D—research and development—the key being that he and all around him had to remain open and flexible to any emerging paradigm. Thus Edison was keenly cognizant of the need not only to utilize all of the four leadership frames described by Lee Bolman and Terrance Deal (1991), but also to seek moderation *within* each of the frames.

Edison often used the invention of the automobile as a metaphor for the need to be situational and far-sighted in responding to anything new or innovative. Although he saw the automobile as having an overall positive effect on society, almost prophetically, he declared, "Automobiles will change every detail of movement in our cities and thus present one of the biggest *problems* in the modern city" (Baldwin 1995, 373).

At that time in history, Edison held that we had only barely begun to envision the monumental impacts of the automobile. In that light, he was the first to suggest "express streets," overpasses and underpasses, and other innovations to relieve traffic congestion. He also anticipated the urban sprawl and global warming that would eventually accompany the automobile. He suggested that we never get locked into a certain paradigm. As a result of his situational thinking, Edison always seemed to have an innovative response for every question that arose (Baldwin 1995).

However, there are indications that Edison acquired his situational mindset the hard way—through unfortunate experiences. For example, while watching phonograph cylinder sales plummet by 90 percent, he stubbornly refused to allow his son to purchase a record-making company, failing to see that the situation had changed and that the phonograph record would eventually replace his phonograph cylinder. A similar instance of not being situational took place regarding Edison's failure to see the advantages of alternating current over direct current. Still, despite these rather minor lapses, Edison was an enthusiastic disciple of situational leadership theory well before it became codified by the likes of Bolman and Deal.

The Structural Frame

Structural frame leaders seek to develop a new model of the relationship of structure, strategy, and environment for their organizations. Strategic planning, extensive preparation, and effecting change are priorities for them.

As noted above, Thomas Edison could be described as the quintessential structural frame leader. He was the author of the often repeated adage that "Those who can, do, and those who can't, teach." There are many examples that show him as an industrious, passionate, and conscientious man not limited by the twenty-four-hour day and his strong preference for structural frame leadership behavior. "I was small and industrious," he wrote. "I could fill the position all right. . . . Night jobs suited me as I could have the whole day to myself. . . . I seldom reached home before 11:30 at night" (Baldwin 1995, 37).

Edison continued to utilize structural behavior in both his professional and personal lives. As a telegraph operator for Western Union in New York City when he was only nineteen years old, Edison began the faithful recording of every technological advancement that he discovered. As a result, Edison is justly known and revered for having registered more than one thousand patents in the course of his sixty-year career.

His use of structural behavior crossed over from his inventor's role to his management role. Edison was a hands-on manager. He refused to leave the telegraph office because he needed to "watch the men and give instructions" (Baldwin 1995, 50). He set very specific and oftentimes unreasonable standards for himself. "Sleep," he said, "was a scarce article" for him at the time (Baldwin 1995, 51).

Nevertheless, Edison's six-day, ten-hours-a-day work week paid off with the invention of the phonograph and incandescent light bulb. Rather than springing fully formed from the workshop of his imagination, however, the phonograph and the light bulb had been gradually developed through many hours of plain hard work. His persistence, industriousness, and other such traits are associated with a structural frame. "Nature contains certain materials which are capable of satisfying human needs," he would say, "but those materials must, with rare and minor exceptions, be won by labor, and must be fitted to human use by more labor" (Baldwin 1995, 127).

When Edison finally developed the long-lasting tungsten filament and patented the light bulb, he distinguished himself from other inventors by monopolizing the production of the dynamos that generated the electricity and the wiring that carried the electricity to his light bulbs. The Edison Electric Light Company (later General Electric) was organized "to own, manufacture, operate and license the use of various apparatus used in producing light, heat, or power by electricity" (Baldwin 1995, 103).

Edison even took a structural frame approach to non-work-related issues. In his later years, the Wizard of Menlo Park was asked about his thoughts on ending wars. He replied that peace conferences and the League of Nations alone would not do it. He believed that the key to ending wars was "prepara- tion." The way to make war impossible, he declared, was for nations to go on experimenting and keeping up to date with inventions, so that war would be unthinkable. In effect, he was forecasting the "atomic age," when leaders would be reluctant to wage war in light of the probable consequences. Suf- fice it to say, there were a plethora of instances in Thomas Edison's life that showed him to be a prototypical structural frame leader (Baldwin 1995).

The Human Resource Frame

Human resource leaders believe in people and communicate that belief. They are passionate about productivity through people. Although human resource leadership behavior could never be construed to be one of Thomas Edison's greatest strengths, there is evidence that he used it when the situation called for it. One needs to remember that during the post–Industrial Revolution era of the late 1800s and the early 1900s, human resource behavior was not as expected by one's followers as it is in today's age of political correctness— the *situation*, indeed, has changed. Still, Edison did not have the reputation for exploiting his employees that many of his counterparts had, the reason being that he frequently applied human resource leadership behavior when appropriate.

Edison began applying human resource behavior and becoming more collegial as his career progressed. While working for Western Union, he joined his coworkers to form the local chapter of the National Telegraphic Union (NTU). The NTU was founded to give the telegraph operators a voice in their industry and a way of addressing the many work grievances that they encountered in this unregulated era. In the process of his union organizing he was to find the love of his life, Mary Stilwell, whom he married on Christmas Day in 1871.

Edison used human resource behavior in cultivating his relationship with Charles Batchelor. Batchelor was one of Edison's first collaborators and friends and remained so for over twenty-five years. Batchelor referred en- dearingly to Edison as "The Old Man," although a number of their coworkers were older than Edison.

While, on the one hand, he maintained a classically hierarchal structure in order to efficiently make what needed to be made and maintain his authority, Edison was "compelled," as he put it, to apply a human resource dimension by democratically wandering up and down the aisles. His ubiquitous pres- ence was encouraging to the welders and die cutters bent over their wooden workbenches (Baldwin 1995, 57).

In a community atmosphere at Menlo Park, where Edison also lived, his colleagues in upper management shared houses on the property. To improve morale and encourage camaraderie, he hired a distant relative to run a boarding house on-site, where the single men would have a home away from home with a family atmosphere.

Edison also practiced human resource behavior in his personal life. Although he somewhat neglected his wife and children because of his workaholic nature, when he was with them, he showed his human touch. Marion, his daughter, loved to make surprise visits to the laboratory, which she saw as an exotic play land. There she doted on her father until he gave her a dime to buy some candy. When his second wife, Mina, made an appearance in the lab, he would conduct whimsical experiments with her.

Many of his closest colleagues were drawn to Edison because of his penchant for human resource behavior. Francis Upton, who was instrumental in the development of the light bulb, being the first to place a filament in a vacuum, was attracted to Edison by his sensitivity toward others. A typical day for Edison would include a good measure of both structural and human resource behavior. He would start at dawn, work through lunch at his rolltop desk, then go on to dinner, and then share more laughs with his crew at Delmonico's in Manhattan.

Compared to the robber barons of his generation, Edison paid his employees well. He also respected his employees, empowering them to be creative and make independent decisions. He constantly pointed out to his audiences that, "When you honor me, you are also honoring the vast army of workers, but for whom my work would have gone for nothing" (Baldwin 1995, 397).

Finally, Edison demonstrated his human resource behavior inclinations in his relationship with his lifelong friend and confidant, carmaker Henry Ford. They had mutual respect for one another. Edison honored the younger Ford for his knowledge of the production process. Likewise, Ford respected Edison for his creativity. Their friendship became so close that they deliberately purchased homes next door to one another in Fort Myers, Florida.

The Symbolic Frame

In the symbolic frame, the organization is seen as a stage, a theater in which every actor plays certain roles, and the symbolic leader attempts to communicate the right impressions to the right audiences. Thomas Edison was quite astute at creating and sustaining his positive image through the thoughtful and strategic use of symbolic leadership behavior. One of Edison's favorite quotes, and the one that we began this chapter with, was Ralph Waldo Emerson's, "If a man can write a better book, preach a better sermon, or make a better mousetrap than his neighbor, though he build his house in the woods, they will make a beaten path to his door." Although he truly believed the sentiments expressed in these words, he was not one to wait patiently for folks to come to his door (Baldwin 1995).

On the contrary, he was very proactive in promulgating his image as the Great Inventor. Even relocating his research facility to Menlo Park was symbolic in that Edison wanted to relocate from Port Huron, Michigan, where he had been bullied as a child, a place where his mother was buried, where he had spent thousands of dollars helping his aimless brother avoid bankruptcy, to the idyllic environs of New Jersey.

Edison frequently used symbolism in his advertisements for his products. For example, an ad for his electric pen, which duplicated letters, was romantically portrayed. The pen was not shown in the ad. Rather, an embracing couple was seen, surrounded by words floating overhead: "Like kissing, every succeeding impression is as good as the first, endorsed by everyone who tried it! Only a gentle pressure used" (Baldwin 1995, 71).

Edison often used symbolic behavior in coining memorable phrases. A classic Edison maxim is, "Genius is 1 percent inspiration and 99 percent perspiration." He also gave this standard advice to young people: "Don't go to college; get into a shop and work out your own salvation," echoing Benjamin Franklin's declaration to the American worker to "Keep your shop and your shop will keep you" (Baldwin 1995, 51).

In his competitive efforts to outdo Bell and other inventors, Edison offered the press an adversarial image that would become all too familiar. He projected the image of a young man so often ridiculed that it had no effect except to motivate him to want to excel even more. In effect, he portrayed himself as the unappreciated underdog.

So, because of his symbolic leadership behavior, it was "Professor" Thomas Edison, the Wizard of Menlo Park, the New Jersey Columbus, the Napoleon of Invention, that the masses were coming to see at Menlo Park, or as it came to be known, Monte Cristo's Cave. Although he would never admit it, Edison had a streak of P. T. Barnum in him.

To add to his budding reputation, Edison became a member of the National Academy of Sciences at an early age. Viewing the stars through the mighty telescope, Edison identified strongly with Galileo and his struggle to have his ideas taken seriously—just as his invention of the phonograph was considered by many to be but a popular toy. On one of his visits to the Observatory in Washington, D.C., Edison was invited to the White House by President Rutherford B. Hayes for a private phonograph session. Of course, in what had become his symbolic frame style, Edison made certain that the press was also invited.

So established had Edison's image become, that his staff at a Christmas party at Menlo Park, in the midst of the development of the light bulb, composed a tribute to their boss, set to the tune of Gilbert and Sullivan's *H.M.S. Pinafore*:

> I am the Wizard of the electric light
> And a wide-awake Wizard, too.
> I see you're rather bright and appreciate the might
> Of what I daily do.
> Quadruplex telegraph or funny phonograph,
> It's all the same to me;
> With ideas I evolve and problems that I solve
> I'm never ever stumped, you see.
> What, never?
> No, never!
> What, never?
> Well, hardly ever! (Baldwin 1995, 114)

Menlo Park, at Edison's direction, now became an electric showplace. Further demonstrating his symbolic frame tendencies, Edison transformed Menlo Park into a sort of proto-Disneyland and a symbol of his huge impact on America and the rest of the world.

Even when immersed in his work, Edison was quick to respond and never too preoccupied with research to engage in image building. In fact, he was one of the first captains of industry to hire a public relations director, John Michels, a former *New York Times* writer (Baldwin 1995).

In an era of atheistic and agnostic scientists, Edison was careful to project the image of a believer. He believed that man's intelligence came from a greater power. When asked if he believed in an intelligent Creator and personal God, Edison replied, "Certainly!" His belief in Intelligent Design was depicted in the opening scene of the MGM classic *Edison the Man*. Spencer Tracy, as Edison, is surrounded by a group of children asking questions, and with great humility he smiles and looks heavenly, saying, "That's the real Inventor!" (Baldwin 1995, 172).

Edison also used symbolic leadership behavior in his running feud with George Westinghouse over whose electric dynamo was better. Once, Westinghouse demonstrated the effectiveness of his dynamo by generating the electricity necessary to execute a criminal in the electric chair. After that, Edison referred to prisoners who were executed this way as "being Westinghoused" or having been "condemned to the Westinghouse" (Baldwin 1995, 202).

In another instance of using symbolic behavior, Edison's name was removed from the Edison General Electric Company letterhead because of corporate infighting. Even though he was still salaried and on the board of directors of General Electric, he led the public to think that the white-haired Wizard of Menlo Park was once again being taken advantage of by the black-hearted robber barons.

Another incident that added to the Edison folklore took place at his winter home in Florida. At Fort Myers, the spring training facility for the Philadelphia Athletics, Kid Gleason challenged Edison to hit his curve ball. Having missed the first pitch, Edison hit a blooper into the outfield on his second try. Gleason yelled, "Sign him up, Connie (Mack)! After missing the first curveball, he must have *invented* a way to hit the second one" (Baldwin 1995, 369).

Edison continued his inventing until he was eighty-five, during which time he created his greatest invention of all—his final persona.

The Political Frame

Leaders operating out of the political frame clarify what they want and what they can get. Political leaders are realists above all. They never let what they want cloud their judgment about what is possible. They assess the distribution of power and interests. As we shall see, Thomas Edison made frequent and intelligent use of the political frame. Even with his earliest underwriters, Edison set the tone and terms for the ways in which he needed to do business and conduct his work. The fact that he held an astounding 1,093 U.S. patents is testimony to his astute use of political behavior.

For example, in 1875, while working for Western Union, Jay Gould offered Edison the staggering sum of $30,000 for the right to his laboratory. Under some financial stains at the time, Edison believed that it was in his best interest to sign the contract, which he did. Out the door went any loyalty to Western Union.

As mentioned earlier, Alexander Graham Bell and Edison were fierce competitors. Edison found that Bell's telephone messages could only be sent a short distance. There had to be a way to make the sound travel further. If Edison could find the way, he could successfully circumvent Bell's patent. Eventually Edison found that way and, outwitting Bell, ended up with the patent for the telephone *receiver*, a version of which is used to this day. However, as was his practice in patent disputes, Edison displayed some human resource leadership behavior and reached a settlement with Bell, to the benefit of both great inventors, resulting in the United Telephone Company of Great Britain.

Edison even outwitted the unions by using political frame behavior. Edison withstood the threat of a strike, whereby all the lights in New York would have been in danger of burning out, by threatening to relocate and consolidate major manufacturing functions outside of the big cities like New York, where unionization was less likely to take place. This tactic worked, as the union capitulated.

Yet another example of Edison's savvy use of political behavior was his relationship with the great inventor Nikola Tesla. Knowing talent when he saw it, Edison moved swiftly to co-opt Tesla, who invented alternating current, and hired him at a low salary before he became famous. Even after he left Edison's employ, Edison maintained a share of his patent. As a result, Tesla became one of Edison's few critics.

And, in true political frame manner, Edison was not beyond ingratiating himself to a potential customer. At the Paris International Exhibition in 1889, seeking French business over his competitors in England, he pointed out to the French that the Eiffel Tower was a great idea. "The glory of Eiffel is in the magnitude of the conception and the nerve of its execution. I like the French," he said. "They have big conceptions. The English ought to take a leaf out of their books. What Englishmen would have this idea? What Englishmen could have conceived of the Statue of Liberty?" (Baldwin 1995, 205).

Finally, Edison's long kiln for making cement turned out to be one of his most profitable and sustained inventions. Into the 1920s, he was receiving a royalty of one cent on every barrel of cement produced by other companies through the long-kiln method. He was happy to point out to anyone who would listen that Yankee Stadium was not really the house that Ruth built. Rather, it was the house that Edison built—after all, it was 180,000 bags of his concrete.

The Moral Frame

The moral frame is my own contribution to situational leadership theory. In my view, the moral frame completes situational leadership theory. Without it, leaders could just as easily use their leadership skills for promoting evil as for promoting good. Leaders operating out of the moral frame are concerned about their obligations and responsibilities to their followers. Moral frame leaders use some type of moral compass to direct their behavior. They practice what has been described a servant leadership and are concerned with those individuals and groups that are marginalized in their organizations and in society. In short, they are concerned about equality, fairness, and social justice.

By all accounts, Thomas Edison was a thoroughly decent man. His leadership behavior is full of instances where he demonstrated an ethic of caring and a concern for the "little guy" (which ironically he considered himself to be) and the more marginalized individuals in society. He was fair to his competitors and sought to arrive at a mutually beneficial outcome to their negotiations. He treated his employees with dignity and respect, compensating them at a higher rate than most of his competitors. In general, Edison seemed to view his leadership behavior through a moral lens that was most likely ingrained in him in his youth. The available evidence indicates that Thomas Edison was as active in the moral frame as he was in the other four frames of leadership behavior (Baldwin 1995).

Conclusion

Thomas Edison's rise to fame as perhaps the most successful inventor and entrepreneur in history was no accident. He practiced situational leadership long before it became popular to do so. Although he was basically a structural frame leader, being a workaholic of major proportions, he effectively utilized the other situational leadership theory frames as required and appropriate.

We saw how Edison was ahead of his time in his application of human resource leadership behavior. He paid his employees considerably more than the competition. He respected his work force, oftentimes complimenting them to the press and crediting them for his success. He was close enough to his employees that they felt comfortable parodying him in their own rendition of *H.M.S. Pinafore*.

Edison's use of symbolic leadership behavior was also prolific. He cultivated his image as the Wizard of Menlo Park, the New Jersey Columbus, and the Napoleon of Invention. He depicted himself as the homespun Professor Edison who was continually victimized by those avaricious robber barons.

Edison also made effective use of political frame leadership behavior, especially among his major competitors like Alexander Graham Bell and Henry Westinghouse. However, he used the political frame in moderation, always trying to create a win-win situation whereby both parties benefited.

Finally, it seems obvious that Edison was also active in the moral frame. He seemed to view his behavior through the lens of the Golden Rule—do unto others as you would have them do unto you. Thus, his credibility and integrity were rarely questioned.

There is much to be learned from studying the leadership behavior of Thomas Edison. Leaders and aspiring leaders would be well served in emulating his ability to balance his leadership behavior both across and within the five leadership frames explored here. In my view, Thomas Edison is an exemplary leader in the situational leadership theory tradition.

II. CHARLES PONZI

A little dollar could start on a journey across the ocean and return home in six weeks, married and with a couple of kids.

—Charles Ponzi

Background

Charles Ponzi was born in Parma, Italy, in 1882 and attended the University of Rome but did not graduate. He arrived in Boston in 1903, learned English quite quickly and held numerous odd jobs including a job as a dishwasher. He was promoted to a position as a waiter but, in a portent of things to come, was fired for shortchanging some of his customers.

In 1907, Ponzi moved to Montreal to work as an assistant teller in the newly established Bank Zarossi, which was established to service the huge influx of Italian immigrants in Montreal, Canada. The bank offered nearly twice the going interest rate at the time and as a result grew rapidly.

But the bank eventually went bankrupt due to bad bank loans, and the owner, Luigi Zarossi, fled. Ponzi, now without a job and penniless, forged a check, and when arrested, admitted his guilt and spent three years in a prison in Quebec. After being released, he returned to the United States and got involved in a scheme smuggling Italian immigrants into the country. He spent two more years in prison for this scheme, this time in Atlanta.

While working for a local company in the months after being released, Ponzi received an envelope from a Spanish company containing an international reply coupon (IRC), something Ponzi had never seen before. He discovered loopholes in the coupon system, which if exploited, could potentially be profitable to him.

An international reply coupon is a coupon that can be exchanged for a number of postage stamps that are used as postage for a priority airmail letter to another country. Ponzi realized that he could take advantage of the different postage costs in different countries to make a profit. For example, he could buy IRCs cheaply in one country, exchange them for more expensive stamps in another, and pocket the difference.

Ponzi would ostensibly send money to agents abroad who would buy IRCs. They would then send the IRCs back to the United States where Ponzi would exchange the coupon for stamps worth more than he had spent on the coupon originally. He would then sell the stamps. The reported net profit of such a transaction could be more than 400 percent. The idea was a form of arbitrage which is not technically illegal.

Ponzi persuaded investors to back the scheme, promising them a 50 percent return in forty-five days, or a 100 percent return in ninety days. He founded a company, the Securities Exchange Company, to run the scheme.

After he repaid his initial investors, word soon spread that there was easy money to be had. In the first six months of 1920 Ponzi made $328,000, which would amount to over $4 million in today's dollars.

When financial analyst Clarence Barron was asked by the *Boston Post* to examine Ponzi's company, he found that in order for Ponzi to be making as much as he did, 160 million IRCs would have to have been in circulation. At the time there were only about 17,000 in circulation, so the numbers did not add up. This story, combined with announcements by the United States Post Office that IRCs were not being bought in bulk anywhere caused a panic and rush to redeem investment funds from Ponzi's company.

On August 12, 1920, Ponzi was arrested on financial fraud charges. Ponzi pled guilty and was imprisoned for fourteen years. He was released in 1934 and lived the rest of his life in poverty, dying in Rio de Janeiro in 1949 (Zuchoff 2005).

The Structural Frame

Structural frame leaders seek to develop a new model of the relationship of structure, strategy, and environment for their organizations. Strategic planning, extensive preparation and effecting change are priorities for them. While Charles Ponzi operated mostly out of the political and symbolic frames, he demonstrated a number of behaviors attributed to a structural leader. For example, by the time he was thirty-eight years of age, Ponzi was able to clearly and confidently explain to reporters and potential customers how he could reap a profit from a simple and unlikely medium, international reply coupons that could be redeemed for postage stamps. He could convincingly describe his company's growth from pennies to millions of dollars in seven months, and could boast of having opened branch offices up and down the East Coast.

Like most structural leaders, Ponzi's moment of success was decades in the making. The thirty-eight years that preceded July 1920 were known mostly for a number of setbacks in pursuit of riches. Nevertheless, Ponzi continued to display structural leadership behavior and those years served as the training ground for his ultimate success—albeit an illegal one.

Concerned by the expense of advertising, Ponzi realized he would be wiped out by mailing fees before he ever made a profit from his postage stamp scheme. Instead he used structural leadership behavior and started his own foreign trade publication, one whose huge circulation would allow him to get the word out and make a profit on selling advertizing space in the magazine. In his usual dramatic and exaggerated style, he had a new sign painted on his door—The Bostonian Advertising and Publishing Company—and set about launching a publication he called the *Traders' Guide*.

Once again utilizing structural frame behavior, Ponzi established his Securities Exchange Company to operationalize his foreign stamp trading scheme. Always the opportunist, his scheme could be traced to his stretches in prison and the men he had met there, his passion for stamp collecting, and his chance meeting with a foreign exchange expert. His analytical mind made it possible for him to see what no one else at that time could.

In typical structural frame style, Ponzi learned his "trade" by astutely observing a banker friend, Luigi Zarossi. Zarossi's bank and others catering to immigrants paid depositors 2 percent interest on their accounts. It was a simple system and one that banks still use. The banks invested in securities and other investments that paid at least 3 percent, then gave two percent to the depositors and kept the remainder for expenses and profits.

Zarossi, however, announced that he would pay the depositors another 3 percent as a bonus, for an unheard-of 6 percent interest on their investments. Zarossi claimed he could do this because he was just sharing the bank's earnings more fairly with his depositors than his counterparts were. The competition was depicted as typical greedy bankers. In reality Zarossi was engaging in the age-old fraud of "robbing Peter to pay Paul," and eventually his bank went bankrupt.

Ponzi used structural behavior in developing a plan to raise the money that he needed to start his stamp redemption business. He pawned four items: three diamond rings that belonged to his wife, Rose, and his own gold pocket watch. Rose, who was unconditionally devoted to her husband, gladly offered her diamond rings to him to pawn.

Ponzi was astute enough to launch his company by seeking small sums from large numbers of people. The big-money types would draw undue attention to his scheme, and almost anyone could spare ten, fifty, or a hundred dollars to invest. He correctly assumed that even if they did not grasp the details of how he could do it, or had doubts about his credentials, the possibility of huge returns on such a small investment in such a short period of time would be too tempting for most to pass up.

Soon Ponzi had sixteen branch offices in nine different towns and cities. He opened a second Boston office and then came two in New Hampshire, two in Vermont, three in Connecticut, two in Maine, three in Rhode Island and two in New Jersey.

Making use of the structural frame he developed a plan to solidify and sustain his new business over the long run. If he could gain control of a bank, it might allow him to weather any storms that came in the form of an investors' run on the withdrawal of their principal. Given enough time, he rationalized, the plan might allow him to transform his unsustainable business into something more permanent—and legitimate.

Being the structural leader that he was, Ponzi began his plan to acquire a bank with the two-pronged strategy of both buying stock in the bank and at the same time increasing his deposits. In this way, the stockholders and board of directors of Hanover Trust, the bank he eventually purchased, would need him almost as much as he needed them (Zuchoff 2005).

The Human Resource Frame

Human resource leaders believe in people and communicate that belief. They are passionate about productivity through people. Despite making victims of unsuspecting investors, Ponzi displayed a strange sort of affinity for others. In this and other ways, he was the proverbial conundrum wrapped up in an enigma. In a typical display of human resource behavior, Ponzi once said to a reporter:

> I get no pleasure out of spending money on myself, but a great deal in doing some good with it. Always I have said to myself, if I can get one million dollars, I can live with all the comfort I want for the rest of my life. If I get more than one million dollars, I will spend all over and above the one million trying to do good in the world (Zuchoff 2005, 7).

Once he reached the million dollar plateau, which he did early on, he claimed he had no need for more investors. But he declared he would continue accepting money out of the goodness of his heart, so his investors could join him and his family in savoring the finer things in life.

In another indication of his human resource tendencies, Ponzi's first act after his initial success was to redeem Rose's diamond rings. And, once he became financially solvent, he wired ten thousand lire, worth about five hundred dollars, to his mother, Imelde Ponzi, in Italy. He continued these payments until he was finally able to pay for his mother's transportation to the United States.

In an incredibly generous display of human resource behavior, Ponzi befriended a nurse at a mining company hospital at which he was working. The nurse, Pearl Gossett, was cooking a patient's meal when the gas stove blew up, leaving her with severe burns. When Ponzi heard about this caring nurse needing a skin graft to save her life, he volunteered to give fifty square inches of his own skin to help her.

It befuddled him, Ponzi said, "to think that any person could be so selfish, cowardly, as to refuse a mere inch of his own skin to save a human life" (Zuchoff 2005, 54). In all, Ponzi donated over 120 square inches of his skin to help save the nurse's life, and he spent more than three months in the hospital recovering.

While waiting to see his mother, who had finally been able to immigrate to America, Ponzi learned that the ship's steerage passengers were left tired and hungry from the long ocean crossing. Remembering his own similar experience, Ponzi handed out cash and provided sandwiches and drinks to as many of the passengers as he could.

Later in life while sitting in jail and learning that he had to have an operation for his painful ulcers that he might not live through, Ponzi indulged in yet another application of human resource behavior. He wrote a letter to his beloved Rose to be opened only upon his death. "I do hope that I may live," he wrote, "because as long as I have you, life seems sweet regardless of our present sorrows. . . . I am leaving forever, but I am bringing with me the most wonderful recollection of your wonderful self, and I am leaving you with kisses from lips which will close with your name firmly impressed upon them, and with a smile of eternal love for you" (Zuchoff 2005, 304).

The Symbolic Frame

In the symbolic frame, the organization is seen as a stage, a theater in which every actor plays certain roles and the symbolic leader attempts to communicate the right impressions to the right audiences. One could argue that the symbolic frame was one of Ponzi's strongest. In typical symbolic frame fashion, Ponzi always made the most of press coverage. He actually had the foresight to hire a publicity man, an ex-reporter named William McMasters.

The strategy bore fruit early on when Ponzi was blessed by an unexpected story on the front page of the *Boston Post* comparing the paltry 5 percent interest that banks were paying to the 50 percent in forty-five days that Ponzi was offering.

Typical of Ponzi's early investors was Fiore Bevilacqua. In a lifetime of hard work as a common laborer and a real estate investor, he had slowly amassed a small fortune of ten thousand dollars. Bevilacqua had entrusted the entire amount to Ponzi, and, as Ponzi fully expected, spent the next few weeks sharing the news with his family and friends, instantly creating new customers for the Securities Exchange Company.

Always aware of the image he presented to the public, Ponzi dressed to impress. In the summer, Ponzi typically wore a new Palm Beach suit with a silk handkerchief hanging stylishly out of his jacket pocket. A starched white collar was held in place by an expensive silk tie tacked to his shirt with a diamond stick pin. He also featured a gold-handled walking stick, similar to that favored by another showman of an earlier age, P. T. Barnum (Zuchoff 2005).

Early on in his career when he worked at Zarossi's Bank, Ponzi's engaging personality and sartorial splendor enabled him to convince customers to invest in his boss's bank in great numbers. He was especially effective with the bank's female customers, flirting and showering attention upon them.

In a very overt use of symbolic behavior, Ponzi modeled what he hoped would be desired behavior on the part of his potential clients. He took out a few notes himself, and his wife, Rose, joined him by coming by the office on its first day of operation for a visit and proudly and publically deposited her pin money of seventy dollars.

Ponzi's list of clients was impressive. In May 1920, 1,525 investors placed more than $440,000 in Ponzi's care. As Ponzi colorfully put it, they all wanted to see how "a little dollar could start on a journey across the ocean and return home in six weeks, married and with a couple of kids" (Zuchoff 2005, 134). Two months later, deposits had averaged an amazing $2.5 million a month.

In typical symbolic leadership style, Ponzi depicted his rags to riches evolution in the form of a parable. He spoke of what at first was a spectacular failure by a fellow Italian that had turned into an unparalleled success. In 1492, Columbus had started out from Spain on what he thought was the western route to China and the East Indies. On the way, he serendipitously discovered America. With characteristic self-aggrandizement, Ponzi assessed his own attributes and concluded that he was a modern-day incarnation of Christopher Columbus.

Ponzi's investors dramatically increased in number starting in the spring of 1920, when he engaged in ever greater symbolic behavior and arranged his first interview with a Boston newspaper. The story on the front page of the *Boston Traveler* was headlined "Dear Old 'GET RICH QUICK' Pops Out of Postal Guide" (Zuchoff 2005, 145). In what for him would be the magical year of 1920, his exposure in virtually all of Boston's newspapers made Ponzi the most popular, sought-after man in all of New England. People began calling Ponzi "a wizard of finance" (Zuchoff 2005, 181).

But Ponzi's use of symbolic behavior in the form of newspaper publicity backfired when his scheme was questioned by Clarence Barron, who was just beginning to establish his name in the world of finance. A headline in the *Boston Post* quoted Barron's attack on Ponzi: "Questions Motive Behind Ponzi Scheme." The subtitle added, "Barron Says Reply Coupon Plan Can Be Worked Only in Small Way" (Zuchoff 2005, 186).

Even at the moment of his ultimate demise, Ponzi engaged in symbolic behavior. Before a marshal led Ponzi out of the courtroom and off to prison, he scribbled a note on a legal pad. He passed the note to the crowd of reporters in the front row. It read, "Sic transit Gloria mundi." The scholars in the press corps duly translated it: "Thus passes worldly glory" (Zuchoff 2005, 290).

The Political Frame

Leaders operating out of the political frame clarify what they want and what they can get. Political leaders are realists above all. They never let what they want cloud their judgment about what is possible. They assess the distribution of power and interests. Being the con man that he was, along with the symbolic frame, Ponzi was most active in the political frame. Ponzi engaged in some political frame behavior when a copycat investment plan called the Old Colony Foreign Exchange Company rented space near Ponzi's Securities Exchange Company to be in a position to attract the Ponzi investor overflow. He decided to scare them into retreating from the premises, so he grabbed the telephone on his desk and loudly asked the operator to connect him with the Boston Police Department, with whom he had made many friends.

Having been supplementing the paltry salaries of the police with what amounted to bribes, Ponzi explained the situation to one of his detective friends, strongly suggesting the competition was deceiving the public. Moments later, the police arrived to conduct a surprise inspection of Old Colony.

Ponzi's years in prison had taught him a few things about the value of political frame behavior. He quickly began calculating a way to improve his meager accommodations. Pretending to be catatonic, he curled up in a corner and chewed a hole in his towel. He was placed in a straitjacket but continued to whoop and holler. It was a crude use of political frame behavior, but it worked as Ponzi was placed in the relative comforts of the prison infirmary.

Ponzi used political behavior in hiring his first salesperson. Wanting someone who would have access to and the trust of the masses, he decided upon Ettore Giberti, a popular grocer near Boston. Ponzi urged the grocer to tell his customers and friends about the Securities Exchange Company and convince them to invest in Ponzi's scheme. Giberti would be entitled to 10 percent of whatever money he collected. In his first week on the job, Gilberti collected almost two thousand dollars, a large sum of money in 1920 (Zuchoff 2005).

Ponzi used political frame behavior once again in creating imaginary characters to make his business scheme plausible. He claimed that a man named Lionello Sarti was his foreign agent who worked aboard a transatlantic liner and purchased postal coupons in Italy and other foreign countries for him. This ruse lasted for almost a year before skeptics began to question if Sarti really existed—of course, he did not.

Knowing on what side his bread was buttered, Ponzi was generous to the right people and groups. "Well," said Ponzi, "you have an excellent police force in Boston, and there are some fine men among them. I desire to make a small contribution to the fund for their relief," he enthusiastically declared. He then placed $250 on the counter, along with his business card. "This is my contribution—for the present" (Zuchoff 2005, 119). Over time, in addition to protecting Ponzi's business interests, several Boston police detectives and hundreds of rank-and-file officers would invest in the Securities Exchange Company.

When his ex-prison mate, Louis Cassullo, showed up at Ponzi's office making it clear that he wanted a piece of the action, Ponzi once again exhibited political frame leadership behavior. If word got out of his prison record, particularly the bank forgery conviction in Montreal, his reputation and financial empire would be in danger of crashing down. Under the circumstances, Ponzi saw fit to capitulate and gave Cassullo a job.

Ponzi used yet more political frame behavior by sending Cassullo on an endless number of fool's errands and wild goose chases. For example, he sent him to the wharves of New York to buy a few bottles of Ponzi's favorite after-dinner drink, Hennessy cognac, from a French ship that was in port. Secretly he hoped that Prohibition agents would catch Cassullo and get him out of his hair by putting him in prison.

Ponzi engaged in political frame behavior in making friends with his fellow Hanover Trust stockholders. Ponzi would eventually control not only his but also the votes that came with their shares. As mentioned earlier, he combined this strategy with his own deposits of over $2.7 million, becoming the bank's largest depositor, and virtually controlling the policy-making decisions of Hanover Trust. Ironically, the Hanover Trust Company, which less than a year earlier had denied him a loan for two thousand dollars, had effectively become his own personal bank.

Furniture dealer Joseph Daniels was the first to challenge Ponzi's scheme in court. Even though Ponzi had paid him his interest and returned his principal in full, Daniels had uncovered the scheme and saw a chance to extort even more money from Ponzi. In the process, Daniels's lawyer threatened to freeze Ponzi's bank accounts. If this were allowed to happen, Ponzi would not have access to the funds he might need for an eventual run on principal by his investors. Once again employing political frame behavior, Ponzi paid Daniels to go away and hedged his bet by also making his Hanover Bank deposits in other people's names.

Ponzi's greatest fear was a court injunction that would shut him down immediately, short-circuiting his plans to legitimize his businesses and to go straight. With his trademark flair, Ponzi decided to be proactive and forestall a court injunction by doing what his enemies least expected. He shut down his operations and took no more deposits, while pledging to pay in full any of his investors who wanted to redeem their certificates. Of course, he was hoping that his display of trustworthiness would preclude any such withdrawals.

He also invited the authorities to engage in a full-scale investigation of the Securities Exchange Company. He flamboyantly waved his $1.5 million certificate of deposit in the Hanover Trust Company at the press and promised that he had more than enough money to meet all his obligations.

In this high stakes poker match Ponzi was betting that his investors would remain loyal and that he would have enough money in both profits and loans from Hanover Trust to met his financial obligations if any of his clients did decide to leave him. Being the political frame leader that he was, he had high hopes in getting away with it. Unfortunately for him, he overplayed his hand.

During this time of crisis and investor doubt, Ponzi employed both political and symbolic frame behavior and established the Ponzi Foundation as a vehicle for his intended philanthropy. In his typically dramatic style, he donated $100,000 to a new orphanage, The Home for Italian Children, scheduled to open the coming weekend.

Casting himself as David in a battle against the Goliath of established bankers and business interests, Ponzi declared, "The issue now at stake is an issue between a man who wants to do all he can for the people and men who want to take as much as they can from the people without giving adequate return" (Zuchoff 2005, 233).

In one of his final uses of political frame behavior, Ponzi accepted a plea bargaining proposal and pleaded guilty in return for the decreased prison term of five years (Zuchoff 2005).

The Moral Frame

The moral frame is my own contribution to situational leadership theory. In my view, the moral frame completes situational leadership theory. Without it, leaders could just as easily use their leadership skills for promoting evil as for promoting good. Leaders operating out of the moral frame are concerned about their obligations and responsibilities to their followers. Moral frame leaders use some type of moral compass to direct their behavior. They practice what has been described a servant leadership and are concerned with those individuals and groups that are marginalized in their organizations and in society. In short, they are concerned about equality, fairness, and social justice.

Ponzi had a convoluted sense of morality. Although he operated out of the moral frame quite often, the moral lens through which he filtered his behavior was often clouded, to say the least. His basic scheme, for example, was based on the purchase of stamps in one country and the sale in another country where, because of the devaluation or inflation of the currency, they were worth more. In and of itself, this was as ethical as any other normal business transaction.

However, he never actually made the stamp purchases that he promised. Instead, he used new investors' funds to pay the interest earned by the past investors—in other words, it was a "rob Peter to pay Paul" scheme. But the more he thought about it, the more he liked it. He would effectively be working under the protection of one of the most trusted institutions in the world—the U.S. Postal Service.

Ponzi showed his inclination to avoid operating out of the moral frame much earlier in his career. While working as a teller for Zarossi's Bank, Ponzi walked into the empty office of the bank manager and found a checkbook from another bank where the company had an account. Ponzi tore a blank check from the checkbook and wrote and cashed a check for over $400. Ponzi served time in a Montreal prison for his indiscretion.

The day the grocer Ettore Giberti gave Ponzi his first fistful of money, Ponzi had to make a moral choice. The way Ponzi put it, an angel sat on one of Ponzi's shoulders and a devil sat on the other. The angel's message was to use the money to determine if Ponzi's theory about legally exploiting fluctuations in foreign currencies could be put into productive practice.

On the other hand, or should we say shoulder, the devil's approach was to follow the notorious "rob Peter to pay Paul" approach. When Ponzi's first investors came looking for their 50 percent, he would pay them with money from later investors, hoping that his earlier investors would leave their principal with him to earn even more profits. By taking the latter approach, he chose the devil's way.

Ponzi's moral philosophy can be summed up in his own words: "Environment had made me rather callous on the subject of ethics. Then, as now, nobody gave a rap for ethics. The almighty dollar was the only goal. And its possession placed a person beyond criticism for any breach of ethics incidental to the acquisition of it" (Zuchoff 2005, 98).

Situational Leadership Analysis

Situational models of leadership differ from earlier trait and behavioral models in asserting that no single way of leading works in all situations. Rather, appropriate behavior depends on the circumstances at a given time. Effective managers diagnose the situation, identify the leadership style or behavior that will be most effective, and then determine whether they can implement the required style.

There is no doubt that Charles Ponzi was a leader in the situational mold. As we have seen, Ponzi was active in all five leadership frames, albeit with considerable deficiencies in the moral frame. We saw his skillful use of the structural frame in devising his insightful scheme to legally exploit the stamp coupon foreign exchange business. We also saw his real love of the human race and his rather frequent use of the human resource frame, once donating skin grafts to a nurse friend who had suffered severe skin burns in a fire.

At first, Ponzi had been skeptical about publicity. But he soon realized that a little symbolic behavior could go a long way in ensuring success. So he became readily available to the press. The same could be said for his prolific use of political frame leadership behavior. He was, after all, a consummate con man, and as such, became an expert in manipulating people and events to his advantage.

His nemesis, however, was his failure to appropriately and consistently utilize moral frame behavior. He never developed a clear moral lens through which he could view his leadership behavior, and as a result, became forever know as the creator of the illegal and infamous "Ponzi Scheme."

Leadership Implications and Conclusion

In the end, Ponzi was a liar and a common criminal. Nevertheless, there was something almost appealing about him which made it possible to believe that he was as credulous and innocent as his victims and deceived himself as much as he did them. When New Yorkers went to the polls a few weeks after Ponzi's conviction, election officials came across the names of two write-in candidates for state treasurer: John D. Rockefeller and Charles Ponzi (Zuchoff 2005, 294).

We need look no further than a couple of years ago to see a contemporary version of the Ponzi scheme—the infamous case of Bernie Madoff, who is profiled later in this book. We also see similar incidents in every profession, including education. As a university dean I was witness to one of our directors falsifying credit card receipts to obtain cash reimbursements for books and other items that were never actually purchased. This is but one of many examples of a leader failing to operate out of the moral frame. Fortunately for all of us, these incidents remain the exception rather than the rule.

Chapter Six

Addams v. Capone

I. JANE ADDAMS

Let us have faith that right makes might, and in that faith, let us to the end dare
to do our duty as we understand it, with malice towards none, with charity for
all, with firmness on the right as God gives us to see the right, let us strive on.

—Abraham Lincoln

Background

Jane Addams was born in Cedarville, Illinois, at the dawn of the Civil War in
1860. She is remembered primarily as a founder of the Settlement House
Movement. She and her friend Ellen Starr founded Hull House in the slums
of Chicago in 1889. She was also the first American woman to receive the
Nobel Peace Prize.

Addams was a pioneer in the areas of labor reform, especially laws that
governed the working conditions for children and women, and was a charter
member of the National Association for the Advancement of Colored People
(NAACP).

Addams's father had a great influence on her. He instilled in her a sense
of tolerance toward others and a strong work ethic. At his insistence she went
on to pursue higher education at the Rockford Seminary for women, where
she was a stellar student who developed strong and effective leadership traits
and earned the respect and admiration of her classmates.

Her parents decided that the best course was to take her and a few of her
friends on a grand tour of Europe for a year or two. Perhaps Addams would
discern a career or vocation for herself.

A couple of years later, Addams headed back to Europe. She did a lot of the usual sightseeing, but just by chance, while in England, she was introduced to the founders and the workings of Toynbee Hall, an all-male settlement house in the slums of London. It did not immediately strike her that social work was to be her calling. After this experience, she and her traveling companion, Ellen Starr, committed themselves to the idea of starting a settlement house in Chicago. Within a few years, Hull House was founded and offered medical care, child care and legal aid to poor immigrants. It also provided classes for immigrants to learn English, vocational skills, music, art, and drama.

Addams realized that there would be no end to poverty unless there was legislation passed to counteract it. Her followers joined Addams to lobby the state of Illinois to reform its child labor, factory inspection, and juvenile justice laws. She and her colleagues had laws passed that limited the working hours of women, recognized labor unions, and provided for safety in the workplace.

Addams helped supplement the Hull House operating budget with revenue that she earned from her lectures and magazine articles. She began to enjoy international acclaim when her first book was published in 1910. Her most significant writing success and the source of her wealth was her autobiography, *Twenty Years at Hull House*.

Addams also became an ardent pacifist. In 1915, at the advent of WWII, she tried to avert war with Germany by launching the Women's Peace Party and the International Congress of Women, both of which advocated a pacifist agenda. In 1919 she was elected as the first president of the Women's International League for Peace and Freedom. She was also a founding member of the American Civil Liberties Union (ACLU). Her positions on the war and human rights led to much enmity, and she was accused at various times of being a socialist, anarchist, and communist.

However, after World War I and especially during the Great Depression, her reputation was reinstated and she received numerous awards during this time including, in 1931, the Nobel Peace Prize. That year her health began to fail, but she continued her work until her death in 1935 (Davis 1973; Diliberto 1999).

Situational Leadership Analysis

Situational models of leadership differ from earlier trait and behavioral models in asserting that no single way of leading works in all situations. Rather, appropriate behavior depends on the circumstances at a given time. Effective managers diagnose the situation, identify the leadership style or behavior that will be most effective, and then determine whether they can implement the required style.

Jane Addams was very adept at adapting her leadership behavior to the situation. Addams's basic and well-known image as a compassionate, self-effacing, and gentle woman could easily be misleading. When necessary, she was very capable of engaging in political frame leadership behavior, for example, in order to gain some advantage for the settlement movement or one of her many other causes.

In actuality, Jane Addams engaged in all five leadership frames. She expressed structural leadership behavior with her considerable business acumen; human resource behavior in her concern for humanity; political behavior as a fund-raiser and with her genius for compromise; symbolic behavior as a persuasive public speaker and writer; and moral behavior in the transformative effect she had on society in the area of social justice.

Jane Addams's lifelong coworker and friend, Ellen Gates Starr, made a great partner because each possessed different but complementary traits that allowed them when working together to adapt their leadership behavior to any given situation. Addams was an introvert, while Starr was gregarious. Jane was more cerebral, and Ellen was more intuitive. Together, they were an amazing team because they balanced their leadership skills so that between them they could respond effectively to virtually every situation they encountered.

Addams believed that the ability to adapt one's leadership behavior to the situation depended at least somewhat on one's gender. According to her, men and women were born with different leadership talents. "Woman," she often declared, "wishes not to be a man, nor like a man, but she claims the same right to independent thought and actions." On the other hand, she continued

> We still retain the old ideal of womanhood—the Saxon lady whose mission it was to bring bread unto her household. So we have planned to be bread givers throughout our lives believing that labor alone is happiness and that the only true and honorable life is one filled with good works and honest toil. We strive to idealize our labor and thus happily fulfill women's highest mission (Diliberto 1999, 74).

Lastly, Addams readily admitted that "life cannot be administered by definite rules and regulations" (Diliberto 1999, 204). In order to address the concerns, dreams, and hopes of an individual or a group, one needs to really know what makes them tick. In other words, an effective leader cannot apply the same behavior in every situation. One needs to adapt his or her leadership behavior to the readiness or maturity level of one's followers. Jane Addams knew instinctively that one size did not fit all.

The Structural Frame

Structural frame leaders seek to develop a new model of the relationship of structure, strategy, and environment for their organizations. Strategic planning, extensive preparation, and effecting change are priorities for them.

Although Jane Addams was primarily thought of as a human resource leader, she made extensive use of structural frame leadership behavior. Upon graduation from Rockford College, Addams wanted desperately to make her mark upon the world. She dreamed of leading her life differently from the stereotypical female of her day. To realize her dream, however, she knew that she had to utilize structural frame leadership behavior and devise a plan to attain it.

There was always an aura around Addams that separated her from other girls of her age. At Rockford College her dormitory room was known as "an available refuge from all perplexities" (Diliberto 1999, 69). There was always a sense of gravitas surrounding Addams.

Displaying structural leadership behavior, Addams was a passionate college debater. In one particularly momentous debate, she finished just behind a fellow named William Jennings Bryan. Bryan, of course, became a U.S. congressman, a presidential candidate, and secretary of state, and would go on to become one of the most famous orators in American history. So Addams was in good company, indeed.

In another display of structural behavior, Addams was named class valedictorian. Her speech topic was Cassandra, the Trojan woman who had the gift of prophesy but was not taken seriously by her countrymen because she was a woman. Addams utilized structural leadership behavior and prepared herself so that she would not suffer Cassandra's fate.

Addams read George Eliot, Victor Hugo, John Ruskin, and Thomas Carlyle. Together these authors influenced her thoughts on society's obligation to address the agonies of poverty and human suffering. As a result, Addams eventually settled in the urban slums of Baltimore and it was her experiences there that led to her interest in social work. In typical structural leadership fashion, she prepared herself for this work by visiting various other charitable organizations, including London's Toynbee Hall, the world's first settlement house, which she had visited when in Europe.

During her second visit to Toynbee Hall, Addams had an epiphany. This experience was the defining moment in her decision to establish Hull House. It seems that while Addams was entertained by the bullfight spectacle she attended, her friends were appalled by it and Addams's seemingly blasé attitude toward it. Almost as a penance for her ambivalence toward violence, Addams decided to dedicate her life to the settlement house movement (Diliberto 1999).

Until the 1880s, most charities and philanthropic endeavors were based on giving relief in the form of food, money, clothes, shelter, and other services, based on the Good Samaritan Bible story. But typical of her structural leanings, Addams decided to approach charity in a very different way. She would go beyond providing the poor with material resources and provide them with the education, skills, and know-how that would allow them to rise above the cycle of poverty. She would not only give them fish, but also teach them how to fish.

In typical structural leadership style, Addams prepared herself well to carry on her social work. She attended Sunday school lectures on the subject, volunteered her services to various missions in Chicago, and taught social work at the Industrial Arts School there. So by the time she opened Hull House she was an expert in her chosen field. At Hull House she immediately established the first kindergarten in the city and started an adult education program that focused on job preparation and training,

Being the pragmatic structural leader that she was, Addams defied her critics and insisted that the Hull House residents fit into the American melting pot as soon as possible, believing that doing so was the immigrants' best chance to be assimilated into the American mainstream and attain the "good life."

As a result of Addams's use of structural leadership behavior, Hull House was a magnificent success, and the settlement movement in the United States flourished. When Hull house was founded in 1892 there were only six settlement houses in the nation. By 1910 there were more than a hundred, and their services were sorely needed in that workman's compensation and social security were still years away.

Perhaps this anecdote about Jane Addams's idiosyncrasies sums up her reliance on structural leadership behavior. It seems that in the preparation of her many speeches Addams had the habit of cutting up her pages of notes and rearranging the paragraphs and then piecing them together with straight pins—all this in the midst of the phenomenal and distracting activity always taking place around her. Thus, we have seen that Jane Addams utilized structural frame leadership behavior quite extensively and effectively.

The Human Resource Frame

Human resource leaders believe in people and communicate that belief. They are passionate about productivity through people. Considering her concern for social justice, it is difficult to imagine Jane Addams not extensively utilizing human resource leadership behavior. She expressed her human resource tendencies when she said, "I am a great admirer of Platonic love or rather pure sacred friendship. I think it is so much higher than what is generally implied in the word love" (Diliberto 1999, 76).

There are myriad examples of Addams's use of human resource behavior. One of them included an instance where she took the side of a person associated with a known criminal. Addams was a friend of Flora Guiteau, whose insane half-brother, Charles, assassinated President James Garfield. After the shooting, Flora became a pariah in the community. Addams, however, demonstrated human resource leadership behavior and remained loyal to Flora.

In another instance, Addams urged an out-of-work shipping clerk to take a construction job that he was reluctant to take because of health and safety reasons. Two days into the job, the man contracted pneumonia and died. The grieving Addams remained in touch with his wife and children and helped fund their living and educational expenses.

In a letter to her college friend and Hull House cofounder, Addams wrote, "I am convinced every day that friendship is after all the main thing in life. And friendship and affection must be guarded and taken care of just as other valuable things" (Diliberto 1999, 99). In still another example of Addams engaging in human resource behavior, upon visiting one of her shelters for African Americans, she observed, "I had such a pleasant afternoon yesterday with the old women in the Colored Shelter. They are so responsive and confidential and begin to know me well enough now to be perfectly free" (Diliberto 1999, 118). Addams was particularly sensitive to race and class distinctions. She was a pioneer in recognizing the value of ethnic pride, which led her to host a number of ethnic-themed dinner parties at Hull House.

Unlike most of the social elite of her time, Addams believed all children, even the poor, had the capacity to be productive citizens. This human resource–type conviction led her into the most successful battle of her early career, the outcome of which was the establishment of the first juvenile court system in the United States. Up to then, juvenile criminals were tried, convicted, and jailed as adults.

Perhaps the way to end this section on Jane Addams's propensity for utilizing human resource leadership behavior is to note what her friend and coworker Ellen Starr once said of Addams's faith in humanity, "Jane, if the devil himself came riding down Halsted Street with his tail waving out behind him, you'd say, 'What a beautiful curve he has in his tail'" (Davis 1973, 115).

The Symbolic Frame

In the symbolic frame, the organization is seen as a stage, a theater in which every actor plays certain roles, and the symbolic leader attempts to communicate the right impressions to the right audiences. Like most successful leaders, Jane Addams made frequent and effective use of symbolic frame leadership behavior. One way Addams used symbolic leadership behavior was to establish her feminist image. Early on it became obvious to her that the only way to significantly impact society was for women to acquire the right to vote. So, after some delay, she became a woman's suffrage exponent.

Addams drew strength in her endeavors from Abraham Lincoln's words at New York's Cooper Union in 1860: "Let us have faith that right makes might, and in that faith, let us to the end dare to do our duty as we understand it, with malice towards none, with charity for all, with firmness on the right as God gives us to see the right, let us strive on" (Diliberto 1999, 211).

Using symbolic leadership behavior, Addams consciously chose to establish Hull House in the middle of an immigrant ghetto. It was to become an oasis in a desert—a place where young females dedicated to social work and poor immigrants could gain refuge from the horrors of the streets.

In another symbolic leadership move, Addams encouraged the publication of a cartoon in the Chicago newspapers depicting the "Hull House Revolution." A series of six black-and-white contrasting drawings showed the after–Hull House transformation of two immigrants, a man and a woman, from disheveled, slack-jawed new arrivals to prosperous, neatly attired citizens (Diliberto 1999, 160).

Addams's generosity became part of her legend. It is said that her seamstress resorted to monogramming everything so she would be less likely to give it away. As a result, she became a nationally and internationally recognized symbol for rich liberal women. And Hull House became the beacon of hope on the hill.

Women felt a common bond with one another and Addams was their icon. In an example of political correctness, 1890s style, Addams struggled to avoid using the term *young lady*, favoring instead *sister*, and apologizing once to a friend for a lapse into "false social distinction, a remnant of former prejudice" (Diliberto 1999, 180).

Addams was careful to use symbolic behavior to build up the image of the settlement house and social movements. For example, she made certain that she was one of the five people chosen to lead the Civic Federation of Chicago to try to settle the famous Pullman Strike of 1894. This appointment was precipitated by a speech to the Ethical Culture Society and published in the prestigious *International Journal of Ethics*. Addams also used this occasion to attack corrupt Chicago alderman John Powers. These two events helped put Jane Addams in the national spotlight.

In 1911, after the John Powers incident, in yet another symbolic move, Addams became keenly aware of the power of the vote and finally joined America's suffrage efforts, becoming vice president of the National American Woman Suffrage Association (NAWSA). In that same year, she starred in a silent movie with Anna Howard Shaw, president of the NAWSA.

Through Addams's effective application of symbolic behavior in her publications and speeches, her reputation began to spread both nationally and internationally to the point where she had no trouble getting an appointment with President William McKinley in 1899 to get her friend Florence Kelly the job of general secretary of the newly formed National Consumers League in New York.

John Dewey, the legendary educator and philosopher, thought so much of Addams that he named his daughter after her. Their respect for one another was mutual, as a newspaper reporter once remarked: "Dewey's faith in democracy as a guiding force in education took on both a sharper and deeper meaning because of Hull House and Jane Addams" (Davis 1973, 97). And, according to most reporters, Jane Addams was the epitome of the nineteenth-century heroine who had "never had a selfish thought," "who was wonderfully gentle" and sexually pure and innocent, and who was thus in a sense superior to men. She was an early version of Mother Teresa (Davis 1973, 103).

Her national reputation grew to the point where, "with a flag-waving, foot-stomping crowd cheering her every word, Addams stood at the podium of Chicago Coliseum on August 7, 1912, to second the nomination of Theodore Roosevelt for president on the Progressive Party ticket." This symbolic leadership behavior was prompted by Roosevelt's running on a platform "calling for the abolition of child labor; an eight-hour, six-day workweek for adults; housing reform; and the vote for women"—"all the things I was fighting for," said Addams (Diliberto 1999, 260).

As a result of her effective use of symbolic leadership behavior, by 1914 her reputation was at its zenith. Her popular speeches and her bestselling books made her the most famous woman in America. Honors came her way from every direction and she became the first woman to be awarded an honorary doctorate by Yale University.

Addams's almost universal popularity temporarily ended, however, when World War I broke out in Europe in 1914 and she strenuously opposed American involvement. As chairperson of the Women's Peace Party she became one of America's most ardent pacifists. Even her old friend Teddy Roosevelt denounced her as "one of the shrieking sisterhood," referring to her as "Poor Bleeding Jane" and "Bull Mouse" (Diliberto 1999, 261).

Another public relations disaster was her support of Henry Ford's ill-fated "Peace Ship." Ironically, even though Addams was sick and did not sail on the Ford Peace Ship, her name was closely associated with the failure. Ford's promise that he'd "get our boys home by Christmas" never happened (Davis 1973, 242). Addams and her friend Woodrow Wilson were now at odds. The country followed Wilson and not Addams. This turned out to be one of the only times that Jane did not use political frame leadership behavior and compromise—and it cost her.

A few years later, when the Red Scare captivated the nation, Addams's reputation lost even more of its luster. Because of her support of labor unions and the right of free speech, she was denounced as a communist. She was first on the list of subversives on the War Department's chart—a precursor of Jane Fonda.

However, Addams's popularity and influence were resurrected in the 1930s. The Great Depression had created doubts about the effectiveness and fairness of capitalism as an economic and political system.

Addams's commitment to the poor during the Depression made her once again an admired figure, and in the last years of her life, she was once again treated like a saint. In May 1931, Jane Addams was awarded the Nobel Peace Prize for her efforts to bring about world peace. Suffice it to say that her reputation as a role model for women everywhere was to a large degree the result of her astutely applied symbolic leadership behavior.

The Political Frame

Leaders operating out of the political frame clarify what they want and what they can get. Political leaders are realists above all. They never let what they want cloud their judgment about what is possible. They assess the distribution of power and interests. Among Jane Addams's considerable leadership skills was the ability to utilize political frame leadership behavior when appropriate. Addams had a natural ability to make friends and influence people. Her lifelong friend Ellen Gates Starr marveled at her ability to get along with almost anyone. Addams protested, "Ellen always overestimates my influence" (Diliberto 1999, 123). But the reality was that Addams consciously utilized political frame behavior in order to forward the goals of the settlement movement and the other causes she championed. She even suddenly decided to join an established church because she knew a baptismal certificate would give her credibility with Chicago's most powerful clergymen, the city's reformists, and those she would need for ensuring the continuing existence of Hull House.

Addams's most notable trait was that of conciliation. She was no unyielding ideologue. She frequently engaged in political frame behavior and almost always sought a reasonable compromise. Her position in the textile strike of 1910 was perhaps typical. The strike began as an unorganized walkout of the Hart, Schaffner, and Marx factories in Chicago and spread to other plants. Addams played an important role in bringing the two sides together, but when the arbitration board was selected, her name was missing because there were those on *both* sides who felt she was too committed to the other side.

Addams was called "the Henry Clay (the Great Compromiser) of Chicago." She was by nature a conciliator who preferred the middle ground. Through her writing and her speaking, she created the image of being a great moral leader. She was credited with being the "feminine conscience of the nation" (Davis 1973, 134).

Addams's political connections allowed her to attract Chicago's leading lights to lecture and support Hull House. Among them were the famous muckraker, Henry Demarest Lloyd, Clarence Darrow, Frank Lloyd Wright, and educator/philosopher John Dewey.

Addams became an intrepid fund raiser for her varied causes. Addams once asked Helen Culver to pay for two new bathrooms and repair of the front piazza of Hull House. Culver sent her one hundred dollars, and Addams responded in another display of political frame behavior by threatening to have the beautiful but crumbling piazza torn down if she did not increase her gift—which she did, of course.

In another example of her political skill, in a widely publicized 1891 internecine battle between women's suffrage advocates Bertha Palmer and Phoebe Couzins, which ended up in court, Addams consciously stayed out of the conflict, maintaining good relationships with all the women involved. Thus, despite their differences regarding suffrage strategies, they all remained ardent supporters of Hull House in particular and the settlement movement in general.

As mentioned earlier, Addams made it her goal to depose the powerful and corrupt Chicago alderman, John Powers. But she was not successful in getting him unseated because of the political favors Powers was able to bestow on his constituents. Powers's greatest power was his ability to bail out constituents from jail, hand out patronage jobs, and provide turkeys to voters at Christmas. Addams learned the valuable lesson that, in order to achieve any political gains, women needed the right to vote. So she engaged in yet more political leadership behavior and at long last became a suffrage advocate.

The Moral Frame

The moral frame is my own contribution to situational leadership theory. In my view, the moral frame completes situational leadership theory. Without it, leaders could just as easily use their leadership skills for promoting evil as for promoting good. Leaders operating out of the moral frame are concerned about their obligations and responsibilities to their followers. Moral frame leaders use some type of moral compass to direct their behavior. They practice what has been described as servant leadership and are concerned with those individuals and groups that are marginalized in their organizations and in society. In short, they are concerned about social justice.

The moral frame is one of Jane Addams's strongest. Even at the early age of fifteen, when she was a devotee of the writings of Ralph Waldo Emerson, his work appealed to her because, like her father, he celebrated "the demise of religious dogma and the rise of religion based on moral duty." She asserted that "the test of righteousness is good works, not divine election" (Diliberto 1999, 52).

As the above quote would indicate, Addams was not necessarily a religious person, but her actions were guided by moral philosophy. In her religious quandaries, Addams was greatly influenced by the works of the humanists John Ruskin, Thomas Carlyle, Matthew Arnold, and Ralph Waldo Emerson. Their advocacy of the Golden Rule moved her.

In this regard, Addams was a typical late-Victorian intellectual who was suspicions of organized religion. She confessed that she could not accept the divinity of Christ. "I can work myself into a great admiration of his life, and occasionally I can catch something of his philosophy, but he doesn't bring me any nearer the deity," she remarked. "I feel a little as I do when I hear very fine music—that I am incapable of understanding" (Diliberto 1999, 68).

Nevertheless, as we have seen, after years of religious questioning, she finally decided to be baptized in the Protestant faith. "At that moment something persuasive within made me long for an outward symbol of fellowship, some bond of peace, some blessed spot where unity of spirit might claim right of way over all differences" (Diliberto 1999, 136).

Addams came to see that addressing the needs of the underserved was a moral issue. Underlying Addams's ideologies was her moral commitment to the basic equality of all human beings. In this, she was ahead of her times in many ways, but especially in her views of diversity and social justice (Davis 1973; Diliberto 1999).

Conclusion

Jane Addams no longer provides an ideal role model for young women. For better or worse, her insistence on the special intuitive nature of women and her Victorian attitudes toward sex have partially separated her from the present generation. Her reform ideas and her attempt to promote peace often seem naive from the vantage point of 2011. Yet her struggle to overcome the traditional image of women as solely housekeepers and her attempts to serve society still have meaning for all of us today.

In addition, those seeking to improve urban schooling and promote social justice and peace in the world can build on what Addams and her coworkers constructed. For educational leaders and others, we cannot help but be impressed by the life of Jane Addams. And one cannot ignore the journeys that led to her being perceived as a saintly heroine and then a villain and then finally a saint again. In all of this, Addams was very much the situational leader. She utilized all five frames of leadership behavior in almost equal measure. There is much to be learned from this "woman of the ages."

II. AL CAPONE

I've been spending the best years of my life as a public benefactor. I've given people the light pleasures, shown them a good time. And all I get is abuse—the existence of a hunted man . . .

—Al Capone

Background

Al Capone is one of the most famous criminals in American history. He was born in 1899 in Brooklyn, New York. Like many European immigrants at the time, his family had migrated from Italy to the United States to "seek their fortune." Still a teenager, Capone became a member of the local gang under the leadership of Johnny Torrio, and when Torrio decided to move his operation to Chicago, Capone went along as his top lieutenant.

It was early in his life of crime that Capone received the scar that gave him the nickname Scarface. It seems that Capone unintentionally insulted a woman while working as a bouncer at a Brooklyn night club. The women's brother, Frank Gallucio came to her defense and slashed Capone's face three times on the left side. Ironically, Capone forgave his attacker and employed him as one of his gang members later in life.

Shortly after Torrio and Capone arrived in Chicago, the reform mayor William Dever took office and began to harass the gang elements within the city limits. This prompted Torrio and Capone to move their base of operations outside the city limits to the suburban town of Cicero, Illinois. Largely as a result of Capone's intimidations and bribes, Torrio and Capone were able to attain full control of the Cicero town government and saw to it that its laws were tolerant of crime.

In 1925, Torrio was mortally wounded in an assassination attempt by the North Side Gang. The shaken Torrio promptly turned over his operations to the younger Capone and left for his native Sicily. Capone became notorious during the Prohibition era for his control of large portions of the Chicago underworld and his influence over mob activities all across the nation. His Chicago gang became nationally known as the Outfit.

Over the next several years, a gang war between the North Side Gang and the Outfit over control of Chicago's underworld activities took place, culminating in the bloody event of February 14, 1929, known as the Saint Valentine's Day Massacre. Capone arranged the most notorious gangland killing of all time when he had seven victims shot to death in a garage on Chicago's North Side.

The massacre was the Outfit's effort to halt the advance of Bugs Moran's North Side gang into Capone's bootlegging trade in Chicago. In fact, Capone thought that Moran would be present at the garage, but he was late in arriving and fortunately for him avoided being killed.

The public outcry over the massacre was such that the local and federal governments had to renew their efforts to convict and punish Capone and the other gangs for their crimes. In 1929, Bureau of Prohibition agent Eliot Ness began a successful campaign to put Capone out of business and in prison. Shutting down many of Capone's breweries and speakeasies, Ness began to bring about the slow demise of Scarface Capone.

Finally, in 1931, Capone was indicted for income tax evasion and various violations of the Volstead Act. Attempting to bribe and intimidate the potential jurors, his plan was discovered by Ness and following a long trial, Capone was found guilty of income tax evasion and was sentenced to eleven years in prison. He was eventually sent to Alcatraz and remained there until his health began to seriously decline due to having contracted syphilis in his youth.

Capone was paroled in 1939 and returned to his home in Palm Island, Florida, where in 1947 he had an apoplectic stroke and died (Kobler 1971).

The Structural Frame

Structural frame leaders seek to develop a new model of the relationship of structure, strategy, and environment for their organizations. Strategic planning, extensive preparation and effecting change are priorities for them. Al Capone would never have had the success that he had in his "business" without having frequently operated out of the structural frame. The nerve center of Capone's criminal activities was his six-room suite at the Lexington Hotel. From there, in structural frame style, he directed, with the guidance of Jake "Greasy Thumb" Guzik, his Russian-born financial manager, a syndicate that owned and controlled breweries, distilleries, speakeasies, warehouses, fleets of boats and trucks, nightclubs, gambling houses, horse and dog racetracks, brothels, labor unions, and business and industrial associations, together producing annual revenue in the hundreds of millions of dollars. He more or less behaved like a CEO of a major corporation.

Early on in his Chicago days Capone exhibited structural frame tendencies. Immediately after James "Big Jim" Colosimos's death, John Torrio, assisted by Capone, designed a grand plan for expansion. First, they successfully sought recognition as Colosimos's legitimate successor. Next, having secured their home base of Chicago, Torrio and Capone proceeded to expand their suburban gambling and brothel interests. In just two years corruption transformed these once model, law-abiding communities into vice pits (Kobler 1971).

In typical structural frame fashion, Torrio and Capone negotiated a tripartite treaty to dominate the rackets in the Chicago area. One gangster received the slot machine operation while another gang won an exclusive beer franchise in several sections of the city and its suburbs. In exchange, Capone and Torrio were granted permission to sell beer anywhere in the suburb of Cicero and to operate gambling houses there.

Once again operating out of the structural frame, when reformers attempted to take back control in Cicero, Capone and Torrio saw it as a challenge, calling for combat rather than diplomacy. Capone's thugs roughed up reform candidates and destroyed their campaign headquarters. When the polls opened, a fleet of black limousines carrying heavily armed Capone gang members cruised the town wreaking havoc with the voters. As a result, the reformers lost the election.

Capone continued his radical structural frame behavior in the form of violence when the Irish O'Banion gang was infringing on Torrio and Capone's territory. They convened a meeting to devise a plan to deal with Dion O'Banion. The resolution became obvious when police discovered O'Banion dead in one of his flower shops.

Capone engaged in more structural behavior in learning from John Torrio how to become a modern-day gangster, one who would forgo personal vendettas, murdering only when absolutely necessary, and leaving the execution to low-level hoods with whom he could not be identified. He would be a person who, guided by corporate counsel, would launder unlawful profits through legitimate businesses until, becoming a multimillionaire, his position in business and society would be indistinguishable from that of reputable businessmen.

When Torrio retired and formally transferred everything to Capone, he knew he must establish his authority with every major gang in the city. He was equipped for the challenge with qualities that made him, by the unique standards of the underworld, capo de capo, a leader of leaders. The Capone gang had discipline among the troops, cohesiveness, and esprit de corps, equaled only by the O'Banion gang under the similarly charismatic Dion O'Banion. In typical structural frame fashion, each man had a well-thought-out plan of action.

Further applying the lessons Torrio taught him, Capone forged a large heterogeneous and disciplined criminal organization. On the top echelon of the hierarchy stood Jake Guzik, his business manager. Frank Nitti had been "promoted" from an able and willing triggerman to treasurer, and Capone's brother Ralph became his director of liquor sales. Indicative of a structural leader, Capone had developed a smooth running organization, albeit an illegal one.

Liquor continued to produce the bulk of Capone's profits. However, in typical structural frame manner, Capone understood the need for diversification. He saw that Prohibition could not last forever. So Capone made racketeering his most profitable alternative to bootlegging. A typical racketeer would be the boss of a supposedly legitimate business association, like a labor union, but in reality was at the service of the gang. Gradually, Capone came to control the great majority of the Chicago rackets. Of the estimated $105 million the Capone syndicate grossed in 1928, about $10 million flowed from the rackets (Kobler 1971).

Capone utilized structural behavior further in establishing the Mafia as a national and international organization. Some authorities date the beginning of modern nationally organized crime to a meeting held at Cleveland's Hotel Statler on December 5, 1928, over which Capone presided. At the Cleveland meeting and one held several months later in Atlantic City, the mob put asunder the old ethnic and national divisions and divided the country up among them.

Capone summed up the three-day meeting by saying:

> I told them there was business enough to make us all rich and it was time to stop all the killings, and look at our business as other men look at theirs, as something to work at and forget when we go home at night. We finally decided to forget the past and begin all over again and we drew up a written agreement and each man signed on the dotted line (Kobler 1971, 258).

The Human Resource Frame

Human resource leaders believe in people and communicate that belief. They are passionate about productivity through people. It is difficult to identify occasions when Capone was sincerely active in the human resource frame. Most often, he used his human resource skills to manipulate his associates, which in effect, is more like political frame behavior than it is human resource frame behavior.

Nevertheless, one is able to find a few instances when Capone engaged in seemingly sincere human resource frame behavior. On one such occasion, Capone knew that Jack "Machine Gun" Magurn, one of his young recruits, was a complete jazz-age fanatic. So, Capone offered Magurn a 25 percent interest in a popular jazz club if he could persuade a popular young comic, Joe E. Lewis, to stay rather than accepting a better offer elsewhere.

Lewis decided to take the better job. A few days later a pair of Magurn's henchmen pistol-whipped Lewis and stabbed him in the face and mouth several times, leaving him a virtual invalid. It took Lewis ten years to fully recover. Capone was so embarrassed that one of his men would do such a horrendous thing that he paid for Lewis's medical bills and gave him $10,000 during his recovery.

On another occasion, when Capone was attacked by Hymie Weiss's gang at a restaurant in the lobby of his headquarters at the Hawthorne Inn, the lobby and restaurant were completely ruined by gunfire, but the only individual wounded was Mrs. Clyde Freeman, and innocent woman who happened to be in the wrong place at the wrong time. When he heard that Mrs. Freeman's injured eye would require major surgery and a long hospitalization, Capone insisted on paying the entire medical bill, which came to over $10,000. He also paid for repairs to the damaged lobby and the adjacent store fronts (Kobler 1971).

The Symbolic Frame

In the symbolic frame, the organization is seen as a stage, a theater in which every actor plays certain roles and the symbolic leader attempts to communicate the right impression to the right audiences. Other than the political frame, the ability to effectively utilize the symbolic frame was one of Capone's greatest strengths. Always aware of his image, he was careful to present the right, scarless side of his face to photographers. Even though he resented them for the nickname they had given him, he nonetheless exploited them into publicizing his feats and publishing his rationalizations for how he conducted his "businesses." He also encouraged the press and his intimates to refer to him as Snarky, which is slang for elegant.

Capone symbolically and morbidly observed the old traditions among gangsters, in particular, hospitality before execution. In one famous instance, Capone was hosting some of his Sicilian rivals at a banquet. At the assigned hour, Capone's henchmen descended upon them, tying them to their chairs and gagging them. In a scene made famous by a motion picture of his life story, Capone got up with a baseball bat and slowly, methodically walked the length of the table and stopped behind each guest. With both hands on the bat he stuck them again and again, breaking bones and drawing blood. One of the bodyguards then shot each man in the back of the head (Kobler 1971, 17).

Early in his career as a gangster, Capone was a bouncer at the Harvard Inn in Brooklyn, where he usually prevailed in most encounters. He suffered one notable defeat, however, at the hands of Frank Galluccio, a petty felon. Capone made an offensive remark to his sister and Galluccio took out his pocket knife and opened the long cut on Capone's jaw that would define him for posterity as Scarface Capone.

Normally vindictive, Capone engaged in symbolic behavior and in a rare show of compassion, decided to forgive Galluccio. Some years later, in one of those magnanimous gestures that he learned could afford him admiration from his peers; he once again utilized symbolic leadership behavior and hired Galluccio as a bodyguard at a very generous $100 a week.

In another symbolic gesture, Capone had some business cards printed describing himself unpretentiously as Alfonse Capone, second-hand furniture dealer, 2220 South Wabash Avenue. Stocking the storefront with junk that he palmed off as valuable antiques, he never really tried to sell any of it. Prospective collectors who made inquiries by phone were told, "We ain't open today" (Kobler 1971, 101). Capone, of course, maintained the shop as a cover for his illegal operations.

In a combination of human resource, symbolic, and political frame behavior, Capone made a dramatic gesture of compassion during a long and severe draught in the Midwest. Ralph Capone, representing his big brother, announced that Al "is feeding 3,000 unemployed every day." A huge sign hanging from the front of a South Side building proclaimed "Free Food for the Workers," and there a soup kitchen, financed by Capone, dispensed 120,000 meals in six weeks at a cost of $12,000. On Thanksgiving Day Capone donated 5,000 turkeys to the poor and at Christmas he sponsored a huge block party for them in Little Italy (Kobler 1971, 308).

Perhaps Capone's most notorious display of symbolic behavior was the bloody St. Valentine's Day Massacre. After the murder of Dion O'Banion and Hymie Weiss, Bugs Moran took on the mantle of Capone's biggest nemesis. The opposition to Capone's reign abruptly ended, however, on St. Valentine's Day, 1929. The slaughter of seven of Moran's henchmen took place in a Chicago warehouse. Moran escaped the massacre by only minutes and observed: "Only Capone kills like that." Not to be outdone, when Capone was asked by the press if he had anything to do with the murder, he replied: "The only man who kills like that is Bugs Moran" (Kobler 1971, 246).

The Political Frame

Leaders operating out of the political frame clarify what they want and what they can get. Political leaders are realists above all. They never let what they want cloud their judgment about what is possible. They assess the distribution of power and interests.

The political frame was Al Capone's most prolific. Because Capone used the political frame in the form of bribery and extortion so liberally in Chicago and its environs in the 1920s and early 1930s, it was a given that Al Capone owned the city. Through the systematic use of payoffs, his hand reached into every department of the city and county government. Among the cities' public enemies, Capone was number one. Yet, in the fall of 1928 when Chicago officials wanted to guarantee a free, honest election, they sought out Capone. They did not go to the governor of the state, an embezzler and protector of felons, nor Chicago's grotesque mayor. They did not go to the police, of whom Capone once boasted: "I own the police." They went instead to Scarface Capone (Kobler 1971, 13).

Only Capone could and did allow an honest election to be conducted in that year. Of course, he did so to ensure that he and his gang would continue to have the run of the city. Frank Loesch, a founding member of the Chicago Crime Commission, went to Capone to entice him into allowing a fair mayoral election to take place in Chicago. "All right," said Capone, "I'll have the cops send over squad cars the night before the election and jug all the hoodlums and keep 'em in the cooler until the polls close." Such was Capone's power in Chicago.

"It turned out to be the squarest and most successful election day in forty years," Loesch said later in a college lecture in criminology, "There was not one complaint, not one election fraud and no threat of trouble all day" (Kobler 1971, 16.)

An early arrest demonstrated the political clout that Capone had garnered. When a taxi driver accidently hit a parked taxi with Capone in the back seat, Capone flashed his deputy sheriff's badge and threatened to shoot the offending taxi driver. When the police arrived Capone was booked on aggregated assault, public intoxication, and carrying a deadly weapon. Any one of these charges would have sent the average person to prison, but like almost every other case that was to be filed against "Deputy Sheriff" Capone during those years, it did not even come to trial and the charges were expunged from the record.

When former judge William Dever became a reform mayor of Chicago, Capone and John Torrio knew they needed a haven beyond his reach. Using some political behavior, they moved their operation to Cicero, just outside of Chicago, and while most of their Chicago establishments continued to thrive, Cicero became the center of their criminal empire throughout Dever's tenure. In the process, Capone virtually took over the Cicero government. All the successful candidates for president of the village board, its trustees, and the police magistrate were Capone's minions.

Capone's control and power ran so deep that when a group of rookie cops raided a Capone-affiliated headquarters searching for an escaped criminal and confiscated the gangster's guns, delivering them to their commanding officer, the officer was so flustered that he declared: "Who gave you such orders? Take the stuff back" (Kobler 1971, 141).

Another incident that showed Capone's political power was when one of his lieutenants was arrested and held without bail. Capone telephoned the offending judge. "I thought I told you to discharge him," he said. The judge explained that he was not on the bench the day the police brought in the prisoner, but had given his bailiff a memo for the alternate judge. The bailiff forgot to deliver it. "Forgot!" Capone roared. "Don't let him forget again" (Kobler 1971, 142).

Because he was not of Sicilian heritage, Capone did not qualify for membership in the Unione Siciliane which ran the rackets in the United States. However, the ever-resourceful Capone used some political leadership behavior and simply had his Sicilian consigliore, Tony Lombardo, named president of the organization.

When Hymie Weiss attempted to have Capone assassinated, in true political frame manner, Capone took it in stride. Capone's mentor, John Torrio, would have been proud of the restraint that he showed. Repressing his natural urge to take revenge, Capone proposed peace talks instead. Weiss stalked out of the meeting because Capone would not "eliminate" two of his young recruits. But Capone could not be faulted for at least trying to use political leadership behavior when appropriate—that is, until he used radical structural and symbolic behavior and had Weiss murdered.

At the conclusion of the 1925 gang wars in Chicago, Capone held a meeting of the surviving gangs and again used political frame behavior in proposing a five-point treaty:

1. All standing grievances and feuds were to be buried—a general amnesty.
2. Arbitration substituted for violence in settling disputes.
3. An end to using malicious gossip to instigate assassination attempts.
4. No encroachment on established territories.
5. The head of each gang was to punish violations committed by any member.

The treaty, of course, was very advantageous to Capone and left him in control of nearly all of Chicago and most of the suburbs, a domain encompassing an incredible 20,000 speakeasies and innumerable roadhouses, gambling dens, and brothels. "Just like the old days," as Capone remarked to a reporter. "They (the O'Banion gang) stay on the North Side and I stay in Cicero and if we meet on the street, we say 'hello' and shake hands. Better, ain't it?" (Kobler 1971, 193).

Capone used political frame behavior combined with structural frame behavior in ensuring that the reform mayor William Dever did not defeat "Big Bill" Thompson to gain a second term. As the voting for the mayor and other local Chicago politicians got under way, Capone's henchmen cruised the polling areas in cars bearing, of all things, "America First" stickers. Like a military general, Capone commanded his battle troops and positioned them strategically so that the legitimate election officials abandoned their posts allowing only the Thompsonites to cast their votes.

Within a month of "Big Bill" Thompson's return to City Hall for his third term as mayor, Capone engaged in political frame behavior once again and took advantage of "Big Bill's" tolerant treatment of gangsters by enlarging his Hotel Metropole headquarters in Chicago to fifty rooms and reserving the Hawthorne Inn for his suburban Cicero operations.

How powerful Capone was during the new Thompson administration became clear when the Italian flier Francesco de Pinedo, circling the globe as Benito Mussolini's goodwill ambassador, landed in Chicago. An antifascist demonstration was expected, and the mayor was not certain how to prevent an impending riot. So he appointed Capone to the reception committee, believing that he could quell any riotous antifascists—ironically, with some fascist activity of his own. Of course, the riot never came to pass.

When Capone realized he was not welcome in California and Florida because of his reputation, he again engaged in political frame behavior to acquire a second home to which he could retreat whenever the political climate in Chicago became too hot. When feelers sent out to several resort communities produced no offers of hospitality, he decided to settle incognito in Miami.

Capone, counting on the profit motive to prevail in his move to Miami, decided he would make a public show of candor and say what was obviously on his potential hosts' minds. In speaking to the Miami chief of police, Leslie Quigg, he said, "Let's lay the cards on the table. You know who I am and where I come from. I just want to ask a question. Do I stay or must I get out?" "You can stay as long as you behave yourself," said Quigg. Taking the offensive, Capone replied, "I'll stay as long as I'm treated like a human being" (Kobler 1971, 212).

He then waxed eloquent (for him) about the natural resource that was Miami. He described Miami as "the garden of America, the sunny Italy of the new world, where life is good and abundant, where happiness is to be had even by the poorest. I am going to build or buy a home here and I believe many of my friends will also join me. Furthermore, if I am permitted, I will open a restaurant and if I am invited, I will join the Rotary Club" (Kobler 1971, 215).

Capone's biggest mistake, however, was placing too much dependence on his political frame ability. He thought he could get away with virtually anything, including never filing an income tax return in his entire adult life. So, in addition to Eliot Ness's Department of Justice attack on his operations, the Internal Revenue Service investigated him. When he was convicted of income tax evasion and sent to prison for the remainder of his life, he found it incredulous that after stealing millions and murdering with impunity, such a severe penalty could be incurred for what he considered the minor crime of withholding tax money owed to the federal government (Kobler 1971).

The Moral Frame

The moral frame is my own contribution to situational leadership theory. In my view, the moral frame completes situational leadership theory. Without it, leaders could just as easily use their leadership skills for promoting evil as for promoting good. Leaders operating out of the moral frame are concerned about their obligations and responsibilities to their followers. Moral frame leaders use some type of moral compass to direct their behavior. They practice what has been described as servant leadership and are concerned with those individuals and groups that are marginalized in their organizations and in society. In short, they are concerned about equality, fairness, and social justice.

To put it politely, Al Capone had some deficiencies in operating out of the moral frame. Apparently, the kaleidoscope through which he filtered his leadership behavior did not include a moral lens. In a typical Capone rationalization, he said: "I violate the prohibition law, sure. Who doesn't? The only difference is I take more chances than the man who drinks a cocktail before dinner and a flock of highballs after it. But he's just as much a violator as I am" (Kobler 1971, 209).

His business, he claimed—and undoubtedly believed—was a boon to his fellow man. In his mind, he spent the best years of his life as a public benefactor.

> I've given people the light pleasures, shown them a good time. And all I get is abuse—the existence of a haunted man. I'm called a killer. Ninety percent of the people of Cook County drink and gamble and my offense has been to furnish them with those amusements. Whatever else they may say, my booze has been good and my games have been on the square. Public service is my motto (Kobler 1971, 210).

Asked whether a gangster had any remorse when he killed another gangster in a gang war, Capone once again rationalized:

> Well, maybe he thinks that the law of self-defense, the way God looks at it, is a little broader than the law books have it. Maybe it means killing a man who'd kill you if he saw you first. Maybe it means killing a man in defense of your business—the way you make the money to take care of your wife and child. You can't blame me for thinking there's worse fellows in the world than me (Kobler 1971, 210).

Situational Leadership Analysis

Situational models of leadership differ from earlier trait and behavioral models in asserting that no single way of leading works in all situations. Rather, appropriate behavior depends on the circumstances at a given time. Effective managers diagnose the situation, identify the leadership style or behavior that will be most effective, and then determine whether they can implement the required style.

As we have seen, Al Capone, whether consciously or unconsciously, utilized situational leadership theory. He was active in all four of the Bolman and Deal frames, albeit hyperactive in the political frame and an extremist in the structural frame. We saw how he engaged in structural leadership behavior in being one of the precursors of organized crime in the United States. And, although he utilized sincere human resource behavior infrequently, there were occasions when he demonstrated human kindness.

Capone was a master in the application of both symbolic and political frame behavior. He established an image that was both menacing and benevolent at the same time. His use of political frame behavior was legendary among his counterparts in organized crime. Thus, for all intents and purposes, he displayed many of the characteristics of the great leaders of his times.

His greatest deficiency, however, and the source of his downfall was his inability to consistently operate out of the moral frame. He was a master of rationalization and could wax eloquent about "not being any worse than the next guy." This failure to filter his leadership behavior through a valid moral lens led to his arrest and imprisonment and also kept him from becoming a truly great and heroic leader.

Leadership Implications and Conclusion

If Al Capone were not found guilty of tax evasion, the forward momentum of organized crime promised to carry Capone to even greater heights. He was only thirty-one when he entered Alcatraz. His organizational skills and personal charisma were recognized throughout the underworld. Lucky Luciano of New York so valued his input that he sent an emissary to Chicago to justify in Capone's eyes the murder of Salvatore Maranzano, his competitor for gang supremacy in the Big Apple. Undoubtedly, there would have been a seat for Capone on the national commission.

But none of this was meant to be because Capone did not see fit to operate out of the moral frame, even to the degree where he would have at least paid his income taxes. This is another instance of an otherwise talented and effective leader not willing or not able to consistently apply the moral frame to his leadership behavior.

I cannot share an anecdote in my experience in education to match Al Capone's excesses—but I can come somewhat close. When I was superintendent of one of the largest school systems in the United States, I woke up to read about one of our teachers, who was also a lawyer, being accused of being integrally involved in a major drug smuggling ring. You can imagine my shock. But over the years I had learned that there were all too many of these unfortunate instances where educational leaders and others never develop and consistently use a moral compass by which to guide their behavior—hopefully, a word to the wise will be sufficient.

Chapter Seven

Dewey v. Mao

I. JOHN DEWEY

When you think of the thousands and thousands of young 'uns who are practically being ruined negatively if not positively in the Chicago schools every year, it is enough to make you go out and howl on the street corners like the Salvation Army.

—John Dewey

Background

John Dewey was a philosopher, psychologist, and educator. As an educational reformer he was the founder of what has become known as progressive education. He was born in Burlington, Vermont, in 1859. He graduated from the University of Vermont with honors and moved on to acquire his doctorate at Johns Hopkins University.

After spending three years as a high school teacher in upstate Pennsylvania, Dewey accepted a faculty position at the University of Michigan, where he taught for ten years. In 1894 he joined the faculty of the fledgling University of Chicago. He spent the better part of his life at the University of Chicago, developing his educational, philosophical, and psychological theories and concepts.

During these years he instituted the University of Chicago Laboratory School, which was one of the first laboratory schools within a university where aspiring teachers could put pedagogical theory into practice. One of the outcomes of the laboratory school was the publication of his first major work on education, *The School and Society*. He also used his laboratory school observations as the basis for his seminal publication on progressive education, *Democracy and Education*.

The constant theme in Dewey's works in education was his undying belief in the values of democracy. As an educational reformer, he decried the traditional belief that the teacher is the sole transmitter of learning, in favor of a more student-centered approach. He believed in a more balanced approach with a much greater emphasis on active, experiential, and hands-on student learning.

In addition to his work in education, Dewey, along with the historian Charles Beard, and economists Thorstein Veblen and James Harvey Robinson, established what came to be known as The New School. The New School made significant contributions to the fields of philosophy and psychology. Dewey's work, *The Reflex Arc Concept in Psychology*, was a critique of traditional psychological theories and practices in favor of his concept of functional psychology. His publication, *Experience and Nature* explored new concepts in philosophy, including pragmatism and instrumentalism. As a result of these and other accomplishments, he was named president of the American Psychological Association and of the American Philosophical Association.

Dewey resigned from the University of Chicago after a disagreement with administration and in 1904 accepted a professor of philosophy position at Columbia University in its Teachers College. He remained there for the remainder of his life. After a long and distinguished career, John Dewey passed away in 1952 at the age of ninety-two.

The Structural Frame

Structural frame leaders seek to develop a new model of the relationship of structure, strategy, and environment for their organizations. Strategic planning, extensive preparation and effecting change are priorities for them. Along with the other four leadership frames, we will find that John Dewey was very active in the structural frame. In a combination of structural and symbolic frame leadership behavior, Dewey helped to create and sometimes lead a number of educational and civic organizations, including the American Civil Liberties Union, the American Psychological Association, the American Philosophical Association, the National Association for the Advancement of Colored People, the American Association of University Professors, and the New York Teachers Union.

Dewey used the structural frame in establishing himself as a public intellectual by distilling his complex philosophical, educational, and psychological beliefs into concepts that were relevant to the average person's day-to-day professional activities. His goal, he said, was to make philosophy "a method . . . for dealing with the problems of men" (Menand 2001, 237).

In typical structural frame style, Dewey researched his positions to be certain that they were substantive. For example, in developing his philosophy of education and life in general, he relied on a physiological textbook written by Thomas Huxley. Huxley's description of the human body as being at once an independent and an interrelated organism inspired Dewey to look at life in the same way. He wrote that this book provided "a kind of type or model of a view of things to which material in any field ought to conform. Subconsciously, at least, I was led to desire a world and a life that would have the same properties as had the human organism in the picture of it derived from study of Huxley's treatment" (Menand 2001, 252).

Dewey used structural frame behavior in accommodating the career interests of both himself and his wife. Since his wife, a former student of his, was interested in a career in social work, he moved from the rather insular suburbs of Ann Arbor, Michigan, and took a position at the University of Chicago to be in a much more urban environment. He arrived in Chicago in the midst of the famous Pullman railroad workers strike, with which both he and his wife would become involved on the side of the union.

To Dewey, the city of Chicago was equivalent to a social science laboratory, with Jane Addams's Hull House and settlement movement in full stride and the Pullman strike wreaking its havoc. Dewey finally had his life's vision. He wrote

> I think I'm in a fair way to become an educational crank. I sometimes think I will drop teaching philosophy directly, and teach it via pedagogy. When you think of the thousands and thousands of young 'uns who are practically being ruined negatively if not positively in the Chicago schools every year, it is enough to make you go up and howl on the street corners like the Salvation Army (Menand 2001, 319).

So, in 1896, Dewey opened the University Elementary School of the University of Chicago to experiment with his educational philosophy and pedagogy. Later called the Laboratory School, it began with only 16 elementary school–aged children. In five years, the enrollment increased to 140 and quickly gained an international reputation. Dewey's school was an educational laboratory in the same vein as Jane Addams's Hull House was a sociological experiment.

Again working out of the structural frame, Dewey took a page out of Maria Montessori's book and was the first in the United States to use manipulatives such as blocks to teach arithmetic and to schedule field trips to learn geography. "Learning by doing" also known as the "hands-on approach" was one of his lasting mantras.

Some of the other educational terms and pedagogies he coined included the unity of knowledge approach, which stressed the relationship that one academic discipline had with another. This concept launched the interdisciplinary movement, which militated against the traditional silo effect that is to this day still ingrained in the nation's educational psyche. At the Dewey school, the young students were involved in workshop-type projects where learning was acquired in the same way that it was acquired in the laboratory of real life—through cooperative activities. He was also famous for insisting that the academic disciplines be made relevant to the students' lives, and in this vein he became the so-called father of vocational education in the United States.

One of Dewey's obsessions, for instance, was cooking. The young students in the Laboratory School would cook and serve at least one meal per week. Of course, Dewey's real genius was the integration of the various academic disciplines in the cooking process. For example, the students would use mathematical principles in weighing and measuring ingredients, and science in the boiling and heating of the food.

Typical of Dewey's consistent use of structural frame behavior, he convinced the University of Chicago to combine the famous Francis Parker Elementary School, which stressed community and citizenship, with his Laboratory School, which emphasized progressive education. Dewey was in charge of the combined schools and every other aspect of the education program at the University of Chicago (Menand 2001).

The Human Resource Frame

Human resource leaders believe in people and communicate that belief. They are passionate about productivity through people. John Dewey had a great love and respect for humankind, so he operated out of the human resource frame almost constantly. Some historians believe that Dewey was as liberal a thinker as the United States has ever produced. As such, he was vitally concerned with democracy and social justice. He abhorred distinctions of any kind, whether due to class, gender, status, or race. He is said "never to have come across a distinction he did not find invidious and wish to break down" (Menand 2001, 236).

Dewey derived much of his love for humanity from his contemporary in Chicago, Jane Addams, the founder of the settlement movement in the United States. His reverence for her and her love of people was made evident in a letter that Dewey wrote to his wife: "Miss A [Addams] said she would give the whole thing up [the Settlement House Movement] before she would ask for policemen; one day a Negro spat straight in her face in the street, and she wiped it off and went on talking without noticing it" (Menand 2001, 314).

Dewey was drawn to a career in education because of his love for children and his great respect for the common man. He saw the intellectuals' preference of thinking over doing as a reflection of their class bias. But in condemning the thinking priority, he was not necessarily trying to reverse the emphasis, as those who branded him as an anti-intellectual claimed. As his friend Jane Addams pointed out in his defense, "He was showing that doing and thinking, like stimulus and response, are just practical distinctions we make when tensions arise in the process of adjustment between the organism and its world" (Menand 2001, 330).

The Symbolic Frame

In the symbolic frame, the organization is seen as a stage, a theater in which every actor plays certain roles and the symbolic leader attempts to communicate the right impressions to the right audiences. Like any successful leader, John Dewey was frequently active in the symbolic frame. Dewey projected the image of an ultra-liberal. Though he was never a socialist, his symbolic frame behavior would lead one to believe that he was much closer to socialism than he was the new liberalism reflected most popularly by Franklin Roosevelt's New Deal. In fact, Dewey engaged in the very symbolic act of supporting and voting for the socialist candidate Norman Thomas, not once, but three times.

Dewey used symbolic frame behavior in expressing his philosophy and ideologies early on in two short articles, "The Metaphysical Assumptions of Materialism" and "The Pantheism of Spinoza." Both were apologias of transcendentalism, which was spawned in his home state of Vermont. In doing so, he positioned himself to take a prominent place in the pantheon of American philosophers.

He burnished his image by exhibiting an equanimity and poise that verged on a certain charisma that gave Dewey a sort of personal authority. His speeches and writings assumed the status of those of a Greek oracle coming down from Olympus.

Dewey exhibited symbolic leadership behavior and polished his ultra-liberal image during the Pullman strike by being a public admirer of Eugene Debs, the leader of the American Railway Union. He wrote to his wife,

> I don't believe the world has seen but few times such a spectacle of magnificent, widespread union of men about a common interest as this strike evinces. The government is evidently going to take a hand in and the men will be beaten almost to a certainty—but it's a great thing and the beginning of greater things (Menand 2001, 295).

Dewey's support of the strikers brought to light the many contradictions that had come to be part of the nation's cumulative psyche. At Dewey and Jane Addams's urging, public policies that were the result of a mixture of Puritan ethics, laissez faire economics, the natural law, and social Darwinism were questioned for the first time. What resulted was a significantly more progressive public.

In Dewey's *The Ethics of Democracy*, he defended democracy against rugged individualism and unregulated capitalism—union against management. He asserted the primacy of "the popular will." "Society in its unified and structural character is the fact of the case," he wrote. "The non-social individual is an abstraction arrived at by imagining what man would be if all his human qualities were taken away" (Menand 2001, 305).

The real meaning of the Pullman strike was not for an academic like Dewey to interpret, he opined. It was for a practicing social scientist like his friend and colleague Jane Addams to dissect. So Dewey displayed symbolic frame behavior by deferring to her. In her Hull House experiences she had discovered that the people social workers try to help almost always have better notions about how their lives can be improved than the so-called professionals do.

Both Addams and Dewey came to the realization that any reform that depended on top-down decisions was doomed to failure. "We must learn," she wrote, "to trust our democracy, giant-like and threatening as it may appear in its uncouth strength and untidy applications." Dewey and Addams saw that the resistance that society displays in social actions like the Pullman strike is not a reflection of a full-fledged conflict of interests. "I don't know as I got the reality of this at all," Dewey concluded, "it seems so natural and commonplace now but I never had anything take hold of me so." He and Addams likened it to King Lear's conflict with his daughter Cordelia in Shakespeare's play—paternalism versus self-determination. So to Dewey and Addams, the right outcome was always the outcome democratically reached (Menand 2001, 311).

In typical symbolic leadership fashion, Dewey used the metaphor of the organic circuit to express his theory of learning in his paper entitled "The Reflex Arc Concept." "There is a circuit in any material," he explained. "The beginning and the end is the individual activity. Knowledge is not the result of experience, any more than a response is the result of a stimulus; knowledge is experience itself in one of its manifestations. The facts and truths that enter into a child's present experience, and those contained in the subject matter of studies, are the initial and final terms of one reality" (Menand 2001, 330).

"The Reflex Arc Concept" paper replicated Dewey's thinking process. It was the metacognitive process he used in approaching any problem, and he believed that most young people engaged in the same process. First he would expose a tacit hierarchy in the terms in which people conventionally think about something. Most people believe that a response follows a stimulus. Dewey taught that there is a stimulus only because there is already a response. We think that first there are individuals and then there is society; Dewey taught that there is no such thing as an individual without society. We think we know in order to do; Dewey taught that doing is why there is knowing. As a result of these beliefs, he adopted his learning-by-doing approach (Menand 2001).

The Political Frame

Leaders operating out of the political frame clarify what they want and what they can get. Political frame leaders are realists above all. They never let what they want cloud their judgment about what is possible. They assess the distribution of power and interests. Even in the apparently benevolent fields of philosophy and education there is a need for leaders to operate out of the political frame on occasion if they wish to be effective. Perhaps Dewey's most obvious use of political frame behavior was in his involvement with the Pullman railway strike. He wrote to his wife,

> The strike is lost and Labor is rather depressed. But if I am a prophet, it really won. The business made a tremendous impression, and while there has been a good deal of violent talk—particularly it seems to me by the upper classes, yet the exhibition of what the unions might accomplish, if organized and working together, has not only sobered them, but given the public mind an object lesson that it won't forget. I think the few thousand freight cars burned up a pretty cheap price to pay—it was the stimulus necessary to direct attention, and it might easily have taken more to get the social organism thinking. My main impression is that I am a good deal of an anarchist (Menand 2001, 297).

In general, Dewey often used political frame behavior to advance in his profession and to promote his programs and projects. He believed, for example, that his Laboratory School should be funded in the same way other laboratories were funded at the University of Chicago, while the president's view was that it had to be self-sufficient. Dewey won the day by demonstrating that the Laboratory School provided intangible benefits, like prestige, to the university. However, as oftentimes happens in these types of negotiations, his winning the day did not enhance his standing with his colleagues in the other academic disciplines.

In another instance of his use of political frame leadership behavior, when opposition arose to his wife being the principal of the Laboratory School, Dewey responded in kind. When his wife was forced to resign as principal, in retaliation he promptly resigned as director of the School of Education. A few days later, Dewey raised the stakes and resigned as chair and professor of the philosophy department and offered his services to the grateful Teacher's College at Columbia University (Menand 2001).

The Moral Frame

The moral frame is my own contribution to situational leadership theory. In my view, the moral frame completes situational leadership theory. Without it, leaders could just as easily use their leadership skills for promoting evil as for promoting good. Leaders operating out of the moral frame are concerned about their obligations and responsibilities to their followers. Moral frame leaders use some type of moral compass to direct their behavior. They practice what has been described as servant leadership and are concerned with those individuals and groups that are marginalized in their organizations and in society. In short, they are concerned about equality, fairness, and social justice.

Dewey was greatly influenced in the development of his moral compass by James March's *Aids to Reflection* and its synthesis of philosophy and faith. It impressed upon Dewey that there was a compatibility rather than a conflict between Christian beliefs and modern scientific thought. March's work, he said many years later, was "my first Bible" (Menand 2001, 252).

Thus, Dewey was not interested in philosophy and education as a form of mental exercise. He was interested in his adopted disciplines as a moral and ethical guide for his leadership and other behaviors. Dewey believed in the Hegelian concept of the "Absolute God." "I suppose, borne in upon me as a consequence of a heritage of New England culture, divisions by way of isolation of self from the world, of soul from body, of nature from God, brought painful oppression, or, rather, they were an inward laceration," he confessed. The remainder of his life reflected his belief in the compatibility of faith and reason, and this seemingly contradictory concept made up the moral code that guided his every action (Menand 2001, 275).

Perhaps James Tufts, a mentee of Dewey's at the University of Michigan put it best in regard to his appropriate use of moral frame behavior when he said: "As a man, he is simple, modest, utterly devoid of any affection or self-consciousness, and makes many friends and no enemies. He is a man of religious nature" (Menand et al. 2001, 288).

Situational Leadership Analysis

Situational models of leadership differ from earlier trait and behavioral models in asserting that no single way of leading works in all situations. Rather, appropriate behavior depends on the circumstances at a given time. Effective managers diagnose the situation, identify the leadership style or behavior that will be most effective, and then determine whether they can implement the required style.

There is no question but that John Dewey was a leader in the situational mold. We saw how he was appropriately active in all five frames of leadership behavior. He used structural frame behavior in establishing his unique

Laboratory School at the University of Chicago. His use of human resource frame behavior derived from his genuine concern for humanity and civil and human rights. The astute use of symbolic leadership behavior established him as perhaps the most famous and prominent American philosopher and educator of his time. We saw how he used political leadership behavior in obtaining special funding for his Laboratory School, and, we observed how he developed a moral compass to guide his leadership behavior.

Leadership Implications and Conclusion

It was no accident that John Dewey became the revered philosophical and educational leader that he was. His influence on both philosophy and education endure to this day. There is much for leaders and aspiring leaders to learn from examining the leadership behavior of this great and heroic leader. His astute and effective use of the five leadership frames was exemplary. The leadership lessons that are his legacy are particularly applicable to educational leaders. In many cases in this book we had to adapt a leader's leadership behavior to have it apply to the field of education. In Dewey's case, we can merely duplicate it.

II. MAO ZEDONG

> People who try to commit suicide—don't attempt to save them! . . . China is such a populous nation, it is not as if we cannot do without a few people.
>
> —Mao Zedong

Background

Mao Zedong was born in 1893 and was a Chinese statesman whose status as a revolutionary in world history is second only to that of Vladimir Lenin. Mao was born in Shaoshan, Hunan, China. By 1918, Mao was already committed to communism. With the rise of the Chinese Communist Party (CCP) in 1921, of which Mao was one of fifty founding members, he pursued his political agenda.

Meanwhile, the major nationalist Chinese political party, the Kuomintang (KMT), was restructured, and a coalition party was formed between the KMT and CCP. Mao was a minor figure in the coalition until he discovered the revolutionary potential of the peasants who had been treated poorly by the Chinese warlords.

Eventually, the Communists took up arms against the government and established rural soviets in central and northern China. One of these soviets served as Mao's home base. Years of struggle occurred between the Communist Party and Chiang Kai-shek's anti-Communist party. Eventually Chiang was able to drive the Communists out of their occupied territories and forced them to retreat on what was called the Long March, a year-long, six-thousand-mile journey through the hills of China.

The various Communist factions were searching for a leader who could rival Chiang in case a civil war broke out. Mao filled this role and his popularity soon soared. The personality cult of Mao grew until his concepts were written into the Party's constitution of 1945. Under Mao's leadership the Communists won one military victory after another.

On January 21, 1949, in a decisive battle, Chiang's forces suffered massive losses against Mao's Red Army. Red Army troops then laid siege to Chengdu, the last Kuomintang-occupied city in mainland China, and Chiang Kai-shek evacuated from the mainland to the island of Formosa (Taiwan).

The People's Republic of China was officially established on October 1, 1949, after two decades of civil and international war. In 1954, Mao took control of the national Communist Party and became known as Chairman Mao. Following the consolidation of power, Mao launched the First Five-Year Plan. The success of the First Five-Year Plan encouraged Mao to instigate the Second Five-Year Plan, called the Great Leap Forward, in 1958. Under this program, land was taken from landlords and wealthier peasants and given to poorer peasants. The program was a colossal failure.

Facing the prospect of losing his place on the world stage, Mao responded by launching the Cultural Revolution in 1966. As part of the Revolution, Mao organized the army and young students in the form of the Red Guards. With their help, Mao began to consolidate his power. Soon there was no official Chinese thought beyond the extent of Mao's thought, which was compiled in the ubiquitous *Little Red Book*.

During the Cultural Revolution, Mao closed the schools in China, and the young intellectuals and many university professors living in the urban areas were ordered to the countryside. For example, one of my Chinese friends was the esteemed chair of the geology department at Nanjing University. He ended up being sent to a farm to perform manual labor. His daughter told me that this humiliation almost led him to commit suicide. The Cultural Revolution led to the destruction of much of China's cultural heritage.

In 1969, after three years of national misery, Mao declared the Cultural Revolution to be over. In the last years of his life, Mao was faced with declining health due to Parkinson's disease. He died on September 9, 1976 (Halliday 2005).

Situational Leadership Analysis

Situational models of leadership differ from earlier trait and behavioral models in asserting that no single way of leading works in all situations. Rather, appropriate behavior depends on the circumstances at a given time. Effective managers diagnose the situation, identify the leadership style or behavior that will be most effective, and then determine whether they can implement the required style.

Although Chairman Mao had a reputation for being a rigid demagogue, there were times when he realized that being more situational in his leadership behavior would be beneficial to the attainment of his long-range goals. Initially, Mao's philosophy toward communism varied somewhat from that of the Russians. Whereas Lenin and Stalin saw the urban workers as the leaders of the communist revolution, Mao believed the farmers and peasants should serve in that role. But being the situational leader that he was, Mao shifted with the prevailing winds. He was not stubbornly attached to his views. "On the peasant question," he said, "the class line must be abandoned, there is nothing to be done among the poor peasants and it is necessary to establish ties with landowners, and gentry" (Halliday 2005, 39).

By nature, Mao was an impulsive man, but as a situational leader he usually was able to control his impulses. He once told staff who commented on his "unruffled calm" and "impeccable self-control": "It's not that I am not angry. Sometimes I am so angry I feel my lungs are bursting, but I know I must control myself, and not show anything" (Halliday 2005, 260). In this instance, he was alluding to the kidnapping of his son by Joseph Stalin. His impulse was to strike back in some way, but upon reflection, he decided to display political frame behavior, and as we will see, it paid dividends.

Terrorization had always been Mao's solution whenever he wanted to achieve anything or was challenged in any way. But in 1956, after Khrushchev condemned Stalin's use of terror, Mao decided to curb the number of arrests and executions. So, in situational leadership fashion, Mao gave orders to his police chief: "This year the number of arrests must be greatly reduced from last year. The number of executions especially must be fewer" (Halliday 2005, 416).

Another indication of his reliance on situational leadership behavior was when the Great Famine occurred during the Great Leap Forward and the Chinese were struggling mightily. Mao decided that the purges would be decreased. As soon as the famine passed, however, the Great Purge and the Cultural Revolution took place, and the Red Guard was revitalized.

The Structural Frame

Structural frame leaders seek to develop a new model of the relationship of structure, strategy, and environment for their organizations. Strategic planning, extensive preparation, and effecting change are priorities for them. It is fair to assert that the structural frame was one of Mao's strongest. In an effort endemic to a structural leader, he was one of the first world leaders to devise a national long-range plan built upon successive five-year strategic plans.

Even as a youth, Mao practiced a combination of structural and political leadership behavior. He was in charge of a bookshop, but he got a friend to run it. An important trait emerged at this time. He had a gift for delegating chores and identifying and convincing people to perform them. He also had an excellent work ethic. He would work himself to exhaustion, but with the adrenalin continuing to flow, he had to rely on sleeping pills to fall asleep. Later in his life, he would almost comically rank the inventor of sleeping pills alongside Marx as one of the greatest men in history.

Mao was partial to the highly structured and hierarchical military approach to management. In 1927, he told an emergency Communist Party meeting, "Power comes out of the barrel of the gun" (Halliday 2005, 50).

Like a prototypical structural leader, he had a well-thought-out plan that included the building of his own army, staking claim to his own territory, and dealing with Moscow and Washington from a position of strength. During World War II, for example, Mao opted not to fight the Japanese or the Chinese Nationalists. With Russia preoccupied with Germany and in no position to intervene, Mao seized the opportunity to consolidate his party and prepare his army for the forthcoming civil war against the forces of Chiang Kai-shek.

In true, albeit extreme, structural leadership style, the Chinese people were pounded into submission at indoctrination meetings, rallies, and interrogations. Consumed in writing "thought examinations," the Chinese people had no time to think of rebellion. "Get everybody to write their thought examination and write three times, five times, again and again," Mao said. "Tell everyone to spill out every single thing they have ever harbored that is not so good for the Party" (Halliday 2005, 245).

Mao succeeded in getting people to inform on each other. After two years of indoctrination and terror, the young volunteers were transformed from passionate champions of justice and equality into robots at the service of Mao. By forcefully operating out of the structural frame, he was able to attain this influence over his followers. Every day, at the interminable party meetings, Mao's simplistic modus operandi was made know to his disciples: "For everything wrong in the party, blame others; for every success, himself" (Halliday 2005, 268).

The use of structural behavior such as this served Mao well in his preparation for successfully managing the Chinese civil war. His nonmilitary intelligence networks provided Mao with precise information about the movements of Chiang Kai-shek's army, which placed Chiang at a huge disadvantage.

Mao used structural frame behavior in seamlessly transitioning China from Nationalist rule to Communist rule. The plan called for the conquering army to replace government workers with young Communist recruits. Another part of the plan was to co-opt the legal system and the news media. Once the state was secure, Mao began systematic terrorization of the population to induce long-term conformity and obedience.

In a combination of structural and symbolic frame behavior, Mao became famous for launching his Five-Year Plans, with various goals like ending poverty, and building worldwide domination. However, the breakneck speed he imposed on the Great Leap Forward, whereby China would have the atomic bomb and become a world leader, spawned a long-term quality-control problem that plagued arms and industrial production throughout his time in power.

Beginning in 1960, the national goal became to propagate Mao Zedong's thought around the world in the form of "Maoism." Mao used structural leadership behavior to formulate the goal and again in bringing the goal to fruition. Thus, as we have seen, Mao utilized structural leadership behavior, albeit very often to an extreme, as an integral part of his overall leadership style.

The Human Resource Frame

Human resource leaders believe in people and communicate that belief. They are passionate about productivity through people. Although he gave lip service to his concern for his countrymen, there was little evidence that Mao thought seriously about employing human resource leadership behavior. Nevertheless, when it served his purposes, Mao was capable of utilizing human resource behavior.

For example, as a means for currying favor with his troops, Mao set up "soldiers committees" to satisfy their desire for input into how to distribute the proceeds of their looting. Still, Mao's relationship with his army was in many ways a remote one. He never tried to inspire his troops in person, never visited the front, and never went to meet the troops in the field. He did not care about them as individuals, just as a war machine to achieve his goals. Other than this one diluted example of Mao's use of human resource behavior, it is difficult to find any substantial evidence that he utilized the human resource frame to any great extent.

The Symbolic Frame

In the symbolic frame, the organization is seen as a stage, a theater in which every actor plays certain roles, and the symbolic leader attempts to communicate the right impressions to the right audiences. One could argue that, along with the political frame, the ability to exploit the symbolic frame was one of Mao's greatest strengths. Even at a young age, Mao went about cultivating his public image as a great scholar and thinker. He spent many hours in the library reading books, including translations of Western writings. In the process, he scorned his fellow Chinese writers. "The nature of the people of the country is inertia," he said. "They worship hypocrisy, are content with being slaves, and narrow-minded" (Chang and Halliday 2005, 12). He took part in book burning. This was an early indication of a theme that was to typify his rule—the destruction of Chinese culture.

Unlike most founding dictators, such as Lenin, Mussolini, and Hitler, Mao did not inspire a passionate following through his oratory or writings. He simply sought willing recruits who were ready to blindly follow his orders.

Mao's use of symbolic leadership behavior was so effective that despite his disdain for the peasants and working class, his image as the champion of the workers survives to this day. Writing to a friend in 1920, in which he complained about his own conditions as an intellectual, he remarked, "I think laborers in China do not really suffer poor physical conditions. Only scholars suffer" (Chang and Halliday 2005, 30). Nevertheless, as a testament to his ability to effectively employ symbolic leadership behavior, he retained the image of the working man's hero.

To help develop his image as a godlike figure, Mao had one of his poems widely circulated:

> Eagles soar up the long vault,
> Fish fly down the shallow riverbed,
> Under a sky of frost, ten thousand creatures vie to impose their will.
> Touched by this vastness,
> I ask the boundless earth:
> Who after all will be your master? (Chang and Halliday 2005, 38)

Mao was famous for taking advantage of every opportunity to create and propagate his image. He did so in dramatic fashion when Chiang Kai-shek decided to purge his National Party of any communist influence. Mao immediately went public in his opposition, once again casting himself as the champion of the common man. In typical symbolic frame fashion, he labeled his opposition to Chiang's army as the Autumn Harvest Uprising.

After one of his early victories over Chiang in the Autumn Harvest Uprising, one of his officers came to offer congratulations: "Mao Zhuxi!" (Chairman Mao), he called out. "You learn really fast," Mao replied. "You are the first person." This officer was the first person to use the title that was to become part of the world's vocabulary: *Chairman Mao* (Chang and Halliday 2005, 100).

In another example of his use of symbolic behavior, Mao was a devotee of public executions. He organized large rallies to view the executions as a way of intimidating the populace into obeying him. In time, he made these viewings mandatory.

In 1934, Mao led some eighty thousand soldiers on what came to be called the Long March. The ten-day long retreat across hundreds of miles of terrain and rivers created one of the most enduring facets of Mao's legend. It was yet another chapter in his becoming the peoples' hero.

In 1937, Mao once again used symbolic behavior by publishing the political pamphlet *Red Star* in a number of languages. In what was now a grand tradition, it painted a favorable picture of Mao as the champion of the workers and had a tremendous influence on his image in the West, including the United States.

Public opinion was further influenced by the publication *Stories of a Journey to the West*. In addition to this book and the Mao Zedong autobiography, a third book was produced from Edgar Snow's material, *Impressions of Mao Tse-tung*. Edgar Snow was a British news reporter and Mao's pawn. These publications helped shape Mao's positive image both at home and abroad.

Mao adroitly exploited his followers' idealism, somehow convincing them that his harsh treatment of them worked to their advantage and was part of "serving the people," an expression he coined. "We were fighting the enemy in the dark," he said, "and so wounded our own people." Or, "It was like a father beating his sons. So please don't bear grudges. Please just get up, dust the mud off your clothes and fight on" (Chang and Halliday 2005, 248). These declarations, of course, were all rationalizations, but nonetheless believable to the Chinese people.

Mao was jealous of Chiang Kai-shek's lingering reputation as the nation builder of modern China. Thus, he set out to debunk that image. In 1944 he ordered the party to be re-educated on the question "Who is the nation-builder of China, the Nationalists or the CCP?" (Chang and Halliday 2005, 251). He developed a strategy whereby the answer would be Chairman Mao. This strategy led to what was to become known as "Mao Tse-tung Thought."

Eventually, Mao was successful in developing his own personality cult. The turning point in this regard occurred when the Chinese people "firmly established in their minds that Chairman Mao is our *only* wise leader" (Chang and Halliday 2005, 268). It was at that time that the deification of Mao had begun.

On October 1, 1949, the symbolic behavior continued as Mao appeared standing on top of Tiananmen Gate, in front of the imperial Forbidden City, and formally established the People's Republic of China (PRC). From then on, Mao would make these appearances on special occasions, a practice modeled after Soviet leaders ascending Lenin's tomb in Red Square to make their political speeches.

In typical symbolic leadership fashion, Mao became famous for coining terms for many of his programs. The "Three-Antis" targeted embezzlement, waste, and bureaucratism or laziness. This campaign was followed shortly by the "Five-Antis": bribery, tax evasion, pilfering state property, cheating, and stealing economic information. Of course, he also coined the terms *Five-Year Plan*, *The Great Leap Forward*, and the *Cultural Revolution* (Chang and Halliday 2005).

The campaign to spread Maoism embraced a great reliance on symbolic behavior, including the carrying of the *Little Red Book*, which contained many of Mao's ideals. Mao's face dominated the front pages of the *Peoples' Daily*, which was required to run a column of his quotes every day.

The Cultural Revolution, which sought to eliminate the remains of past Chinese cultures, was characterized by such symbolic behavior as book burnings, condemnation of the intelligentsia, and confiscations of land. Mao wanted to create a society of robots that, devoid of any ideological foundation, would mindlessly obey his orders. Through the prolific use of symbolic and political behavior, he was able to achieve this goal—at least temporarily.

The Political Frame

Leaders operating out of the political frame clarify what they want and what they can get. Political leaders are realists above all. They never let what they want cloud their judgment about what is possible. They assess the distribution of power and interests. Mao's capacity to operate out of the political leadership frame effectively was also one of his strengths. Mao learned the effectiveness of astutely applied political behavior at an early age. He was fond of telling the story of having an argument with his father over his laziness. He ran out of the house, and his father pursued. He told his father that he would jump into the pond in the backyard if he came closer. "My father backed down," he said. "Old men like him didn't want to lose their sons. This is their weakness. I attacked at their weak point and I won" (Chang and Halliday 2005, 6).

One of his first significant uses of political frame behavior came when he was not invited to a communist congress while he was serving as party boss in his hometown area, Hunan. Not being invited meant that he might lose his job as the head Communist in Hunan province. So he decided to be proactive and schedule very visible visits to the lead and zinc mine and the coal-mining center. He also led a number of demonstrations and strikes in support of the Communist Party. Mao also infiltrated the Nationalist Party and undermined Sun Yat-sen's leadership.

This success lead to Mao's power struggles with Sun's successor, Chiang Kai-shek, the new commander of the Nationalist Party army. As mentioned earlier, when Chiang gave orders to cleanse the Nationalist Party of communist influence, Mao saw a chance to make a name for himself by keeping the communist influence alive. It marked his political coming of age.

By 1944, Mao had anticipated that Russia would soon join the Chinese and the United States and enter the war against Japan. After Japan was defeated, Mao would need "friends" in his fight to unseat Chiang Kai-shek, so he engaged in political behavior once again in beginning to tone down the terror so that he would be perceived in a better light by Russia and the United States. He would also recognize the Nationalist Party as the legitimate government and place the Red territory and Red Army under Chiang Kai-shek.

Mao's basic plan for the Sino-Japanese War, therefore, was to preserve his forces and expand the sphere of the Communist Party. So, when the Japanese pushed deeper into China, in exchange for relinquishing Red-held territory, Mao got Chiang to agree that the Red Army would not be put into any battles and would operate only as auxiliaries to the government troops. This way, Mao could preserve his army for the civil war that would come *after* the Sino-Japanese War.

Thus, Mao played both the United States and Soviet Russia like a proverbial fiddle. He convinced Stalin to invade China in 1945, thus creating the conditions for Mao to seize power. At the same time, Mao carefully exploited the fact that U.S. officials were becoming increasingly disenchanted with Chiang. Mao carefully fostered the delusion that the CCP was a moderate agrarian reform party that would be a friendly ally of the United States. After the war, Mao continued to use political behavior to enhance his power and influence. While an armistice was being negotiated to end the Korean War in 1953, Mao once again used political behavior to further his agenda. President Eisenhower mentioned the possibility of using the atom bomb to hasten the talks toward a peaceful conclusion. Mao immediately exploited Eisenhower's threat by pushing Russia to give him nuclear weapons and information on how to build an atomic bomb.

In the era of de-Stalinization that followed Stalin's death, Mao once again engaged in political frame leadership behavior. In what he called the Hundred Flowers Campaign, he invited people to speak out against the evils of communism so that it could be reformed. Once the reform fad had passed, he arrested and in some cases executed those who had spoken out. In effect, he used the occasion to identify his political enemies.

By 1970, Maoism had waned. Ever resourceful, Mao came up with yet another political strategy that would get him back on the world stage. He decided that he would convince the president of the United States to visit China—enter Richard Nixon. After Nixon's historic visit, Mao had a rebirth, and world leaders from every country around the world were anxious to get an audience with the great and powerful Chairman Mao.

The Moral Frame

The moral frame is my own contribution to situational leadership theory. In my view, the moral frame completes situational leadership theory. Without it, leaders could just as easily use their leadership skills for promoting evil as for promoting good. Leaders operating out of the moral frame are concerned about their obligations and responsibilities to their followers. Moral frame leaders use some type of moral compass to direct their behavior. They practice what has been described as servant leadership and are concerned with those individuals and groups that are marginalized in their organizations and in society. In short, they are concerned about equality, fairness, and social justice.

Chairman Mao is another of example of a great leader who was not a *good* one. There is little in his leadership behavior to indicate that he gave even one iota of consideration to acting out of the moral frame. Mao's attitude toward morality consisted in one core value, the self. "I do not agree with the view that to be moral, the motive of one's action has to be benefiting others. People like me want to satisfy ourselves to the full, and in doing so automatically have the most valuable moral codes. Of course there are people and objects in the world, but they are only there for me," he declared (Chang and Halliday 2005, 13). As a result of this credo, Mao will be remembered in history primarily as a leader who was responsible for the deaths of millions of his own people.

Conclusion

There is an abundance of evidence that Mao Zedong was a situational leader. We saw how he utilized structural frame leadership behavior and developed a strategic plan to achieve his goals, and he popularized the term *Five-Year Plan*. Once his plans were set in motion, he made good use of symbolic and political frame leadership behavior. For example, he labeled many of his movements in creative ways so as to gain attention. *Great Leap Forward*, *Cultural Revolution*, and the *Hundred Flowers Campaign* are but a few of the catchy terms that he used to derive maximum impact.

We saw that he was a master at utilizing the political frame, especially in his dealings with the United States, Nationalist China, and the Soviet Union. He convinced the Soviet Union to support him in his efforts to displace the

Nationalist government of Chiang with his Chinese Communist Party, and when his reputation was flagging, he enticed Richard Nixon to visit China, thereby resurrecting his image as a world leader.

However, there were two frames, human resource and moral, in which Mao displayed little or no activity. The lack of practicing any significant leadership behavior in these two frames led to Mao's place in history as a notorious leader who caused more evil than good. He is often mentioned in the same breath as Adolf Hitler, Joseph Stalin, Vladimir Lenin, and Benito Mussolini—not the best of company, indeed!

Chapter Eight

Montessori v. Stalin

I. MARIA MONTESSORI

By nature a child has an instinct to explore its surrounding world and become independent of adult help. Just as the mother bird does not hinder, but encourages her young to fly, we should cultivate our children's instincts to be independent.

—Maria Montessori

Background

Maria Montessori was born in 1870 in Chiaravalle, Italy, and became a renowned medical doctor and educator who developed a system of Montessori schools that utilized her progressive method of education—the Montessori Method. Innumerable Montessori schools have been established in North America and in virtually every other continent in the world.

Montessori was the first woman to graduate from medical school in Italy. As a member of the University of Rome's Psychiatry Clinic, she became intrigued with children with special needs and how they might be educated. After giving a lecture at which she outlined her ideas on educating students with mental disabilities, she was appointed director of the Scuola Ortofrenica (School for Mentally Retarded). When a number of her students took the state examinations and outscored the regular students, she and her method became famous and began taking root in Italy and other countries.

The Montessori method was based on a number of fundamental beliefs, among which was the notion that the teacher should serve only as a guide in the learning process and that children should be left alone to learn at their own pace. Montessori also believed that children have "sensitive periods" when they are particularly able and motivated to learn certain types of aca-

149

demic disciplines. The Montessori Method greatly influenced the work of Jean Piaget and his "stages of development" theory that, much like Montessori, posits that children's learning of certain subject matter comes more easily to them at certain chronological ages.

The Montessori Method flourished throughout Europe during the first four decades of the twentieth century. It had such a formative effect on Italy's children that Benito Mussolini felt it necessary to exile Montessori because she refused to compromise her principles to include military training in her schools. She lived in Spain until the Spanish Civil War broke out, whereupon she moved to the Netherlands where she spent the remainder of her life. After a lifetime devoted to the study of child development, Montessori died in 1952 at age 81 (Lubienski 1999).

The Structural Frame

Structural frame leaders seek to develop a new model of the relationship of structure, strategy, and environment for their organizations. Strategic planning, extensive preparation and effecting change are priorities for them. Being the educator that she was, it is not surprising to find that the structural frame was one of Maria Montessori's dominant frames. As is typical of a structural frame leader, Montessori developed a primary goal and a vision and articulated them in one sentence. It is simply to provide young people with "a guide to achieving a positive attitude of mind in all circumstances of life." This principle was to apply to the entirety of the Montessori system from its nursery schools to its elementary schools and to lifetime learning (Lubienski 1999, 6).

To achieve this positive attitude, Montessori demanded that children in her schools would be encouraged instead of reprimanded, stimulating their positive impulses instead of repressing the negative ones, looking for their good intentions rather than dwelling on their misbehavior and believing in human nature's preference of good over evil.

Montessori's idea was that by changing the educational process from one of restraint, imposition, and recrimination to one of freedom and cooperation, she could help transform the attitudes of the adults who interacted with her children and eventually transform the attitude of society as a whole.

In the training of her teachers, Montessori showed them how to reverse the usual negative attitudes and pessimistic outlook on life that they may have had and instead fostered in them a faith and trust in the younger generation. In particular, she engrained in them the value of scientific, research-based methods that developed self-disciplined, optimistic, joyous, and creative minds by basing their teaching styles to the child's nature and inclinations.

Montessori is best known, of course, for the effectiveness of her approach at the pre-school and elementary levels of education. What is not as well-known is her use of structural frame leadership behavior in strongly encouraging educational policy makers to extend her methods to higher levels of education. And to a great extent, she was successful. The current trend to make education at all levels an enjoyable process rather than drudgery is one of her many lasting influences.

Although Montessori frequently used the structural frame, she prided herself on doing so in moderation. The educational theories of our age seem to drift from one extreme to the other. At times there is an emphasis on back-to-basics rigidity, and at other times a stress on freedom that verges on chaos. Because it is based on both sound educational theory and effective practice, the Montessori method offers freedom without anarchy and discipline without rigidity.

Once again operating out of the structural frame, Montessori used her ingenuity and whatever material resources that were readily available to produce the rudimentary didactic "tools" used in her method, thus enabling even the poorest of communities to provide a Montessori-inspired education.

Montessori used structural frame leadership behavior in developing a training and licensing program for teachers who would be establishing and/or instructing in Montessori schools. This licensing and training process is still in existence today.

As we have seen, Montessori used structural frame behavior to develop the theory and practice of her method. One of the Montessori schools' unique practices is the teaching of foreign languages at an early age when children were learning their native languages, because they are at a point in their cognitive development where they are very facile in their ability to learn languages. This basic intuition has evidently eluded those school districts that even today delay the teaching of foreign languages until middle or high school.

No structural frame leader would be without a set of principles, values, and beliefs. And neither was Montessori. Her principles included the following:

1. Never touch a child unless invited.
2. Never speak ill of a child either publically or privately.
3. Strengthen what is good in a child so there is less space for evil.
4. Prepare an environment conducive to learning.
5. Be sensitive to every child's need.
6. Respect the child who makes a mistake but corrects it. But stop firmly any misuse of the environment that might endanger the safety and welfare of the child or his classmates.
7. Respect the child who takes a rest or watches others working.

8. Help those in search of an activity and cannot find it.
9. Be untiring in repeating instruction until the child absorbs it.
10. Always treat the child with respect. (Lubienski 1999, 78)

One final instance of Montessori's use of the structural frame was in her development of what we now refer to as cooperative or collaborative education. Based on the concept that one only really knows something if he or she can teach it to someone else, Montessori believed that children more fully learn and understand a concept if they can explain it to their classmates—thus the birth of collaborative learning (Lubienski 1999).

The Human Resource Frame

Human resource leaders believe in people and communicate that belief. They are passionate about productivity through people. With her love of children and those who taught them, it is obvious that Maria Montessori was a people person. Human resource frame behavior was at the very foundation of Montessori's beliefs and practice. She believed that children who have not been properly integrated into their miniature society at an early age will likely continue in the same vein as adults. She contended that some of the results of this failure to properly socialize children would be divorce, dissension among siblings, materialism, a declining work ethic, and employers being indifferent to the well-being of their employees.

In summary, Montessori's life's work was dedicated to enhancing the well-being and the quality of life of others. Her frequent use of human resource frame leadership behavior is a testament of her concern and sensitivity toward others (Lubienski 1999).

The Symbolic Frame

In the symbolic frame, the organization is seen as a stage, a theater in which every actor plays certain roles and the symbolic leader attempts to communicate the right impressions to the right audiences. Any accomplished leader must spend time operating out of the symbolic frame, and Montessori was no exception. Symbolic of Montessori's leadership and influence is that her name is almost universally known, and there is a vast network of Montessori schools throughout the world. Her set of beliefs included the God-given right of children to be afforded the knowledge necessary to be happy members of a peaceful society. Given these favorable conditions, a child's virtuous qualities would fully develop and many of society's ills would be precluded.

Montessori used symbolic frame behavior to separate her schools from the pack. When a visitor enters a classroom that uses her method, the visitor will find the children working on a painted line around the room or sitting motionless during a lesson on silence or deeply immersed in some calculation with the help of seeds or stones, and the visitor will immediately recognize that the Montessori method is being used. In all Montessori classrooms there is a brightly painted line around the perimeter of the room upon which the students are instructed to work. It is Montessori's way of adding a certain structure and discipline to the educational process.

The essence of her method was beautifully summarized symbolically in the form of a series of six speeches she presented and later published at the Montessori International Conference in Amsterdam, Holland, in 1933. One of her primary principles is that by nature a child has an instinct to explore his or her surroundings and become independent. Describing this principle in symbolic terms, Montessori likened the child's development to that of a bird. "Just as the mother does not hinder, but encourages her young to fly, we should cultivate our children's instincts to be independent," she said (Lubienski 1999, 14).

If these instincts are curtailed, children become frustrated, bored, and even angry. The way to prevent these so-called deviations according to Montessori, would be to provide them with an environment conducive to independent learning and less dependency on the teacher and other adults.

Another of Montessori's founding principles is that neither the teacher nor the parent should be an autocratic figure, using coercion to impose their will on the children. According to Montessori, a teacher is like a food server who offers the customers a menu with many options and makes recommendations on what might be the best dish for them.

Perhaps Montessori's primary principle is to provide the children with a sense of freedom. In order to accomplish the fine balance between granting the students freedom and still teaching them what they need to know to become productive citizens, the Montessori method creates a structured environment that leads children indirectly or symbolically, instead of directly toward their goals.

Montessori used symbolic frame behavior in accomplishing her principles. For example, to foster freedom and to make learning enjoyable, she strongly emphasized that the classroom and the entire school and its surroundings be attractive, welcoming, clean, and bright. She even mandated that the children be consulted regarding the desk arrangements, wall pictures, and the other materials and decorations in the classroom.

Another of Montessori's principles as enunciated in her Amsterdam speeches included the fact that children should not be given complicated exercises and tasks without any relation to real life. Teachers were directed to use concrete materials that she called "manipulatives," a term that is still used today, to get their points across.

Engaging in both symbolic and structural frame behavior, Montessori established a publication called *Montessori Notes* in which she elaborated on the details of her method. In one of the issues, entitled "Advice to Teachers" she wrote: "She must give her lessons; plant the seed in the soil, and then slip away; observe and wait expectantly, but not interfere. She should point out every detail of the action with absolute clearness, and then leave the child the means of perfecting himself, without correcting him, even if he does badly" (Lubienski 1999, 50).

In her book, *The Montessori Method*, she again added some flesh to the skeleton of her method. One of the matters that she addressed was the apparent contradiction between freedom and discipline in the classroom. "Once the habit of work is formed, we must supervise it with scrupulous accuracy. In our effort to establish discipline, we must rigorously apply the principles of the method. It is not obtained by words; no one learns self-discipline through hearing another man speak," she declared. She believed that the concentration that it took for the students to freely discern what materials they should use would lead to the ability to discipline themselves (Lubienski 1999, 53).

Again displaying symbolic frame thinking, Montessori believed that a teacher should be like a salesperson. In effect, the teacher is selling knowledge and skills to the students and like a successful salesperson, the teacher must make knowledge attractive to the customers. If the teacher is successful in making learning attractive to the students, very few of them will not "buy" it. Like the aphorism that concludes that there are no bad soldiers, just bad generals, Montessori held that there were no bad students, only bad teachers (Lubienski 1999).

The Political Frame

Leaders operating out of the political frame clarify what they want and what they can get. Political leaders are realists above all. They never let what they want cloud their judgment about what is possible. They assess the distribution of power and interests. Even a leader with the kind and gentle reputation of Maria Montessori needed to use at least a modicum of political frame leadership behavior to be successful. The Montessori method has freedom at its foundation, which in and of itself has political implications. In Montessori's view, the purpose of education should be to develop the sense of freedom in children so that they know what they want to do and what they want to be. In effect, she was promoting democracy because she believed that once children experienced true freedom they would be disinclined to accept totalitarianism in later life. "The child is the whole of future humanity," she wrote. "The social question of the child leads naturally to a desire to try to find out the laws of man's formation, so helping us to create a new conscience and giving a new direction to our social life" (Lubienski 1999, 10).

Since her field was education and not politics, Montessori did not feel that she was in a position to unilaterally determine the political aims of educational development in a country. However, she felt compelled and qualified to indicate the most effective and psychologically sound method for raising well-balanced and happy human beings who would be capable of informatively choosing the type of social organization of which they would want to be a part. But would the children educated in the Montessori schools chose freedom over oppression? Montessori thought they would and thus was very optimistic about the future of children educated in her schools.

Nevertheless, Montessori was careful not to suggest that her method was a panacea for all the world's ills. Rather, she recommended that any of her materials that proved ineffective or became outdated be replaced by those that had been scientifically proven to increase learning and bring about the full development and independence of the student. So although some Montessori teachers and principals shy away from using any commercially developed materials to replace the Montessori materials, Montessori herself was much more open to doing so. Her use of political frame behavior in the form of compromise helped to gain almost universal support for her movement. She urged her followers to take a balanced approach whereby they were free to use commercially developed textbooks but not rely on them so exclusively that they were inhibited from being the reflective practitioners they need to be (Lubienski 1999).

The Moral Frame

The moral frame is my own contribution to situational leadership theory. In my view, the moral frame completes situational leadership theory. Without it, leaders could just as easily use their leadership skills for promoting evil as for promoting good. Leaders operating out of the moral frame are concerned about their obligations and responsibilities to their followers. Moral frame leaders use some type of moral compass to direct their behavior. They practice what has been described as servant leadership and are concerned with those individuals and groups that are marginalized in their organizations and in society. In short, they are concerned about equality, fairness, and social justice.

Maria Montessori's life story reflects a strong devotion to moral frame behavior. She believed that in addition to an education in the secular subjects, students should be exposed to moral education. Her primary objective was to educate people to live peacefully within modern society. She insisted that her method be evaluated not only for academic progress, but also on its effectiveness in character formation in its students. She believed that it was of paramount importance to care about the children's hearts as well as their minds.

Situational Leadership Analysis

Situational models of leadership differ from earlier trait and behavioral models in asserting that no single way of leading works in all situations. Rather, appropriate behavior depends of the circumstances at a given time. Effective managers diagnose the situation, identify the leadership style or behavior that will be most effective, and then determine whether they can implement the required style.

After reviewing examples of her leadership behavior, it becomes obvious that Maria Montessori was a leader in the situational mold. She was appropriately active in all five of the leadership frames and used each of them in moderation. In this light, it is particularly illuminating to read Montessori's observations about the changes occurring in the child at the end of the preschool period and the need for a very different instructional approach after that age. At ages seven through sixteen, the child's awakening moral sense has to be cultivated, its wider interests developed, and his or her growing feeling of being a productive part of society needs to be supported and nurtured. In other words, as a child moves through the different stages of development, a situational or contingency approach to instruction needs to be applied.

The balance that Montessori used in her approach to leadership should be an inspiration to all of us. She used each of the five leadership frames when appropriate and behaved in moderation within each frame. Thus, she was truly exemplary in her application of situational leadership theory.

Leadership Implications and Conclusion

Reminiscent of the words of the great football coach and leader Vince Lombardi, to Montessori the child is not the important thing in education; the child is the only thing. The words that she uttered in the latter part of the nineteenth century still ring true today.

> Man meets no obstacles now in reaching any part of the globe, right to the most remote corners of the earth; neither mountains nor seas can stop him, because he can fly above them. Who will sound the trumpet that will wake them? What will man do, he who now lies asleep on the surface of the globe, while the earth is about to engulf him? The answer is clear: it is the children, the new children, who will wake him, the ones freed from the shackles that until now have prevented them from working spontaneously, according to their nature (Lubienski 1999, 115).

The implications for educational leaders are clear. Educators need to cultivate and encourage their students to be free and independent thinkers and people. For educational leaders, one of the ways of nurturing this sense of freedom is to teach and practice situational leadership theory. Educational leaders should encourage aspiring leaders to avoid the inclination to settle on one singular leadership style and experience the freedom that comes with operating at various times and in different situations out of all five of the leadership frames. In doing so, we can strive to be truly heroic leaders in the mold of Maria Montessori.

II. JOSEPH STALIN

> Joseph Stalin is an outstanding mediocrity.

> —Leon Trotsky

Background

Joseph Stalin was born Iosif Vissarionovich Dzhugashvili in Georgia in 1878 and after he played a significant part in the Lenin-led Bolshevik Revolution, he became the first general secretary of the Communist Party of the Soviet Union's Central Committee from 1922 until his death in 1953. He became famous as the man who turned the Soviet Union from a backward czarist country into a world superpower, but at incredible human cost.

Stalin attended the seminary in Tiflis, the capital of Georgia, to study to become a priest. But Stalin never completed his education there, instead dropping out to become a political activist and revolutionary. Never an intellectual in the Lenin or Trotsky mold, Stalin acted as the "enforcer" of the Bolshevik Revolution. He also distributed illegal literature, robbed trains and banks, and engaged in terrorism to support the cause. Although Lenin found Stalin's heavy-handedness embarrassing at times and often excessive, he valued his loyalty and thus appointed him to various leadership positions in the new Soviet government.

After Lenin's death in 1924, Stalin methodically engaged in revisionist history regarding his relationship with Lenin and his part in the founding of the Bolshevik Party. He then perpetrated a character assassination of his competitors for the leadership of the party. At first, they were simply relieved of their posts and exiled for their alleged political crimes. But later, Stalin engaged in a reign of terror and conducted show trials during which the founding fathers of the Soviet Union were exposed as "enemies of the people." The particularly troublesome and persistent Leon Trotsky, who continued to agitate and criticize Stalin from his exile in Mexico, was finally murdered there by Stalinist assassins in 1940.

Domestically, Stalin pursued an aggressive industrialization program so that Russia could successfully compete with the capitalistic world powers. He instituted several Five-Year Plans to consolidate all investment and production in Russia. As a result, the Soviet Union could boast that its economy was booming while the capitalist world was experiencing the Great Depression. In foreign affairs, with the winds of war practically blowing in his face, Stalin negotiated a nonaggression pact with Adolf Hitler in 1939, in which they agreed to divide Poland and not invade one another's homeland. Stalin had such faith in Hitler's word that he at first refused to heed his military advisors' warnings in 1941 that Germany was mobilizing its troops to invade the Soviet Union. As a result, when the attack did come, the Soviet army was almost completely unprepared and suffered over one million casualties in the first days of the battle. The tide eventually turned at Stalingrad in 1943, when the winter weather helped the Soviet Army achieve the final victory.

During the Yalta and Potsdam Conferences, Stalin proved to be an effective negotiator, every bit the equal of Franklin Roosevelt and Winston Churchill. He managed to keep the countries that Russia liberated as part of the Soviet Union and secured three seats for his country in the newly formed United Nations. The Soviet Union was now a recognized world superpower, with its own permanent seat on the United Nations Security Council.

After several unsuccessful assassination attempts, Stalin passed away of natural causes in 1953. He remained a hero to his people until Nikita Khrushchev's famous "secret" speech to a Party Congress in 1956, in which Stalin's excesses were made known and he was officially denounced and publicly disgraced.

The Structural Frame

Structural frame leaders seek to develop a new model of the relationship of structure, strategy, and environment for their organizations. Strategic planning, extensive preparation and effecting change are priorities for them. Although Stalin was not an intellectual in the mold of a Lenin, he was very much the pragmatist and, as such, was very active in the structural frame. As a pupil in the theological seminary he attended, Stalin revealed considerable cognitive abilities and a phenomenal memory. He reportedly outperformed his classmates in his knowledge of both the Old and New Testaments, and would surely have been at or near the top of his graduating class if he had chosen to remain there.

Like the structural leader that he was, he was said to have had a strong tendency to systematize, categorize and intellectually compartmentalize any form of knowledge. However, his religious education fostered a tendency to be dogmatic and self-righteous. As is common among strongly structural leaders, he was inclined to canonize his beliefs, and this inflexibility sometimes led to disastrous results.

Like many structural leaders, Stalin was a workaholic and preferred to remain at headquarters, working in the center of control rather than traveling through the Soviet Union spreading communist doctrines. Because of his overreliance on structural frame behavior, he was not a strong creative thinker. For example, early on he was almost oblivious to the symbolic and political frames of leadership behavior that Lenin was so effective in applying during the pre–October Revolution period.

During the Russian civil war, Stalin's structural frame style was particularly disquieting to many of his fellow commanders, who even then sensed that this man had a stubbornly iron will and that it would be difficult for him to make spontaneous decisions or to change his mind when necessary regarding his battle plans.

Lacking an appreciation for strategic and tactical knowledge, Stalin relied mainly on discipline and blind loyalty among his troops. His operational commands were oftentimes primitive. For example, when a commander asked for reinforcements to recapture a town, he replied: "The point of our last order was to give you the opportunity to reassemble these regiments into a single group in order to destroy the opposition's best regiments. I repeat, to destroy, because what we are talking about is destruction" (Volkoganov, 1991, p. 41).

Stalin's structural leadership ability, albeit extreme at times, showed indisputably that he could effectively contribute to the restructuring of the Soviet society. His elevation to the post of general secretary after Lenin's death came as no surprise. He was thought to be the perfect man to implement and operationalize the vision developed by Marx, Lenin, and Trotsky.

Faithful to his structural frame leanings, Stalin was a supreme pragmatist. To him the world was black and white and whatever and whoever did not correspond to the party line was harmful. His preferred form of reasoning was binary logic, yes and no. His style in notes, speeches or reports was cryptic. But Stalin's structural frame style was very popular among his countrymen. They saw him as very businesslike, a dutiful man without sentimentality, and a man ruled by reason rather than emotion.

Being the structural leader that he was, Stalin was very deliberate in all that he did. For example, his stenographer typed out one 1927 speech that he made to the railway workers while Stalin was beating time with his hand and slowly expounding: "We are completing the change over from a peasant country to an industrial one without help from the outside world. We have our own way, and that is to accumulate our own. There will be shortcomings . . . but they will not be important in the end" (Volkoganov 1991, 111).

It should be noted that, in typical structural leader style, Stalin authored his own articles and speeches. Various assistants who were employed in his secretariat at times have testified that, despite the great workload he carried, Stalin nevertheless did an enormous amount of reading and writing for himself.

Having once set a goal, he was capable of the most amazing persistence in reaching it. This was evident in his written work. Basically he repeated his points over and over, producing a kind of didactic or preaching approach. Some consider the will to be the muscle of the mind, and a strong will was Stalin's forte.

Often taking the structural frame to the extreme, Stalin was cognizant of the famine and starvation that was prevalent in the countryside but was unwilling to alter his plan. Once, when he uncommonly felt a pang of doubt about his choice of policies, he recalled the works of the old anarchist rebel Nikolai Bakunin: "The will is almighty; nothing is impossible for the will." Despite severe harvest failures, the government's quotas for grain and other produce deliveries remained the same (Volkoganov 1991, 169).

Marshal Vasilevsky, one of his generals, recalled Stalin's traits in this way: "I never met anyone who could remember as much. He knew by names all the army and front commanders, of whom there were more than one hundred, and he even knew the names of some corps and divisional commanders." All through World War I Stalin had the composition of the strategic reserves in his head and could name any formation at any time (Volkoganov 1991, 234).

Despite believing that Hitler would honor the peace pact that they signed and not invade Russia, being the structural leader that he was, Stalin still set about building up Russia's defenses, albeit not nearly enough. The USSR now had one of the most powerful industrial machines in the world. However, since he industrialized too rapidly, the quality of the products suffered. It was fortunate that the Soviets had an inexhaustible amount of manpower and the Russian winter, because their weaponry was oftentimes inferior to that of the Germans

Whatever one thinks of Stalin, by his persistent and emotionless application of structural leadership behavior, he did accomplish a significant leap forward for his country. The American nuclear monopoly was broken, and the USSR was now a major player on the world stage.

The Human Resource Frame

Human resource leaders believe in people and communicate that belief. They are passionate about productivity through people. With the individual being subordinate to the state in the communist ideology, one should not be surprised that Stalin saw the use of human resource frame behavior as a weakness rather than strength. Stalin had virtually no friends, certainly none with whom he maintained warm relations throughout his life. Political calculation, low emotional intelligence, and moral apathy made it impossible for him to form and keep friends. In my historical research on Stalin, albeit somewhat limited, I was not able to find any real evidence that indicated that he ever used human resource leadership behavior for non-politically driven reasons.

The Symbolic Frame

In the symbolic frame, the organization is seen as a stage, a theater in which every actor plays certain roles and the symbolic leader attempts to communicate the right impression to the right audiences. Although he was not particularly articulate and put pen to paper in the form of the printed word very infrequently, Stalin found a number of alternate ways to engage in symbolic frame behavior.

The reserve that was a noticeable dimension of the Stalin image in his early years, became in time a total lack of compassion. He nevertheless learned to wear a mask when he was among people, and he utilized symbolic frame behavior to give the impression that he was a composed and even outgoing person.

Stalin realized at an early age that he had to fight for what he wanted. His comrades had often said, "Koba [his nickname], you've got a strong will." He liked what he heard and decided to make that aspect of his character his hallmark, even by changing his name to reflect it. From as early as 1912, he began to sign his name "Stalin," or "man of steel" (Volkoganov 1991, 7).

Perhaps the image that Stalin valued the most was his perceived ideological invulnerability. He assumed the position of the official interpreter and commentator on Lenin's ideologies so people would believe that he stood alongside Lenin as a founding father of the Soviet Union. The resulting Stalin cult became a social, historical, spiritual, moral, and psychological phenomenon—all this despite the fact that it was built on a lie. Lenin actually preferred Trotsky over Stalin (Volkoganov 1991, 74).

Aware of Lenin's preference for Trotsky, Stalin attempted to discredit Trotsky at every opportunity. For example, in a Kremlin speech in 1924 which he entitled "Trotskyism or Leninism," he viciously attacked Trotsky. "The motivation," behind Trotsky's recent speeches Stalin claimed, "is that Trotsky is making yet another attempt to prepare the ground to substitute Trotskyism for Leninism. Trotsky badly needs to dethrone the party and the cadres that went through the uprising, so that, having dethroned the party he can proceed to dethrone Leninism." Thus, Stalin set himself up as the only true defender and interpreter of Leninism (Volkoganov 1991, 109).

Engaging in more symbolic behavior, Stalin wrote "Questions of Leninism" and "The Foundations of Leninism." He made certain that these publications were broadly distributed and used as dogmatic quote sources by the Stalinist propagandists.

Stalin's autocratic rule was gradually reinforced by a host of cult acts and rites. There were "Stalin Stipends," and "Stalin Prizes." The "Lenin Prize" was discontinued. Even the national anthem reflected his role in the destiny of the Fatherland: "Stalin has raised us to loyalty to the people. To labor and to heroic feats he has inspired us," the Soviets intoned (Volkoganov 1991, 222).

Lion Feuchtwanger, a German writer visiting Moscow in 1937 commented:

> The worship and boundless cult with which the population surrounds Stalin is the first thing that strikes the foreigner visiting the Soviet Union. On every corner, at every crossroads, in appropriate and inappropriate places alike, one sees gigantic busts and portraits of Stalin. The speeches one hears, not only the political ones, but even on any scientific or artistic subjects are peppered with glorification of Stalin, and at times this deification takes on tasteless forms (Volkoganov 1991, 237).

In another display of symbolic behavior, Stalin and the leaders of the Bolshevik revolution made a point of living very modestly. When Stalin died, an inventory of his possessions included no antiques or valuable objects of any kind. His clothes consisted of only a couple of suits. However, the thrifty image was only skin deep, as Stalin also had the use of several villas in Moscow and in the countryside as well as a large staff of servants. His every wish was fulfilled, but he did everything possible to project the proletarian simplicity of his lifestyle and to a great extent, he did.

Knowing that blatant dictatorship was anathema to the proletariat, Stalin used symbolic behavior to dispel any "misunderstandings." Stalin frequently spoke about equality and social justice as the basic principles of socialist democracy. "Our democracy must always put general interests in first place. The personal counts for next to nothing compared with the social. As long as there are still idlers and enemies and theft of socialist property, it means there are still people who are alien to socialism, and that means we must keep up the struggle," he pontificated (Volkoganov 1991, 187).

His effective use of symbolic frame behavior enabled Stalin to be one of the few in history to accomplish what he did—to exterminate millions of his own countrymen and receive in return the whole country's cult-like adulation and support. Saying one thing and doing another became Stalin's modus operandi, publically condemning the Stalin cult while privately reinforcing it; talking about democratic leadership while reducing it to totalitarianism was typical of Stalin.

Stalin's propaganda mill stipulated two simple propositions. First, the leader of the party and the nation is a wise man whose every thought is immutably true. Secondly, he is the total embodiment of absolute good and cares for every person. In short, he is that grandfatherly man with the mustache in all the posters, who is carrying the little girl waving the Soviet flag.

Stalin astutely used the Allies' victory in War World II to bolster his image even further. He used his newfound world status to convince his people and the world of the indestructibility of the Soviet Union and its social institutions. Stalin used victory consciously and resolutely to expand the Communist Party agenda in general and the USSR in particular. Through the clever use of symbolic frame leadership behavior, world communism was no longer beyond his reach (Volkoganov 1991).

The Political Frame

Leaders operating out of the political frame clarify what they want and what they can get. Political leaders are realists above all. They never let what they want cloud their judgment about what is possible. They assess the distribution of power and interests. It can be argued convincingly that Stalin spend much of his time operating out the political frame. Yet, as astute as Stalin was in effectively utilizing the political frame, he was never able to have success in using it with his ideological archenemy, Leon Trotsky. Despite Vladimir Lenin's efforts to smooth relations between Stalin and Trotsky, they remained distant and guarded. Stalin found Trotsky's rising popularity painful to endure and thought that it was grossly undeserved. Their bitter rivalry lasted until Trotsky's death in 1940. In fact, there is much evidence that suggests that Stalin ordered his murder.

But Stalin's use of political frame behavior was never more evident than in his relationship with Lenin. For example, probably no one visited Lenin during his illness as often as Stalin. Sometimes he was invited to be brought up to date on current affairs, but more often he came on his own initiative, knowing that Lenin would be naming his successor from his deathbed. Also, at the end of Lenin's life Stalin increasingly took it upon himself to limit the information flowing to Lenin so that he would have little impact on the current situation and Stalin's own position on the issues would prevail.

To Stalin's advantage was the fact that Leon Trotsky was almost inept as a politician. Stalin seized on Trotsky's political naïveté in true political frame style by constantly pointing out Trotsky's apparent lack of party loyalty, knowing that Trotsky was oblivious to the need to at least occasionally apply a little political leadership behavior. For example, Trotsky's absence from Lenin's funeral and his frequent absences from Politburo meetings were used by Stalin to strengthen his position in the party as contrasted to that of Trotsky.

In the pre–World War II days, Stalin used political frame leadership behavior and approached Britain and France several times in an effort to obtain a five- or ten-year agreement on mutual assistance against Germany. Stalin lost patience after he received no official response from these two countries, and in true political frame fashion finally signed a nonaggression pact with Germany.

Both the Soviet Union and Germany entered into the nonaggression pact with ulterior motives, however. For Germany, the pact ensured that Germany would be left free to attack France and Britain among others and not have to be concerned about Russia on the Eastern Front. For the USSR, the pact bought them time to mobilize for the inevitable conflict.

Being the political animal that he was, Stalin had no problem compromising his principles when it became necessary. For the sake of the antifascist coalition to defeat Hitler, Stalin set aside ideological postulates and ignored the long-standing anticommunist sentiments of many of the Western democracies, taking a totally pragmatic approach in aligning himself with the Allies.

Another area in which Stalin applied political frame behavior was in his treatment of the Russian Orthodox Church, an institution the former seminarian had initially disdained. For example, in 1925, by his initiative, the church had been prevented from electing a new patriarch. Suddenly in 1943, however, Stalin invited Russian Orthodox officials to meet with him at his dacha. There they discussed the role of the church in the war effort. In exchange for their cooperation, he promised to relax the constraints that he had enacted. Stalin took this step because of the patriotic and cultural value of being perceived as aligning with an institution that was well-respected and popular with both the Russian people and the other Allied countries.

Thus, Stalin's use of political frame behavior garnered recognition not only within the USSR but also throughout the world. For example, the new U.S. president, Harry Truman, remarked in a letter to him that he had "demonstrated the ability of a peace loving people, with the highest degree of courage, to destroy the evil forces of barbarism" (Volkoganov 1991, 497).

Since Russia suffered an astounding thirty million casualties and vast areas of Soviet land were occupied, something none of the other Allies endured, Stalin lobbied successfully for a peace treaty especially advantageous to the Soviet Union. As we have seen, he was able to negotiate the reinstatement of all the Soviet republics and acquire a permanent seat on the United Nations Security Council.

Given the United States' nuclear advantage at the conclusion of the war, Stalin once again employed political frame leadership behavior at the World Peace Congress of 1949 when he officially coined the term "peaceful coexistence" and used it for the first time. The concept placed the Soviet Union on the same level as the United States and other superpowers.

Finally, Stalin used political frame behavior in dealing with Mao Zedong. Given the persistent hostility that Mao had with the United States, it was a natural for Mao and Stalin to befriend each other. After the Chinese revolution, relations developed rapidly on numerous fronts, culminating in Mao being invited to Moscow in a place of honor to join the celebration of Stalin's seventieth birthday, thus allowing Stalin to gain even more leverage in his dealings with the United States.

The Moral Frame

The moral frame is my own contribution to situational leadership theory. In my view, the moral frame completes situational leadership theory. Without it, leaders could just as easily use their leadership skills for pivoting evil as for promoting good. Leaders operating out of the moral frame are concerned about their obligations and responsibilities to their followers. Moral frame leaders use some type of moral compass to direct their behavior. They practice what has been described as servant leadership and are concerned with those individuals and groups that are marginalized in their organizations and in society. In short, they are concerned about equality, fairness, and social justice.

No one could legitimately claim that Stalin was a good person. He manifestly lacked the moral qualities that one normally associates with virtue. There are numerous instances of his lack of the use of a moral compass to guide his behavior.

In 1922, for example, Lenin had written his "Letter to Congress," recommending the removal of Stalin from the post of general secretary. Stalin conveniently "lost" the letter, and it never became public. Lenin had finally come to the conclusion that Stalin's moral failings were repugnant in a leader of the Communist Party. "I am appalled by . . . the connivance of Stalin," he wrote (Volkoganov 1991, 74). Of course, Lenin was not one to talk.

In 1932 when Stalin's wife committed suicide, he was shattered. But even here he remained true to his a credo: He did not feel at all responsible for his wife's act but saw it as treachery to himself. It never seemed to have occurred to him that it was his callousness and lack of love and attention that could have hurt her so profoundly that she took such an extreme step.

Stalin's contempt for normal human values had long been evident. He saw the emotions of sympathy and mercy as psychological weaknesses. He valued only reason and power. The identification of a colleague as "an enemy of the people" was the noblest of acts in his mind. For him the moral parameters of society were a hegemonic invention of the elite classes to keep the common people in line (Volkoganov 1991, 155).

Even on his deathbed, Stalin perpetuated his image as the merciless tyrant. In speaking to an aid about his physicians not being frank with him regarding his illness, he asked: "Have the doctors confessed? Tell Ignatiev that if he doesn't get full confessions out of them, we'll reduce his height by a head" (Volkoganov 1991, 571).

Situational Leadership Analysis

Situational models of leadership differ from earlier trait and behavioral models in asserting that no single way of leading works in all situations. Rather, appropriate behavior depends on the circumstances at a given time. Effective managers diagnose the situation, identify the leadership style or behavior that will be most effective, and then determine whether they can implement the required style.

Skilled in the art of political survival, Stalin was quite adept at being situational when necessary. He presented one face to the Politburo, another at congresses, and yet another when he was relating to factory workers. And during the October Revolution, Stalin was a centrist who knew how to sit and wait and adapt himself to the constantly changing situation.

Stalin demonstrated his situational leadership skills in dealing with Leon Trotsky. Perhaps earlier than most, Stalin noted Trotsky's strong and weak sides. Taking Trotsky's enormous popularity into account, Stalin at first tried some human resource behavior and tried to establish if not friendly, then at least stable relations with him. On one occasion, Stalin turned up unannounced at Trotsky's home to congratulate him on his birthday. In his public speeches Stalin talked glowingly of Trotsky's role in the revolution and civil war, but that did not improve Trotsky's aloof attitude towards him. Hence, Stalin resorted to structural frame behavior and he openly opposed Trotsky.

Stalin had the ability to move rather facilely from one leadership frame to another. In the privacy of his study, Stalin routinely and without emotion signed off on lists of names to be arrested and executed and approved all types of inhuman sentences; while on the rostrum, waving and gesturing in an embracing way, another Stalin declared that the new Constitution "is not limited by the fixing of formal civil rights, but it shifts the center of gravity to the question of guarantees for those rights" (Volkoganov 1991, 276).

Leadership Implications and Conclusions

Stalinism exploited to the fullest the Russian revolutionaries' readiness to sacrifice everything including their history, culture, and their lives, for the sake of an ideology. But the deification of the state turned into indifference toward human beings. Stalin's embracing of these ideals made a mockery of moral philosophy and is yet another instance of an otherwise talented leader going asunder because of a failure to engage in moral frame leadership behavior.

In this book I frequently refer to conscience and morality. It is said that people like Stalin regard conscience as a chimera or foolish fancy. One cannot speak of conscience when speaking of a dictator like Stalin. He simply did not have one.

Just this morning I read in the *Philadelphia Inquirer* of a principal of one of the local public middle schools who was being accused of falsifying test scores resulting in an almost miraculous test score gain at a school where nine of ten students dwell in poverty and significant acts of violence occur virtually every day. The school's test scores rose an astonishing fifty-two points in math and fifty-one points in reading on the statewide assessments known as the PSSAs. If guilty, one wonders whether this principal, like Stalin, lacked a moral lens through which he or she could filter his or her leadership behavior.

Chapter Nine

Freire v. Jones

I. PAULO FREIRE

People cannot be liberated as long as they are unable to obtain food and drink,
housing and clothing in adequate quality and quantity.

—Paulo Freire

Background

Paulo Freire was born in 1921 in Recife, Brazil. Having lived through the
Great Depression, he formed a great sensitivity and concern for the plight of
the poor, and his solidarity with the poor greatly affected his view on education and learning.

After graduating from college, Freire enrolled in the University of Recife
Law School. He was admitted to the bar but never practiced law, deciding
instead to enter the field of education as a high school foreign language
teacher. In 1944, he married one of his teacher colleagues and together they
formulated his unique approach to education.

Immediately after World War II, Freire was appointed director of the
Department of Education and Culture of the Social Service in his local state.
While working primarily with poor illiterates he began to develop his unor-
thodox philosophy of education with undertones of liberation theology.

Fifteen years later Freire was appointed director of the Department of
Cultural Extension of Recife University, and in this capacity he ran the
University's part-time night school. When a cohort of more than 300 sugar-
cane workers learned to read and write in a month and a half, Freire's method, labeled "cultural circles," began being utilized all over Brazil.

A few years later, a military coup gained power and expelled the former regime's employees, including Freire. After being imprisoned briefly in Brazil, Freire fled to Chile where he continued his career in education. It was in Chile that Freire published his first book, and that was followed by his seminal work, *Pedagogy of the Oppressed*, which became an international best seller.

As a result of the international popularity of his book, Freire was offered a visiting professorship at Harvard. He later moved to Geneva, Switzerland, to work in special education for the World Council of Churches. Freire subsequently returned to Brazil and continued his work in education, this time with adult literacy. He became renowned for having been one of the founders of what is known as critical theory—an educational theory that concerns itself with equity and social justice implications for education. Freire was an active contributor to the field of education until he died of heart failure in 1997 at the age of seventy-five.

The Structural Frame

Structural frame leaders seek to develop a new model of the relationship of structure, strategy, and environment for their organizations. Strategic planning, extensive preparation and effecting change are priorities for them. Paulo Freire was very active in the structural frame, especially in the development of his unique educational pedagogy. To Freire, education has to have a humanizing effect or it is deficient. To be humanizing, education has to be critical or questioning; dialogical or interactive; and practical or relevant. To educate in the Freirean sense is to use education to build a better society by actively resisting both overt and covert oppression on the part of the dominant culture.

As director of the Cultural Extension Service at the University of Recife, Freire used structural frame leadership behavior to develop what he called "culture circles," whereby the goal of education was to teach students to read and write while at the same time fostering a more critical understanding of oppressive social conditions. His successful methods, used primarily with illiterate adults, quickly spread throughout Brazil and other countries in South America.

Contrary to the view of many of his critics who depicted his approach as "anything goes," Freire demanded that in order to be effective, educational dialogue needs to have a purpose, a sense of structure and a direction—all structural frame characteristics.

Also, like many strong structural leaders before and after him, Freire remained very active right up to the end of his life. For example, there were three distinct periods in his publishing career starting with the early period when he published his seminal work, *Pedagogy of the Oppressed*. That was followed by a less active period when he published only *Pedagogy in Progress: The Letters to Guinea-Bissau*. But he ended his life with a flourish, publishing a number of works, including his second-most-famous book, *A Pedagogy of Liberation*, when he was sixty-five years of age.

In another demonstration of his structural frame leanings, Freire was a great proponent of dialectical thinking. According to him, thinking dialectically required one to look for and uncover the contradictions in social reality. This concept led to what is now called critical theory and critical pedagogy, which implies an investigation beyond the surface to ascertain the social implications of one's actions. Thus social problems are not merely studied in the abstract, but rather as part of a gestalt and theorized in global terms.

Thus, for Freire, present knowledge is by definition incomplete. It is always open to questioning and further adjustment. Acquiring knowledge is an everlasting process of discovery with no real end in sight. Hence, Freire considered the acquisition of knowledge to be akin to constant traveling with no final destination. In the process, he helped inspire a generation of scholars who adopted critical theory and critical pedagogy as a way of thinking and as a theoretical basis for their research.

Being the structural frame leader that he was, Freire sought a theoretical underpinning to guide his acquisition of knowledge or learning. That underpinning was his basic belief that every person seeks liberation or freedom. Those who are oppressed seek liberation more forcibly, which sometimes leads to the transformational action of reform and even rebellion. According to Freire, "people cannot be liberated as long as they are unable to obtain food and drink, housing and clothing in adequate quality and quantity" (Roberts 2000, 45). This understanding was at the foundation of all of his educational efforts.

In both a structural and moral frame display, Freire summarized his philosophy in three underlying principles: "(1) All aspects of reality are constantly changing as is the process of knowing; (2) humans, unlike animals, are rational and need to utilize this capacity in the process of humanization, both for themselves and others; and (3) humans live in a social world, interacting with other humans in their mutual struggle for liberation" (Roberts 2000, 49).

Further, at least five key principles derive from this philosophy: "(1) People ought to pursue their vocation of becoming more human through engaging in critical, dialogical praxis; (2) no person ought to oppress another; (3) we ought to collectively determine a social setting in which all people are enabled to pursue their humanization; (4) all people ought to transform existing structures that impede the pursuit of humanization; and (5) educators and others who have positions of responsibilities ought to be in solidarity with the oppressed in seeking to promote a better world" (Roberts 2000, 50).

Freire offers us what he calls "liberating education" in place of "banking education." Liberating education, which is child centered, is contrasted with banking education, which is teacher centered. Banking education treats the learners as empty vessels into which the teacher makes "deposits," while liberating education is student centered, respects earlier learning, and subjects itself to continuing critical analysis.

But in true structural frame fashion, Freire does not advocate an "anything goes" classroom philosophy. Liberating education is structured, goal-oriented, didactic, and rigorous. The primary difference in his approach as compared to the traditional approach is that in liberating education the teacher serves as the guide to learning rather than the source of learning (Roberts 2000).

The Human Resource Frame

Human resource leaders believe in people and communicate that belief. They are passionate about productivity through people. As we have seen, Paulo Freire was exceptionally concerned about the welfare of humankind. He was a champion of the oppressed and spent his entire life fighting for human rights and social justice.

In the same way that Freire sees knowledge as forever incomplete, he sees human beings in a continuous state of "becoming." The ideal that he fosters is one of humanization, or becoming more fully human, and he dedicated his life's work to that process. He also believed that what distinguishes human beings from the animals and other beings is their ability to reason and place learning into reflective practice, or praxis. In all of this, his concern for the welfare of humanity was eminently evident.

In that light, Freire argued that caring for students is essential to the practice of teaching. He believed that teachers should not only have high standards, but also be concerned for their students' welfare, especially the neediest. In his own practice, he modeled the use of both cognitive and emotional intelligence.

The Symbolic Frame

In the symbolic frame, the organization is seen as a stage, a theater in which every actor plays certain roles and the symbolic leader attempts to communicate the right impressions to the right audiences. A number of instances can be indentified in which Freire utilized symbolic frame leadership behavior. Few educational thinkers have been more globally influential than Freire. His seminal book, *Pedagogy of the Oppressed*, spawned the international movement called critical theory and has been greatly influential among liberation theologians and social theorists.

Part of the explanation for Freire's popularity among educators is in his use of symbolic frame leadership behavior in the form of hope. Both his teaching pedagogies and his written works exhibit a profoundly hopeful image. For example, the title of one of his last books was *Pedagogy of Hope*. In this work, published in 1994, he attests to the importance of hope in his own and in other teachers' theory and practice. Even in the most oppressive situations, Freire never gave in to the temptation to despair. He always retained what he called the "utopian dream," the hope that through constant opposition a more democratic, less class-, gender- and race-discriminating society would emerge.

Another one of Freire's endearing characteristics was his humility. People who met him or heard him speak often remarked that humility was one of his distinguishing characteristics. Despite the awards and recognition that he received during his lifetime, he never claimed anything spectacularly insightful in his teachings. Instead, he often depicted himself as a "vagabond of the obvious" (Roberts 2000, 16).

Freire also made much use of the symbolic frame in the form of coining a number of terms that remain a part of his continuing legacy. His concept of "conscientization," for example, quickly became perceived as a panacea for curing the social ills in society. As a result, Freire became an internationally recognized guru of adult education, this despite his insistence that his philosophy was effective but not the be-all and end-all of educational pedagogy. By way of explanation, conscientization is Freire's way of describing the movement toward critical consciousness and away from either magical consciousness, whereby everything is explained by its being "God's will," or naive consciousness, whereby one blames the individual rather than the system for oppression (Roberts 2000).

The Political Frame

Leaders operating out of the political frame clarify what they want and what they can get. Political leaders are realists above all. They never let what they want cloud their judgment about what is possible. They assess the distribution of power and interests before they act. In order to have the worldwide impact on education that he had, and living in the oppressed societies that he did, Freire was compelled to operate out the political frame often to be an effective leader. Freire's approach to adult literacy education was considered to be subversive by the military government in control of Brazil in 1964, and as a result he was censured for instigating a riot. He was subsequently jailed and exiled to Chile; all of this because Freire believed and taught that widespread illiteracy among the poor reinforced a wider imbalance in power and control. This was very reminiscent of Southern slavery, where the plantation owners kept the slaves uneducated for fear of possible insurrection if they "learned too much."

Freire saw the existing schools in Brazil and other totalitarian states as primarily transmitting and reproducing rather than resisting existing social and economic inequalities. He correlated literacy with the process of social transformation, and as a result was treated like a pariah by the government.

Thus, to Freire, all education is political. This insight is perhaps his greatest contribution to the body of knowledge in education. According to Freire, there is no such thing as a "neutral" education. "This is a great discovery, education is politics," he proclaimed. "After that, when a teacher discovers that he or she is a politician, too, the teacher has to ask, What kind of politics am I doing in the classroom? In favor of whom am I being a teacher (the child or the establishment)?" (Roberts 2000, 57).

The Moral Frame

The moral frame is my own contribution to situational leadership theory. In my view, the moral frame completes situational leadership theory. Without it, leaders could just as easily use their leadership skills for promoting evil as for promoting good. Leaders operating out of the moral frame are concerned about their obligations and responsibilities to their followers. Moral frame leaders use some type of moral compass to direct their behavior. They practice what has been described as servant leadership and are concerned with those individuals and groups that are marginalized in their organizations and in society. In short, they are concerned about equality, fairness, and social justice.

According to Freire, preventing an individual from engaging in praxis, that is, learning critically and placing that learning into reflective practice, is dehumanizing and therefore immoral. Since oppression hinders learning, it is by nature both dehumanizing and immoral. Freire believes that oppression keeps us from being ethical beings. Being ethical, he says, is "our capacity to intervene, to compare, to judge, to decide, to choose, to desist. These behaviors render us capable of acts of greatness" (Roberts 2000, 45).

Thus, Freire's philosophy envisions a social world characterized by relationships based on liberation rather than oppression—a world where everyone has the opportunity and means to engage in humanizing praxis through open dialogue with his or her counterparts.

In this light, Freire believes that teachers have every right and even an obligation to express their political views in their educational practice. They should openly reveal their beliefs and debate them with the students. Of course, this approach implies that the teacher's belief system is ethically desirable. Thus, Freire is suggesting that teachers and others develop what I have been referring to as a moral compass that they can share with their students and use as a guide to their leadership behavior (Roberts 2000).

Situational Leadership Analysis

As we have seen, Paulo Freire was a leader out of the situational mold. He was careful to operate out of the structural frame in delineating the three principles and five beliefs that undergirded his philosophy of education and of life. His primary interest was the welfare of humankind, and as such, he operated out the human resource frame on a constant basis.

Freire utilized the symbolic frame frequently enough to establish himself as the world's foremost expert on liberating education, while coining such terms as cultural circles, conscientization, and critical theory (see chapter 2) in his book *The Pedagogy of the Oppressed.*

We saw that Freire believed that all education was political in nature and taught that teachers and non-teachers alike should develop a moral compass as a guide to their leadership and other behavior. In summary, then, we can reasonably posit that Freire was a devoted and effective practitioner of situational leadership theory.

Leadership Implications and Conclusion

There is much for us to learn from examining the leadership behavior of Paulo Freire. He debunked the notion that imbalances in comparative wealth; widespread hunger both home and abroad; exploitation; class, race, and gender discrimination; and oppression are acceptable and inevitable as the price we pay for the freedoms afforded by a free-market economy. Freire responds to this notion by proclaiming, "The freedom of commerce cannot be ethically higher than the freedom to be human" (Roberts 2000, 118). By revealing that the hidden agenda of schooling is often the sustaining of the dominant culture, he opened the path to resistance—and he did so through the astute and intuitive if not conscious use of situational leadership theory.

Freire's leadership behavior reveals an appropriate balance of all five leadership frames and moderation within each frame. His use of the moral frame is particularly exemplary. Freire can be considered the "poster child" for leading with conscience and, in my view at least, is an example of a truly heroic leader.

II. JIM JONES

Anyone in America who is poor, white, brown, yellow, or black, and does not admit that he is a nigger, is a damn fool.

—Reverend Jim Jones

Background

The Reverend Jim Jones was born in 1931 in Indiana and was best known as the founder of what he called the Peoples Temple. On November 18, 1978, at Jones's urging, more than 900 Temple members took part in a mass suicide in Jonestown, Guyana. Nine others were murdered at an airstrip outside the Jones compound. One of those killed at the airport was Congressman Leo Ryan, who was on a fact-finding mission of the Peoples Temple branch in Jonestown.

Jones was a child prodigy and studied the works of Stalin, Marx, Gandhi, and Hitler at an early age. He graduated from high school with honors and attended Indiana University in Bloomington. He moved to Indianapolis where he completed his undergraduate education at Butler University, receiving a secondary education teaching certificate.

He subsequently became a member of the Communist Party in the United States, and was prominent enough to have had Senator McCarthy investigate his relationship with actor and singer Paul Robeson. In addition to his interest in communism, Jones had a fascination with religion. In 1952, he became a student pastor at a Methodist Church in Indianapolis but resigned when his congregation voted not to admit blacks. Jones then began his own church, which ultimately became known as the Peoples Temple Christian Church Full Gospel, or Peoples Temple for short.

During the 1960s, Jones helped integrate churches, restaurants, and other public places in and around Indianapolis. He became a prominent civil rights figure in the area and eventually served in a number of social welfare positions in the city.

Jones and his wife adopted a number of children of different colors and creeds, referring to them as his "rainbow family." In 1961, Jones and his family travelled to Brazil with the intent of establishing another Peoples Temple location. However, on his way there, he made a side trip to Guyana where he also decided to establish a Peoples Temple site. Subsequently, he set up a location in both Rio de Janeiro and Guyana, making three Peoples Temple locations in all.

With his original location in Indianapolis foundering, Jones returned there to rehabilitate it. But Jones became convinced that the world would soon become engulfed in a nuclear war and decided to seek refuge in Redwood

Valley, California. He subsequently established Peoples Temple locations in Santa Rosa, Sacramento, San Francisco, Fresno, Bakersfield, and Los Angeles.

In San Francisco, Jones made a national name for himself while becoming involved in the mayoral election victory of George Moscone. As a reward, Moscone appointed Jones as the chairman of the San Francisco Housing Authority Commission.

Over time, Jones's atheistic communistic views became more widely known and pressure was being placed upon the United States Congress by a group of relatives of church members to investigate the activities of the Peoples Temple. The Concerned Relatives, as they called their group, accused Jones of brainwashing some of his young followers and engaging in illicit sex acts with several of them.

The accusations came to a head in 1978 when U.S. Congressman Leo Ryan led a fact-finding mission to Jonestown, Guyana, to investigate allegations of human right abuses. After the visit was concluded, Ryan and four others were killed on an airstrip by Peoples Temple guards. Later on that day, fearing the negative results of the investigation, 909 inhabitants of Jonestown, many of them children, committed mass suicide by drinking cyanide-laced Kool-Aid. Jones was also found dead in a deck chair with a gunshot wound to his head (Hall 1987).

The Structural Frame

Structural frame leaders seek to develop a new model of the relationship of structure, strategy, and environment for their organizations. Strategic planning, extensive preparation and effecting change are priorities for them. There are several examples of the Reverend Jim Jones being active in the structural frame. Jones often indicated that he admired his mother for teaching him some of the traditional structural frame virtues like thrift, saying at her death in 1977 that she knew "how to make a dollar stretch, and it's a damn good thing, or we wouldn't all be eating right now" (Hall 1987, 8).

Jones wanted to fulfill his mother's ambitions for him and became increasingly studious and upwardly mobile. He was a voracious reader and developed an interest in philosophy, religion, and medicine. It took him ten years, but he finally earned his bachelor's degree from Butler University. He would have to pull himself up by the bootstraps and live by his wits in order to fulfill his mother's hopes for him. So he took the route that so many rural mid-Southerners took, he became a minister.

Demonstrating an early tendency toward structural frame behavior, albeit to the extreme, Jones developed an aggressiveness that was almost palpable. "I was ready to kill by the end of third grade," he declared. "I mean, I was so f—ing hostile and aggressive. I was ready to kill." When he found a "rich kid" bullying kids at the swimming hole by holding their heads under water, Jones intervened and "damn near drowned him" (Hall 1987, 12).

Jones utilized structural behavior in developing the infrastructure for his success as a minister. He organized a small church, Community Unity, in Indianapolis as a foundation for his work and as soon as he built a loyal following at that church, he immediately engaged in some symbolic behavior and established himself as an important player in the human rights movement in that city. The so-called Laurel Street Tabernacle incident provided him with such an opportunity.

After having success with the Community Unity congregation and making a well-publicized speech in Detroit on human rights, the Laurel Street Tabernacle in Indianapolis asked him to become its pastor. But when the board made it known that blacks would not be welcome, Jones very publically refused the appointment. "I will not be a pastor of a Black Church or a White Church," he said. "Wherever I have a church, all people will be welcome" (Hall 1987, 42).

In another structural frame move, Jones founded Wings of Deliverance, the corporate vehicle for what was soon to become the Peoples Temple. He had the corporation established in such a way that it promoted expansion so that the Peoples Temple could someday encompass several hundred branches.

Like most structural frame devotees, Jones was a workaholic. He sought a strong-willed, loyal commitment from his followers and modeled that desired behavior. He was willing to work long hours to achieve his goals. He may have denied what he called a "sky god" (God in Heaven), but he had a Protestant work ethic. He often reflected on the view that "waste of time is the first and in principle the deadliest of sins." This work ethnic fueled an ever-expanding body of activities (Hall 1987, 45).

In typical structural frame fashion, Jones capitalized on his wife's nursing skills, establishing what would become a home care fiefdom. It seems that one day Jones and his wife visited a follower in a nursing home. When the old woman begged them to move her out of this depressing environment, they took her home with them and she became the first "resident" of what would become a burgeoning group of nursing homes. Eventually, Jones formed the Jim Lu Mar Company to operate the group of nursing homes, which were widely regarded as the best-run nursing homes in Indianapolis.

While operating out of the structural frame, Jones made certain that he was thoroughly prepared for any new endeavor. When he wanted to expand his operations to include a special mission to help African Americans, he built a relationship with the self-styled Black messiah of that era, Father M. J.

Divine. Jones visited Father Divine's Peace Mission headquarters in Phila-delphia several times and ultimately modeled his mission after that of Father Divine.

Jones eventually built a unique alliance that brought together distinct churches and civic organizations united by their common commitment to the goals of alleviating poverty and racism. As a result, he became a local leg-end, enabling him to expand well beyond the Indianapolis area.

By 1965 plans to expand beyond the Indianapolis area were well under-way. The Indianapolis environment was polarized to the point where even the blacks preferred their own segregated communities as opposed to Jones's interracial approach. Operating out of the structural frame once again, Jones sought an area where his approach would be accepted and where "they could develop freely." He found such a place in Redwood Valley, California (Hall 1987, 62).

Although his flock experienced only small increases in California, they were important ones. Jones recruited some key new members that fundamen-tally changed the social relationships in the congregation, making them feel like one big family. In addition, the social prominence and wealth of the new recruits helped propel the Peoples Temple to a new level of acceptability.

This transformation in the culture and organization of the Peoples Temple came primarily in the person of an intelligent, ambitious young Stanford Law School graduate named Tim Stoen. Stoen was from a prominent and wealthy Colorado family and added a badge of legitimacy to the Peoples Temple movement.

Jones exhibited ever more structural frame behavior in initiating his San Francisco expansion. By 1970, the California efforts of the Peoples Temple could boost of a growing number of followers, with branch churches up and down the California coast. The expansion had more than doubled the congre-gation's membership and provided for a successful human services ministry that operated a string of homes for juveniles and the elderly while promoting the family or communal orientation of the Peoples Temple.

It was in California that Jones's more radical ideas took root. But he could not resist the urge to move to a place even more open to his convictions than California. He was preoccupied with getting "out of Egypt . . . out of Baby-lon," and relocating where his ideas of interracial socialism could truly flour-ish and not be dominated by the white establishment. So, in 1973, Jones engaged in more structural frame behavior and began to plan for another migration. This time he decided to found a colony outside of the United States. He decided upon Guyana on the Caribbean cost of South America. By 1976, he had cleared the land, planted crops and constructed facilities so that the Peoples Temple was able to move its headquarters from Redwood Valley to San Francisco and finally to Jonestown in Guyana.

Throughout the 1970s, Jones's fund-raising efforts really bore fruit. He devised an arrangement whereby he was the sole legal trustee in charge of investing the millions of dollars that had been raised. In doing so successfully, he was able to cushion against any unforeseen circumstances that might affect the future financial health of the Peoples Temple. He was also able to obtain the funds necessary for building the colony of Jonestown in Guyana.

The success of the Peoples Temple movement reflects the competence of Jim Jones to astutely apply modern management techniques to his organization. The most significant organizational innovation of his was the creation of a social welfare advocacy network that was client based, whereby, because of Peoples Temple representation, its members, especially the Spanish-speaking, would not be treated inhumanely by faceless and insensitive bureaucrats.

Even at the end, with his empire crumbling around him, Jones utilized structural leadership behavior by attempting to establish yet another haven for the Peoples Temple in case the situation in Jonestown became untenable. His discussions for another home took place with the Soviet Union and centered on the island of Cuba.

The Human Resource Frame

Human resource leaders believe in people and communicate that belief. They are passionate about productivity through people. There are frequent instances when Jim Jones utilized the human resource frame effectively. Jones showed indications, even as a child, of sensitivity to the plight of others less fortunate. He was always bringing home stray animals and endeared himself to his most needy classmates by preventing them from being bullied. So, later in life, when he and his wife came across a ten-year-old girl whose mother had abused her, they invited the youngster to reside with them. The girl received considerable attention to her need for speech therapy, and she was eventually legally adopted by the Joneses. At about the same time, an older woman, Esther Muellar, came into the Jones household seeking their love and care. In effect, she was the first resident of what would become a full-blown nursing-care business that the Joneses established.

At first, many of Jones's followers were skeptical of his ministry. In time, however, they found Jones to be very different from many of the other ministers they had encountered. "Nobody else had ever taken them and looked them in the eye and said, 'I love you,' which Jones would do," recalled Peoples Temple lawyer Tim Stoen (Hall 1987, 72).

Lastly, in an industry notorious for its poor care and financial improprieties, Jones's nursing home operations were a reflection of his penchant for human resource frame behavior. For the most part, they were managed without significant financial malfeasance and provided excellent facilities that were well organized and clean. The residents were always well fed and well clothed, with exceptional attention being given to their personal hygiene (Hall 1987).

The Symbolic Frame

In the symbolic frame, the organization is seen as a stage, a theater in which every actor plays certain roles and the symbolic leader attempts to communicate the right impressions to the right audiences. One could argue that the symbolic frame was one of Jim Jones's strongest. An early incident depicted by his mother is an indication of Jones's instinct for the dramatic. It seems that one Sunday Jones walked into church "half naked and with all his dogs and other animals behind him." In the process, he distributed hand-picked flowers to the congregation, whose laughter at the gesture filled the room. The preacher observed, "There's more religion in one little finger of this child than there is in the whole town" (Hall 1987, 11).

Of course, being the symbolic frame leader that he became, he was strongly drawn to the Pentecostal church and their stress on the emotional rather than the rational side of religious practice. He saw the Pentecostals as a haven from the alienation that he would experience from the traditional religions and from conventional society.

Jones used symbolic behavior to indirectly operationalize his ideologies. He became a communist sympathizer after he went to a rally featuring Communist Party notable Paul Robeson, the African American singer and actor. Wondering how he would demonstrate his newly acquired Marxism, he decided to "infiltrate the church" (Hall 1987, 17).

As a preacher, Jones used symbolic frame behavior in the form of the stock evangelist tricks of staged healings and prophesies. He was better at this than most of his counterparts, especially his gift of prophesy concerning human rights. He predicted the concern many would have over social injustice and fashioned his brand of Christianity to focus on the central concerns of the modern age, namely, race and class distinctions and nuclear holocaust.

Reflecting the communist credo, "from each according to his ability and to each according to his need," Jones portrayed the Peoples Temple as a religious communistic movement as a counterbalance to secular communism. He used symbolic behavior in the form of his dynamic and electrifying evangelical sermons to deliver his revolutionary religious message.

In one particularly well-covered sermon in 1964, he made one of his more dramatic statements and one that was quoted at the beginning of this chapter. "Anyone in America who is poor, white, brown, yellow, or black and does not admit that he is a nigger, is a damn fool," he told his audience. "Because niggardly means to be treated cheatedly. You've been cheated," he declaimed. Then, going into a dramatic pause, he said in a quiet voice, "I turned that word around and I made it the proudest word for the chosen people; I said, yes, we're niggers, and we're proud" (Hall 1987, 30).

Once again using symbolic frame behavior, Jones lived a very modest lifestyle. For the life of his ministry he had a very modest residence and a ten-year-old car. Whatever else one could say about him, no one could credibly claim that he lived an extravagant life style.

Jones even used symbolic behavior in naming his son, Stephan. When his wife gave birth to their only biological child, the Jones gave him the middle name Gandhi to honor the nonviolent but confrontational leader of India's independence movement. Two years later they would take an even more dramatic step and adopt a little black baby, becoming the first white couple in Indianapolis to adopt a black child. As was noted in his background section, Jones began referring to this family as the "rainbow family," after having adopted children of other races.

As mentioned earlier, Jones became great friends with the black minister, Father Divine, and fashioned much of his symbolic behavior after that of the charismatic Divine. Jones often told the story of Father Divine's trial in 1931 on charges that he was living with a woman other than his wife. Three days after Divine began serving a one-year sentence, the judge who heard the case died of a heart attack. From his jail cell Father Divine advanced his claims to be a messiah by exclaiming, "I hated to do it" (Hall 1987, 51).

In 1961, Jones was appointed to the position of executive director of the Indianapolis Human Rights Commission. Taking a page out of Martin Luther King's book, he utilized a combination of symbolic and political behavior in covertly sending out neatly dressed, racially integrated teams from the Peoples Temple around to the various businesses and churches to see if they were employing racially discriminating practices.

Jones used an incident at Methodist Hospital in Indianapolis to his advantage to add to his budding reputation of being a champion of civil rights. Because he had a black doctor admitting him, the hospital assumed that Jones was also black. As a consequence, they placed him in a room with other blacks. When the hospital found out that he was white, they immediately reassigned him to the "white patients' room." Of course, in his typically symbolic way, Jones refused to be reassigned and insisted that the hospital be integrated immediately. Knowing the connections that Jones had with the media, the hospital quickly capitulated.

However, Jones's application of symbolic behavior was not always effective. In his usual iconoclastic style, he used his weekly radio broadcasts to confront conservative Christians and their clergy with how outdated their religious practices were and how Mahatma Gandhi had the right idea with his ecumenical approach. In what was to be the final nail in his coffin, Jones asserted that he "couldn't see a loving heavenly Father condemning to hell persons because they wouldn't accept some Christian doctrines." The negative reaction to this statement helped to bring his Indianapolis evangelical career to an end and necessitated his flocks' migration to Redwood Valley (Hall 1987, 62).

Never one to let good works speak for themselves, Jones developed a capacity to reinvent stories with only minimal factual basis and raise them to the level of legend among his followers and the mass media. He even portrayed his departure from Indianapolis as a protestation of the racial prejudice of the city.

To his credit, Jones rejected a terrorist approach to change, preferring instead his vision of collectivism and migration as the ways to avoid persecution, capitalist exploitation, racism, and the other societal ills in the United States. In time, however, Jones included the ultimate and radical symbolic act of mass suicide as a tactic to make his points and to liberate his people from the Philistine world.

To Jones, of course, suicide was a form of symbolic behavior. In his mind, mass suicide was sort of a penance for failing to succeed in convincing society of the righteousness of the Peoples Temple movement. Jones was greatly influenced in this worldview by Huey Newton's *Revolutionary Suicide*. Newton's idea that mass suicide could lead to a rebirth of their ideological views, resonated perfectly with Jones (Hall 1987, 136).

Jones even had a "practice session" for undertaking revolutionary suicide. At one of his strategy meetings, he insisted that some thirty people in the planning commission meeting drink wine from the Peoples Temple vineyards that he claimed was blessed. Little did his congregation know that he was preparing them for the "real thing" that would happen only a year later. In a further display of symbolic frame behavior, he depicted the Jonestown suicide as "living for principle and now dying for principle" (Hall 1987, 254).

Jones built his image in California the same way that he did in Indiana by engaging in both symbolic and political behavior in cultivating his emergence as a civic leader. After only two years in Redwood Valley, he had been appointed to the Mendocino County grand jury, and served on the Juvenile Justice Commission, the Legal Aid Foundation, and the school board.

So the Peoples Temple image derived from its social work and political orientation. Its slogan was: "The highest worship to God is service to our fellow man." In later years, the word "God" was abandoned and a greater sensitivity to gender discrimination was added so that the new slogan read: "the highest form of worship is service to our fellow man, woman and child" Hall 1987, 149).

Jones even used symbolic behavior in justifying his illicit relationships. In addition to cultivating an image of omniscience, he also projected an image of vulnerability. He led his followers to believe that they were in danger of losing him if they did not treat him with tender loving care. Because he had sacrificed so much for them, they could hardly deny him the few privileges that he took to "replenish his spirit" (Hall 1987).

Toward the latter part of his ministry, Jones was charged by the Concerned Relatives group with brainwashing his disciples and holding many of them captive in Jonestown against their will. The investigation of the Peoples Temple movement eventually led to the final symbolic act, the mass suicide in which over 900 people died.

Before that final symbolic act, however, Jones engaged in symbolic behavior by hiring the conspiracy lawyer of JFK assassination fame, Mark Lane, to represent the Peoples Temple. This was Jones's way of fighting fire with fire, with Lane expounding the view that the federal government was conspiring to bring down Jones and his followers because the Peoples Temple represented an unwanted source of social change in the nation. As Lane made his speeches, the civil rights battle hymn, "We Shall Overcome," was being played over the public address system (Hall 1987).

The Political Frame

Leaders operating out of the political frame clarify what they want and what they can get. Political leaders are realists above all. They never let what they want cloud their judgment about what is possible. They assess the distribution of power and interests. Jim Jones was a politically savvy leader. As we have already noted, Jones was an avowed communist. But he did not want to be labeled with the negative connotations of communism, so he employed political frame behavior and worked covertly in furthering his communist ideals.

In a similar use of political frame behavior, Jones abandoned the poorly organized Pentecostal movement in favor of the more established and credible Seventh Day Baptist/Disciples of Christ Church but took along with him the healing services that were so much a part of the Pentecostals' services. His reasoning was, "You can get the crowd, get some money, and do some good with it" (Hall 1987, 18).

In another politically astute move, Jones followed a common technique among religious groups in attracting new members. He offered services on days and times when the more established churches were not meeting. For example, his followers would fan out across a neighborhood, especially the black ones, inviting the unchurched to join them at a 2:30 PM service on Sunday afternoon, after, of course, they had already attended their own Peoples Temple service that morning.

As mentioned earlier, Jones modeled his mission after that of Father Divine in Philadelphia, who presided over an operation that was based more on the economic and political principles of redistribution of wealth than it was on religious orthodoxy. Consequently, both men indulged in political wheeling and dealing in order to better the lives of their respective congregations.

When the brilliant young lawyer and Peoples Temple recruit, Tim Stoen sought Jones's advice regarding whether he could serve the movement better as the assistant district attorney of Mendocino County or as the attorney for the Peoples Temple, Jones advised him to take the more politically effective secular position, once again demonstrating his political frame inclinations.

Jones was even able to use his migration from Indiana to California to his political advantage. When he learned that the Mendocino County State Hospital was in the process of being privatized, he had many of his congregation apply for jobs there. Eventually, at least eight of the top executives of the psychiatric hospital were Peoples Temple members.

When the *San Francisco Examiner* published a negative article about Jones and the Peoples Temple, he immediately engaged in political leadership behavior and had his followers picket their offices for two days until the negative television publicity prompted the paper to apologize and print a positive interview about Jones.

As we can see, Jones understood the political game and played it to the hilt. He convinced such notables as Vice President Walter Mondale to endorse the work of the Peoples Temple. Of course, Mondale was mortified when the Jonestown suicide took place and he realized that he had made a decision to support Jones based on his image rather than his actions.

Perhaps Jones's most effective, albeit devious use of political frame behavior was in deceiving the public into thinking that the Peoples Temple was a conventional church interested only in service to humanity. In reality, the Peoples Temple was used by Jones to promote his vision of socialism that verged on communism. Paradoxically, he used religion to further the cause of a movement that believed that religion was the "opiate of the people."

Emblematic of Jones's political approach to many issues was his managed letter writing campaigns. He was notorious for prompting his congregation to flood the newspapers, politicians, and others with letters supporting one or another of his causes. Tim Stoen, for example, wrote a letter to President Richard Nixon during the Watergate break-in, describing how "heartsick and outraged" the Peoples Temple members were over the mistreatment he was receiving from the media (Hall 1987, 151).

It perhaps his most effective use of political frame behavior, Jones had his followers march in defense of four *Fresno Bee* reporters who were imprisoned for not revealing their news sources after writing an article that the government claimed endangered some of its agents. The ultimate payoff for this astutely applied political frame behavior was the 1977 Freedom of Press Award that was bestowed on Jones by the National Newspaper Publishers Association.

Jones was especially adept at exploiting his followers for political purposes. For example, he had his followers join the NAACP en masse so that they could vote him in as a member of its national board. In a similar instance, Jones and his disciples appeared at a press conference urging amnesty for Eldridge Cleaver after he disavowed the Black Panther credo and wanted to return to the United States. He also had his flock protest at the California Supreme Court against the *Bakke* decision, which disallowed the setting of racial quotas as part of medical school admission policies. In another example, he had the Peoples Temple support a boycott of Florida Orange Juice because their spokesperson, Anita Bryant, was making antigay speeches across the country.

In a final display of political frame behavior, Jones bused in Peoples Temple members to Rosalynn Carter's speech opening her husband's Democratic campaign headquarters so that she would not be embarrassed by speaking to a half-filled hall. As a result, Jones was one of the few nonpoliticians who had access to the president and vice president (Hall 1987).

The Moral Frame

The moral frame is my own contribution to situational leadership theory. In my view, the moral frame completes situational leadership theory. Without it, leaders could just as easily use their leadership skills for promoting evil as for promoting good. Leaders operating out of the moral frame are concerned about their obligations and responsibilities to their followers. Moral frame leaders use some type of moral compass to direct their behavior. They practice what has been described as servant leadership and are concerned with those individuals and groups that are marginalized in their organizations and in society. In short, they are concerned about equality, fairness and social justice.

Jim Jones is a good example of the importance of not only operating effectively *among* the five leadership frames, but also operating effectively *within* each of the frames. Jones definitely used moral frame leadership behavior, for example, but one could argue that instead of doing so in moderation, he did so to the extreme. We might assert that he viewed his behavior through a moral lens, but for whatever reason, that lens was tragically warped.

To Jones's credit, given the large sums of money that the Peoples Temple raised, the vast real estate holdings that it accumulated, the enormous network of nursing homes, and the many Temple locations, it is noteworthy that the Peoples Temple never succumbed to the illegal practices in which many of its counterparts in the evangelical movement did.

Jones also demanded that the Peoples Temple community members adhere to a moral code. Children were expected to be punished for stealing, lying, acting irresponsibly, bullying, discriminating against the disabled, and fighting. Illicit sexual activity was also verboten. Unfortunately, this last precept did not always apply to the movement's founder.

So there is much evidence that Jim Jones often acted out of the moral frame and developed a moral compass to guide his leadership behavior. However, he sometimes used it to the extreme—for example, in justifying the mass suicide at Jonestown.

Situational Leadership Analysis

Situational models of leadership differ from earlier trait and behavioral models in asserting that no single way of leading works in all situations. Rather, appropriate behavior depends of the circumstances at a given time. Effective manages diagnose the situation, identify the leadership style or behavior that will be most effective, and then determine whether they can implement the required style.

There is much evidence to suggest that Jim Jones was a leader in the situational mold. Many would consider Jones to be an organizational genius in light of the multidimensional empire that he built. When we look closely at his leadership behavior, we find that he accomplished what he did by being very active among the five leadership frames. Point to any one of his successes and we see that he was involved in several institutional spheres at the same time. One event might simultaneously involve administrative practice (structural frame behavior), public relations (symbolic frame behavior) and the promotion of social justice (human resource, political, and moral frames).

So Jim Jones was very facile at moving among the various leadership frames. For example, after eight young recruits wanted to leave the Temple community, Jones reasoned that "My love isn't working. I guess I'll have to start getting hard on people; they seem to respond to it better." In this case, the situation had changed, so it was time for Jones to move out of the human resource frame and into the structural frame (Hall 1987, 132).

Leadership Implications and Conclusion

To many historians, Jim Jones was the personification of the Antichrist. He used his considerable leadership skills to manipulate and dominate his followers. Like a puppeteer, he pulled the strings of his disciples to the point where he had them convinced murder and mass suicide were viable and moral ways of exacting revenge against the enemies of the Peoples Temple.

From a situational leadership point of view, we saw how Jones was appropriately active in all five of the leadership frames. He operated out of the structural frame to develop a vast and efficiently run organization that any business person would envy. The motive behind his movement was a sincere concern for humanity that shows evidence of his human resource frame tendencies. To reach his socialist and communistic goals, he used his talents as a preacher to inspire his followers, which was a form of symbolic leadership behavior. He used political frame behavior to gain public office, thus acquiring the power to influence public policy. Finally, his concern for social justice was an obvious outgrowth of his moral philosophy. However, in applying his moral code, he took the position that the end justifies the means.

Jones's life story personifies the theme of this book in that he is a perfect example of an otherwise outstanding leader who went astray because he did not act in moderation within the five leadership frames, especially the moral frame. Although he developed a moral code to guide his leadership behavior, he often practiced it to the extreme, resulting in a self-righteous attitude that ultimately justified murder and mass suicide to achieve the goal of universal socialism. What possessed Jones to follow this leadership path is open to question, but from a strictly analytical viewpoint, his inability to act in moderation within a particular leadership frame seems to have been his fatal flaw.

To see how Jim Jones's moral leadership flaws are reflected in contemporary times, we need only look to the sexual abuse scandals that are all too prevalent in today's society. Many of the priest pedophiles who have recently been exposed are educators. The fact that, as religious clergy, they have dedicated their lives to spreading Christ's message of love is an indication that they have developed a strong moral code, just as Jim Jones did. But like Jones, they have a warped idea of how to appropriately place it into practice, most likely rationalizing in their own minds that their behavior is somehow justified. Hopefully, the good that will come out of this human tragedy will be that it serves as a teachable moment for leaders and aspiring leaders everywhere.

Chapter Ten

Paterno v. Milosevic

I. JOE PATERNO

The purpose of college football is to serve education, not the other way around.

—Joe Paterno

Background

Joe Paterno was born in Brooklyn, New York, in 1926. He is the head football coach at Penn State University, having held the position since 1966. Paterno has won over 400 football games, more than any other Division I coach in history. He also has more bowl game wins and more undefeated seasons than any other coach in college football history.

Paterno is a graduate of Brown University. There he played quarterback on the football team, and after graduation in 1950, joined Hall of Famer Rip Engle at Penn State as an assistant coach. Paterno became head coach at Penn State in 1966 and is one of the most famous and recognizable coaches in any sport in the United States.

Paterno's loyalty to Penn State was such that he turned down offers to coach the Pittsburgh Steelers in 1969, and the New England Patriots in 1972. Overall, Paterno has led Penn State to two national championships (1982 and 1986) and five undefeated, untied seasons. In 2007 Paterno was inducted into the College Football Hall of Fame. In addition to his reputation as an outstanding football coach, Paterno is admired for his monetary contributions to the academic and student life at Penn State. This was not surprising in that upon his hiring in 1966 Paterno publically announced that he would be conducting what he called a "Grand Experiment" among big time football

schools in integrating athletics and academics and stressing more significantly the student part of the term student-athlete. As a result, Penn State's
football players have consistently surpassed their Division I-A counterparts
in academic achievement, and over the past thirty years, the Nittany Lions'
graduation rate has consistently exceeded that of its Division I-A football
counterparts.

Paterno and his wife, Sue, are also renowned for their charitable contributions to Penn State. They have contributed over $4 million toward various
departments and colleges, including support for the Pasquerilla Spiritual
Center and the Penn State All-Sports Museum. After helping raise over $13.5
million in funds for the 1997 expansion of Pattee Library, the University
named the expansion after him (Paterno and Asbell 1989).

The Structural Frame

Structural leaders seek to develop a new model of the relationship of structure, strategy, and environment for their organizations. Strategic planning,
extensive preparation and effecting change are priorities for them. Joe Paterno has a well-earned reputation for the extensive use of structural frame
leadership behavior. He is known as a coach who is always well prepared and
is demanding of his players both on the field and in the classroom. One of the
reasons for his great success in postseason bowl games is that with the extra
two or three weeks he has to prepare, he almost always out-coaches his
opponents.

Paterno learned the value of structural leadership behavior in his formative years. He often alludes to the fact that his father drilled two important
attitudes into him: (1) Education is very important, and (2) winning isn't as
important as having fun. However, while his father's carative approach
shaped Paterno to some extent, he attributes his drive and intensity to his
mother. His mother never took a backseat to anyone, any place, any time,
according to Paterno. She couldn't abide coming in second. "So, as her first
son, in anything I did I had to be at the top. If we had a classroom spelling
bee, I was expected to win it," he remembered (Paterno and Asbell 1989, 29).

Paterno speculates that he got his sense of rigid discipline from his mother, also. He recalls a day at school when he got into a little "chalk-throwing"
contest while the nun's back was turned. As was the custom in those days,
the nun gave him a crack across the knuckles with her ruler. When he got
home, his mother wanted to know why his hand was so red. "Sister hit me,"
was his reply. "Sister hit you?" "Yeah, but I didn't do any—" His mother
gave him a slap across the head. "That's for giving Sister problems," she said
(Paterno and Asbell 1989, 30).

The value of structural behavior was further drilled into Paterno in high school at Brooklyn Prep. Starting with his first day, his Latin teacher, Father Bermingham, always encouraged his students to get started with what he called the most important task in education—their self-education. *The Aeneid* by Virgil was their first project. Paterno complained that translating the four hundred Latin pages was impossible to cover in one semester. "What's important," Father Bermingham said, "is not how much we cover. In fact, I don't like that word, 'cover.' It's not how much we do, but the *excellence* of what we do that counts" (Paterno and Asbell 1989, 41).

It was at that point that Virgil's hero, Aeneas, the founder of Rome, entered Paterno's life. Aeneas led his people out of Troy into Italy after the Greeks conquered Troy. Paterno decided to model his life after that of Aeneas. Aeneas endured battles, storms, shipwrecks, and the rages of the gods. But the worst storm is the one that raged within. He yearned to be free of his tormenting duty, but he knew that his duty was to others, to his men. Through years of hardship and peril, Aeneas relentlessly carries on until he founds Rome. Paterno sees Aeneas not as a grandstanding superstar but as a humble hero. His first commitment is not to himself but to others. He lives the life not for "me" and "I" but for "us" and "we." According to Paterno, "Aeneas is the ultimate team man" (Paterno and Asbell 1989, 46).

This initial tendency toward structural behavior was reinforced later in life. At Brown University, Paterno was enamored by the Romantic period of literature. He considers himself a "romantic," dreaming of gladiators and knights winning battles. He was a fan of the movie *Patton*, which depicted General George Patton as a tough-minded lover of poetry and military epics, believing that he was reincarnated and in his past life was a Roman general. "My kind of guy," says Paterno (Paterno and Asbell 1989, 49).

Paterno credits his predecessor at Penn State, Rip Engle, and his high school coach, Gus Zitrides, with teaching him to analyze a problem and put down a specific plan for how to get from here to there, step-by-step, in the time that is available. The best teacher, according to Paterno, is not the person who has the most knowledge, but the one who has the knowledge best organized and who knows how to state what he or she knows in coherent ways. If a student doesn't get it when it is taught one way, you've got to teach it another way, he believes. Sometimes a great player who becomes a coach doesn't understand that he is there not because he knows how to do it, but because he knows how to teach it.

According to Paterno, most football fans minimize the importance of structural leadership behavior. They have a tendency to think they know more about the sport than the coach does. Paterno has observed, however, that most of them don't know and really don't want to know the importance of preparation, of having a clear focus on a goal, of sustained discipline, of systematically building self-confidence, and of each player taking responsibility for his own play. Paterno takes a page out of Vince Lombardi's book by pointing out that practice doesn't make perfect; perfect practice makes perfect.

In typical structural leadership fashion, Paterno welcomes improvements in his opponents as a motive for improving his organization. "When in some seasons, we're way ahead of the pack, we get careless. Doesn't everybody?" He points out further, that "the human tendency, when the competition is better, is to get better" (Paterno and Asbell 1989, 63).

Along these lines of respecting one's opponent, Paterno opines that football is played, above all, with the heart and mind. It's played with the body only secondarily. A coach's first duty is to coach minds. If the coach doesn't succeed in that, the team will not reach its potential. Athletes look at their coaches for examples in struggling to learn poise, class, respect, and the handling of adversity. If confidence and poise are essential to great players, they are at least as important to coaches, according to Paterno. "We cannot convince a football team that they have greatness in them unless they smell self-confidence in us." Paterno recalled that when Bear Bryant, among the great coaches of all time, walked out on the football field, self-confidence hung in the air around him like a fine mist (Paterno and Asbell 1989, 82).

Paterno is a realist, however, regarding the limits of structural leadership behavior. People often ask Paterno if he concurs with Vince Lombardi's idea that "winning isn't everything, it's the only thing." His response is that he believes in playing as if winning is the only thing, but he never forgets that the opposing coach and the other team are thinking the same thing. They cannot control all the vagaries involved in a game and neither can he. So, despite wanting to have control, he knows that many things are not in his control, and he has to learn to cope with that. He harks back to the words of his Brooklyn Prep teacher, Fr. Bermingham, who used to say: "Always work as though everything depended on you. Yet always pray knowing that everything depends on God" (Paterno and Asbell, 1989, 120).

In typical structural leader fashion, Paterno often describes sloppiness as a disease. No one ever built a great organization just worrying about the big things. It's the little things that give you the edge, he points out. If the equipment man in the locker room, for example, doesn't check his equipment properly, the players sense it and the lack of attention to detail becomes part of the team's culture and the disease spreads.

As a result of his structural leadership leanings, Paterno can be a difficult and demanding coach. In a rather humorous observation, Joe Lally, one of his star players, came back to campus after ten years to attend an alumni golf outing. As a memento of the event, all the golf balls had Paterno's face printed on them. Lally said, "I could hardly wait to tee up so I could hit Joe. But you know, it was just like when he was on the practice field. I just looked at the ball—and it started to yell at me" (Paterno and Asbell 1989, 221).

The Human Resource Frame

Human resource leaders believe in people and communicate that belief. They are passionate about productivity through people. Although he is basically a structural leader, Paterno knows the value of utilizing human resource leadership frame behavior when appropriate. For example, the former All-Pro linebacker, Jack Ham, recalled that "Joe Pa" was always in his face. But, when he was inducted into the Football Hall of Fame in 1988, "It only took me about five seconds to decide on Paterno to present me" (Paterno and Asbell 1989, ix).

It was this lack of the human touch that dissuaded Paterno from accepting a professional football coaching job. "I don't like the pros," he said. They play only to win. There is no other reason to play. Even more than pro players are compelled to win; coaches are compelled to win" (Paterno and Asbell 1989, 12).

Paterno learned the importance of human resource leadership behavior as a very young man. He says that nothing was more important to his parents than family. His father would barely manage the means to send the children to summer camp for a couple of weeks, and his mother would say, "We can't send Joe and George without sending cousin Nicky" (Paterno and Asbell 1989, 28). Nicky's parents could not afford to send him to camp that year, so Paterno's parents found a way to "foot the bill" for him, also.

Paterno attributes much of what he learned about the appropriate application of human resource leadership behavior to his predecessor and mentor at Penn State, Rip Engle. Engle often pointed out to Paterno that people usually don't mind not always getting their way, but they almost always resent not getting their say. Engle also taught him that part of being a good teacher is sensing when to get off their backs, when to say, "Let's knock off today and have some laughs, and tomorrow we'll start all over again—from a higher plateau" (Paterno and Asbell 1989).

Eventually, through trial and error, Paterno found out that there were different ways to handle different people. He remembered saying to Rip Engle that he could not understand how one player could have such a different outlook on football than another player even though they both came from the same high school and the same football program. How can one be so "gung ho" to practice while the other one can't get himself out of first gear? Rip said, "Joe, the longer you're in this business, the more you're going to realize that everybody's different" (Paterno and Asbell 1989, 84). But Paterno still had trouble understanding this until he had his own family. Then he saw for himself: same home, same parents, different outcomes. So Paterno learned what Vince Lombardi always preached. Coaches who can outline plays on a blackboard are a dime a dozen. The ones who win "get inside their players and motivate them" (Paterno and Asbell 1989, 92).

It did not take Paterno long to see the results of the astute application of human resource leadership behavior. By 1971 and 1972, he began to see more clearly, more specifically, how an emerging Penn State style of football was enriching his players far beyond winning and losing. It had to do with pride; it had to do with caring about their teammates as people, as a community. It had to do with love. The difference is difficult to put into words, but just before every game he has a need to touch each player—physically touch them. He needs to do it to assure each player that he knows how hard that player has worked and that the game and its outcome belong to all of them collectively.

In this light, Paterno observes that to some coaches graduation is a disaster, the enemy. That's when they lose all of their good players. However, with Paterno, all the things he believes in force him to celebrate graduation as achievement, as victory.

Yet another example of the benefits of Paterno's continuous use of human resource leadership behavior in his football program was the celebration after his first national championship at Penn State. He and his team went on a whistle-stop tour of Pennsylvania on a train. The towns along the way sent out their fire engines to greet the team. With emergency lights circling, each town's engines escorted the team up the highway to deliver them to the care of the next town's engines on a hundred-mile relay of joy and pride. In Paterno's own words, "I never saw such love between people who didn't even know each other" (Paterno and Asbell 1989, 232).

The Symbolic Frame

In the symbolic frame, the organization is seen as a stage, a theater in which every actor plays certain roles and the symbolic leaders attempt to communicate the right impressions to the right audiences. Like most of his coaching colleagues, Joe Paterno makes frequent use of symbolic frame leadership behavior. From his insistence on understated uniforms with no names on the back or logos on the helmets, to reinforce Penn State's "team" approach, to his attire on the sidelines, Paterno is a master at getting his points across symbolically. As a result, Paterno is one of the most respected, beloved, and certainly most recognizable college football coaches in America.

Patrolling the sidelines in signature dark glasses and tie during a game, he wears his trousers rolled up, with white athletic socks and football cleats helping to define the differences between his football program and others. In adopting this philosophy, Paterno harkens back to his high school literary hero, Aeneas. "A hero of Aeneas' kind does not wear his name on the back of his uniform. He doesn't wear Nittany Lions on his helmet to claim star credit for touchdowns and tackles that were enabled by everybody else doing his job" (Paterno and Asbell 1989, 46).

In a not-so-veiled critique of another prominent football program, Paterno once recalled how at Brown the football players weren't locked away in a deluxe, carpeted athletic dorm like the one Bear Bryant built at Alabama. He speculates that Bryant might have believed in protecting his Red Tide from the mental distractions of a university, but in Paterno's opinion, Bryant sheltered his squad of stars from an important part of college life—relating to all kinds of people.

Paterno thanks God that he wasn't "protected" in that way at Brown, and at Penn State he wouldn't for one minute think of segregating his players from the rest of the student body that way. Paterno wants his players to discover themselves—by discovering all the different kinds of people his players encounter among the thirty-seven thousand students at Penn State. According to him, the purpose of college football is to serve education, not the other way around. Practicing symbolic behavior, he called it his "Grand Experiment."

When Paterno is asked to name the best team that he ever coached, he alludes to a quote from Knute Rockne: "I'll find out what my best team is when I find out how many doctors and lawyers, good husbands, and good citizens have come off of each and every one of my teams" (Paterno and Asbell 1989, 17). Like every coach, Paterno loves winning games. But while committing everything they've got to play their very best game, they have been coached to know that there's something that counts more than winning.

Paterno recalls receiving a letter of recommendation from Libby McKinney, and English teacher from Pineville, West Virginia. The teacher wrote about a boy that she taught and how she was impressed with his "natural brightness." She urged Paterno to look at his football talents for a scholarship to Penn State, where she knew athletics would not be permitted to overshadow his education. The student/athlete turned out to be Kurt Warner, one of the most prolific running backs in Penn State football history (Paterno and Asbell 1989).

Paterno used symbols in communicating his football philosophy to his players and the broader public. For example, it is common practice among football coaches to use aggressive terms in describing players' roles. A "blood end" was a defensive man who lined up in a certain way. A "monster back" was a secondary player playing the field. Paterno, in his own inimitable style, renamed these terms. For example, he renamed the monster back the "hero back."

This symbolic behavior has helped Paterno define what the chant "We are Penn State" means. To his players, the students, and the alums, those words remind them of the special symbols associated with Penn State. Those black shoes, those plain uniforms with no glitter and no names. A Penn State player doesn't have to let the whole world know by putting six Nittany Lions on his helmet that he made six big plays. When he scores a touchdown, he doesn't dance and go berserk in the end zone. Rather, when a Penn Stater goes on that field, he *expects* to score a touchdown.

Finally, Joe Paterno shows his respect and gratitude to Penn State in a symbolic way. He and his wife are renowned for their charitable contributions to academics and student life at Penn State. They have contributed over $4 million toward various departments and colleges, including support for the Pasquerilla Spiritual Center and the Penn State All-Sports Museum. As mentioned in his background, after helping raise over $13 million in funds for the Pattee Library, the university named the expansion in his honor. In Joe Paterno's mind, however, his gifts "were peanuts" compared to the benefits that he and his family received from Penn State. "Three of our kids have graduated from Penn State" (Paterno and Asbell 1989, 205). Enough said!

The Political Frame

Leaders operating out of the political frame clarify what they want and what they can get. Political leaders are realists above all. They never let what they want cloud their judgment about what is possible. They assess the distribution of power and interests. Paterno is one of the more astute college football coaches in using political frame leadership behavior. In 2002, Paterno chased down referee Dick Honig in a dead sprint following a 42–35 overtime home loss to Iowa. Paterno saw Tony Johnson catch a pass for a first down with both feet in bounds on the stadium's video replay board, but the play was ruled an incompletion; Penn State had rallied from a 35–13 deficit with nine minutes left in the game to tie the score at 35, and were driving on their first possession in overtime for a touchdown to tie the game at 42. Penn State failed on fourth down and Iowa held on for the win.

Just weeks later, in the final minute of the Michigan game, the same wide receiver, Johnson, made a catch that would have given Penn State a first down and put them in range for a game-winning field goal. Although Johnson was ruled out of bounds, replays clearly showed that Johnson had both feet in bounds, making the catch legal. Paterno used these two instances to reinforce his longtime efforts to engage instant replay in college football.

In 2003, as a direct result of Paterno's political frame behavior, the Big Ten Conference became the first college football conference to adopt a form of instant replay. The previous two incidents, along with Paterno's public objection and statements, are often cited as catalysts for its adoption. Within the next year, almost all of the Division I-A conferences adopted a form of instant replay.

Paterno used political leadership behavior to impact a number of other college football issues. He has long been an advocate for some type of college football playoff system. The question has been posed to him frequently over the years, as only one of his five undefeated teams has been voted national champions. The awarding of the National Championship to the team that wins the designated bowl game in a particular year was instituted largely because of Paterno's insistence on a playoff system.

Paterno also believes that scholarship college athletes should receive a modest stipend, so that they have some spending money. As justification, Paterno points out that many scholarship athletes are from poor families and that other students have time to hold down a part-time job. By contrast, busy practice, conditioning, and game schedules prevent college athletes from working during the school year. He constantly uses his influence with the National Catholic Educational Association (NCEA) to promote this view.

Paterno often used his numerous professional coaching offers to his political advantage. He was once being wooed by the New England Patriots and seriously considered leaving Penn State, even announcing his acceptance of the position, only suddenly to change his mind the next day. This sudden switch in decision had at least two happy results. Later in the morning after the news conference announcing that he would stay at Penn State, his athletic director, Bob Paterson, called and "ordered" Paterno to fly with him immediately to Pittsburgh to see a lawyer. Penn State didn't want any more close calls. That day, they agreed to the first formal contract that Paterno and Penn State ever had. The other happy result had to do with his good friend, former Oklahoma coach Chuck Fairbanks, who got the Patriots job that he turned down.

In another instance of Paterno using political frame leadership behavior, he recalls the time when Tommy Prothro of UCLA beat Penn State 49–11. With only two minutes left in the game and with this huge lead, Prothro called for an onside kick as a surprise tactic to recover the ball for an additional score. After the game reporters asked Paterno what he thought of the maneuver? Even though he was fuming, he decided to utilize some political behavior and said, "Oh no! I think coach Prothro had something he wanted to try out with this team (Paterno and Asbell 1989, 92).

Paterno's attitude is that if political leadership behavior can accomplish something good for his team, so be it. If a team needs new facilities as a condition of success and the coach has the power to get them, according to Paterno, he needs to use it. He patterns his use of political behavior after that of Bear Bryant. According to Paterno, Bryant could get summer jobs for his players with just a phone call because he had established many influential relationships. Rather than raw power, he exhibited a personal charm that made people want to do what he wanted.

Former President Richard Nixon was once the recipient of Paterno's political frame behavior. In 1969, when Penn State was undefeated and vying with Alabama for the National Championship, Nixon had been quoted as agreeing with the pollsters that Alabama was the best team in the country that year and deserved the National Championship. Several years later as a Penn State graduation speaker, Paterno seized the opportunity to get back at Nixon. "How come," he wondered, "a President who knew so much about college football in 1969 could have known so little about Watergate in 1973?" (Paterno and Asbell 1989, 166).

After Paterno's first National Championship as coach of Penn State, he spoke to the university's board of trustees. He advised them to stop complaining about the state not supporting the university and to use the recent success to lobby the lawmakers for more state aid, once again demonstrating Paterno's penchant for using political frame leadership behavior to his and his university's benefit.

Paterno learned to use his political leverage in negotiation of his salary at Penn State. When Jackie Sherrill was lured away from Pittsburgh with a huge contract to coach Texas, the senior vice president at Penn State, Steve Garban, was nervous that Paterno would be lured away by a big contract. He asked Paterno if Penn State was paying him enough. Paterno used the opportunity to say, "I don't know. Find out what Bo Schembechler is making at Michigan" (Paterno and Asbell 1989, 249). Paterno got himself an instant $25,000 raise.

The Moral Frame

The moral frame is my own contribution to situational leadership theory. In my view, the moral frame completes situational leadership theory. Without it, leaders could just as easily use their leadership skills for promoting evil as for promoting good. Leaders operating out of the moral frame are concerned about their obligations and responsibilities to their followers. Moral frame leaders use some type of moral compass to direct their behavior. They practice what has been described a servant leadership and are concerned with those individuals and groups that are marginalized in their organizations and in society. In short, they are concerned about equality, fairness, and social justice.

Paterno's attitude toward morality affected his views on racial, religious, ethnic, and class prejudices. At Brown University, athletes were pariahs at this academically prestigious Ivy League institution. "What I felt in those days from some Brownie snobs was exactly what I feel today from some people who clamp shut their white jaws in the presence of a black stranger, silently, eloquently, scarily expressing their superiority" (Paterno and Asbell 1989, 52). His being taken at times for a "football animal" was what sensitized him for his lifelong empathy with black people.

However, Paterno also recalls his lack of the application of moral frame behavior, which he has since corrected. He remembers when he first became athletic director at Penn State and was very condescending about women's new interest in competitive sports. He said at the time that their participation would be a "fad" that would soon dissipate. His attitude was "throw them a crumb and they will go away." He admits now that he was wrong. Today women compete at the highest levels and have proven they are very capable.

Paterno recalls a number of situations where the effective use of moral frame behavior made a difference in peoples' mind-sets. Paterno started Mike Cooper as the first black quarterback in Penn State history. When he received complaints and threats from some of the alumni, he decided to "make a statement" by starting Charlie Pittman, Franco Harris, Lydell Mitchell, and Mike Cooper, all African Americans, in the backfield all at the same time.

In another instance, Paterno faulted himself for not using moral frame and human resource frame behavior when it was appropriate. It seems that Franco Harris was three minutes late for practice one day. Paterno reamed him out in front of the team. Afterward, Paterno felt that he had mishandled the situation. In retrospect, instead of popping off in front of the team that he felt Harris had offended, he wished he had held his peace, and spoken to Harris privately later and tried to determine what was bothering him.

Paterno knew he was doing something right at John Cappeletti's acceptance speech for the Heisman Trophy as the best college football player. Upon receiving the trophy Cappeletti said that he would like to dedicate it to the many who had touched his life and helped him, but especially to the youngest member of his family, Joseph, who was very ill. He had leukemia. Cappeletti said it would mean the world to him if he could dedicate the trophy to Joseph that night and give him a couple of days of happiness. He said for him, as a football player, it was a "battle" on a field and only in the fall. For Joseph, it was all year round. Cappeletti said that the Heisman was more his brother's than his "because of the inspiration" his brother had been to him.

Bishop Fulton J. Sheen was on the dais that night. When he got up to give the benediction, he said, "Maybe for the first time in your lives you have heard a speech from the heart and not from the lips. Part of John's triumph was made by Joseph's sorrow. You don't need a blessing. God had already blessed you in John Cappeletti." Joe Paterno's reaction to all this was, "Do you see now why I could never leave for a professional coaching job?" (Paterno and Asbell 1989, 172).

Situational Leadership Analysis

At age eighty-four, Joe Paterno has been criticized for being too set in his ways and for not being situational in his leadership practice. The evidence, however, challenges this observation. For example, one of the perennial objections to the sport of football is that youngsters are susceptible to serious injuries. Today, however, fatalities are very rare and very seldom the direct result of football. Even injuries have declined because the equipment is better, the coaching is better, the rules protect the players, and the coaches do a better job in getting the kids in condition to play. Paterno has been at the forefront of initiating these changes. "In the old days," he says, "we'd never even give a kid water. It's amazing that more kids didn't die of heat exhaustion (Paterno and Asbell 1989, 61).

He used the situational approach to leadership in disciplining two of his players. It seems that he caught them drinking at a hotel bar after a bowl game victory over Miami. In the case of one of the players who had been in trouble in the past, he summarily dismissed him from the team. To the other player he said, "This is the first trouble I know about. You get one more chance, but you're suspended for the next two games" (Paterno and Asbell 1989, 115).

Paterno became aware of the need to be situational in one's leadership approach early on in his career. Upon assuming the head coaching position at Penn State, he inherited his predecessor's approach to coaching, which had been successful for him. However, after using Rip Engle's coaching philosophies in his first year at the helm, Paterno experienced a losing season. He immediately knew that it would be futile to follow the same philosophy and expect different results. So it would be imperative for him to change. With disaster starring him in the face, he decided that if he wanted to survive in the competitive world of college football, he had to do something radical. He had to do no less than rethink and redesign how a football team ought to play defense. As a result, he created a novel defensive strategy at the time called "rotating coverage," whereby he had his defensive backs rotate to the ball, similar to the way baseball players back each other up when they field the ball and the way basketball players "help" their teammates guard their opponents.

Paterno became famous for adapting his game to his personnel, identifying the unique talents that his players had and placing them in a position where they could be successful in utilizing those individual talents—even when it meant changing their positions. For example, when the great college linebacker Jack Ham showed up at Penn State as a big 198-pound freshman in 1967 after playing offensive guard in high school, Paterno converted him to linebacker because he saw the talent in him for it. After having an All-American career at Penn State, Jack Ham ended up in the Pro Football Hall of Fame as a linebacker. John Cappelletti was another example of Paterno's practicing situational leadership. Cappelletti was recruited as a linebacker and ended up being a Heisman Trophy–winning running back.

However, Paterno sometimes learned the hard way about the appropriate application of situational leadership behavior. In a 1979 game against Alabama University for the National Championship, faced with a fourth and goal, his assistant coaches recommended a conservative approach. Paterno's initial reaction was, "That's a lot of crap. This is the time to surprise them and throw the football" (Paterno and Asbell 1989, 215). Unfortunately, Paterno capitulated and ran the ball, and Penn State was stopped on the one-yard line.

But Paterno was a quick learner. Four years later, faced with a similar situation, this time he called for a pass that won the game. "That moment's decision had come easier for me than on New Year's Day, 1979, because I was not the same person I was then" (Paterno and Asbell 1989, 231). He believed that when he had faced Bear Bryant four years before on the very same spot, he wasn't "big enough, strong enough, grown enough" to face the ridicule if they had thrown the ball and it was intercepted and they lost the game. This time, as he said, he was not that same person.

Another instance of Joe Paterno's use of situational leadership behavior occurred after Penn State had three poor seasons immediately following an undefeated season. In addition to a lack of success on the field, team discipline was eroding in that several players got into off-field trouble. This situation told Paterno that he had to reexamine his role as surrogate father to many of his players. He admitted that one reason for the losing seasons and lack of discipline was that he had relaxed because he had softened his intensity and the "kids had lost fear and respect of Joe Paterno" (Paterno and Asbell 1989, 216).

Paterno came to understand that in the cycle of leadership style, there is a time for letting go, for giving people room to move, to make their own mistakes and grow—and there is a time for tightening the reins and getting a team into a single, unified rhythm. Over a span of years, therefore, the more his staff of assistant coaches grew, the more he released his grip and gave them room to develop the players according to their instincts, to analyze the opponents for themselves, and to call their own plays on the field. Paterno had learned the art of situational leadership.

Finally, although he was accused of never adjusting to the changing times, the reality is that he almost always did. The "situationality" of his leadership behavior accounts for the fact that despite having some "down" times, his teams have always come back to their former glory. As recently as two years ago, his team was contending for the National Championship, after having seen several years of futility when the conventional wisdom was that "the game had passed him by."

Leadership Implications and Conclusion

Joe Paterno's enduring success in college football is no accident. He has sustained his reputation as one of college football's most revered coaches largely because he is able to adapt his leadership behavior to the ever-changing situation. He could be described as the poster child for the effectiveness of situational leadership theory.

He engages in structural frame leadership behavior by always being well organized, disciplined, and prepared. Additionally, although sometimes wrongly criticized for not doing so, he has adapted his structural behavior to the changing situations and times. His offense, for example is not static but dynamic, and varies according to the personnel available.

Paterno's use of human resource frame and moral frame leadership behavior is well documented. His former players are very loyal to him and recognize the fact that he is sincerely concerned with their well-being long after they graduate—which, unlike in many big-time college football programs, they almost always do.

Symbolically, Paterno consciously projects an image of a coach who is competent at his craft, who cares about the individuals entrusted to his care, and who is intent on having them obtain a good education to go along with their athletic prowess. We documented a number of instances where Paterno nurtured this image, including his donation of several million dollars to the Penn State Library.

Obviously, this profile was written before the Penn State child abuse scandal broke. However, the scandal serves to illustrate the point of this book, that is, it takes but one lapse in a leader's application of the moral frame for a lifetime of good to be damaged.

II. SLOBODAN MILOSEVIC

> Serbia will be whole or it will not be anything at all—fulfill my wishes or I will destroy everything.
>
> —Slobodan Milosevic

Background

Slobodan Milosevic was born in 1941 and was the president of Serbia (1989–1997) and Yugoslavia (1997–2000). He was born and raised in Pozarevac, Yugoslavia, during World War II and suffered a very traumatic childhood when both his father and mother committed suicide.

He studied law at the University of Belgrade. While there he befriended Ivan Stambolic, who was instrumental in getting Milosevic involved in the Communist Party in Serbia. However, he initially pursued a life in business and became a successful banker before becoming involved in politics.

Milosevic became a force in Serbian politics after he made a famous speech supporting the Serbs in Kosovo, who claimed that they were being mistreated by the Kosovo government. From that point on, he became known as a strong Serbian nationalist and a hero to the Serbian people.

In 1989, after orchestrating an overthrow of the president of Serbia, Milosevic took his place. Milosevic then instigated a revolution that led to the resignation of the leaders of two of Serbia's neighbors, Vojvodina and Montenegro. Milosevic had two of his allies elected to leadership positions in both countries with the ultimate goal of nationalizing them and making them part of a new Yugoslavia.

In 1992, Milosevic co-opted the Bosnian and Herzegovinian populations, convincing them to vote in favor of secession from the former Yugoslavia and agree to join the new Yugoslav federation called the Federal Republic of Yugoslavia, of which Milosevic would eventually become president.

Milosevic's government policies as president of Serbia and then Yugoslavia were extremely authoritarian. The government exercised control and censorship of the media and the laws provided immunity to government officials, thus placing Milosevic and his henchmen above the law.

During the 1990s Milosevic took advantage of the political instability in the region and consolidated his power by exploiting Serbian nationalism and instigating wars in Slovenia, Croatia, Bosnia, and Kosovo. As the former Yugoslavia collapsed, Milosevic was able to keep his ex-communist socialist regime in power and expand Serbian influence throughout the region.

Milosevic was known as a political opportunist whose ultimate goal was to take control of the new Yugoslavia and become a modern-day Marshal Tito. He took advantage of the growing ethnic tensions between his fellow Serbs and the Albanian-dominated government in Kosovo and systematically eliminated them from power. He did the same thing in the other countries that made up the former Yugoslavia until his power reached its peak in the 1990s, and he became president of the newly organized Yugoslavia.

By the late 1990s, while Milosevic was president of the new Yugoslavia, reports of atrocities in Kosovo led NATO to launch a series of raids on Yugoslavia in an effort to force him into a cease-fire. By the year 2000, Milosevic had been defeated for a second term as Yugoslavian president and was arrested on charges of corruption, genocide, and abuse of power. A protracted trial ensued, and before it could conclude, Milosevic was found dead in his prison cell of a heart attack on March 11, 2006 (Stevanovic 2004).

The Structural Frame

Structural frame leaders seek to develop a new model of the relationship of structure, strategy, and environment for their organizations. Strategic planning, extensive preparation and effecting change are priorities for them. There is a good amount of evidence that Slobodan Milosevic spent a considerable amount of his time operating out of the structural frame. Milosevic engaged in structural frame behavior when he came to the United States for several months to attend a business conference and learn the intricacies of the banking business. While in the United States, he also became proficient in the English language and seemed to become known as a respectable banker almost overnight. Upon arriving home, he was immediately appointed president of the Belgrade Chamber of Commerce.

In typical structural leadership fashion, Milosevic was a workaholic who openly manifested the communist credo, never missed a party meeting, and carried out his duties with precision. He attacked Serbian nationalism in favor of the Marxist ideology of collectivism. He banned the books of anti-communist writers, identified and expelled liberals from the party and the universities, and insisted on communism being a stand-alone subject in public schools.

After Marshal Tito died, the dictatorial power structure gave way to a diffusion of power among the republics and provinces in Yugoslavia. In true structural leadership style, Milosevic sought to resurrect the Tito "pyramid," whereby power was concentrated at the top in the person of Milosevic, with everyone else below. Paradoxically, Milosevic was encouraging totalitarianism at the same time the Soviet Union was stressing glasnost (openness).

Soon after establishing himself as the Serbian leader, Milosevic developed a plan to gain the favor of the Serbs, who made up the bulk of the population in most of the countries that were a part of the former Yugoslavia. His ultimate goal, of course, was to consolidate his power and become president of the new Yugoslavia. His immediate target was the sitting president, whom he proceeded to portray as the antithesis of Marshall Tito and a conspirator in the desecration of the popular former president's name and image. As a result, Milosevic won the election as president of Serbia, in which Belgrade, the key city and capital of Yugoslavia, is located.

Milosevic continued to utilize structural frame behavior as president of Serbia and made certain that he quelled any opposition by strategically declaring his intention to preserve the policies of the Tito regime, reassuring all the stakeholders that they would retain their positions of power and influence. He ingratiated himself to the remainder of the population through the savvy use of the mass media. He took control of the media by nationalizing it and replacing the news editors and journalists with his own people.

Milosevic furthered strategized that in order to realize his plan to establish a Serbian-dominated Yugoslavia, he needed to convince his fellow Serbians that the world was against them in some kind of giant conspiracy. When the Western powers imposed economic and other sanctions on Serbia, they unwittingly played right into his hands.

To the outside world, Milosevic appeared to be placing himself in problematic situations with little or no forethought. The perception was far from the truth. The fact was that he and wife were cunning strategists who had their fingers firmly on the pulse of the situation. He realized, for example, that he was militarily defeated well before the nationalists and the generals did. He then moved from the structural frame to the political frame in order to obtain the best possible settlement (Stevanovic 2004).

The Human Resource Frame

Human resource leaders believe in people and communicate that belief. They are passionate about productivity through people. Suffice it to say that Slobodan Milosevic is not your warm and cuddly type. It is difficult to find instances when he displayed human resource frame behavior where there was not an ulterior motive. In fact, in my rather extensive research on him, I failed to come upon even one instance of him sincerely operating out of the human resource frame. Even with his wife, there seemed to be more of a political or business type relationship than a truly caring one. He is said to have considered "a smile a sign of weakness and politeness the first step towards a loss of authority" (Stevanovic 2004, 47–48).

The Symbolic Frame

In the symbolic frame, the organization is seen as a stage, a theater in which every actor plays certain roles and the symbolic leaders attempt to communicate the right impressions to the right audiences. Like many of his political counterparts Milosevic was very active in the symbolic frame. He utilized symbolic frame leadership behavior in establishing his image as the champion of true communism in Eastern Europe. He was careful to publically reprimand the younger generation of communists for not attending a rally to pay tribute to Marshall Tito's contribution to the revolution. As a result, the party regulars began to see Milosevic as the man to restore true communism, devoid of compromise and excess.

For the hardliners, Milosevic's ascendency was providential. He was seen as the antithesis of the liberal Mikhail Gorbachev. The party regulars believed that Milosevic's totalitarian nature was far better suited to governing the various difficult-to-control republics and provinces that made up Yugoslavia.

Milosevic burnished his strongman image even further in dealing with Kosovo, where the Albanian majority was oppressing the Serbian minority in what was the heartland of Serbian culture and tradition. In a famous incident where Milosevic had attended a rally in Kosovo at which the mostly Albanian police force attacked the Serbians while brandishing their weapons, he dramatically ascended the podium and declared, "No one has the right to beat these people! They will never defeat you again." As luck would have it, the rally was being covered by the media and Milosevic's words and image were broadcast across all of Yugoslavia. As a result, he immediately became a Serbian hero (Stevanovic 2004, 29).

Milosevic used symbolic frame behavior in establishing his image with the young intellectuals in Yugoslavia. He knew that they would be crucial to his ascendency, as they had been in Tito's time. So he made sure that they were given a special place at his rallies and treated with deference. Thus, he could count on them to market his domineering image as the savior of the "Greater Serbia" movement. As a result, his revolution became personal rather than ideological.

By the 1990s, despite a vague platform, Milosevic had developed almost an animal attraction among his followers. Serbs all over the world, including those in the United States, rallied around him and his call for Serb unity. The old Communists were convinced that he would restore communism to its self-denying roots, while his nationalist followers counted on him to place his identity as a Serb above his ideology. Even the Orthodox Church, which had been no friend of communism, perceived him as a closet believer who would return the Church to its rightful place in Yugoslavian society. In short, his savvy use of symbolic behavior had each group believing he was their savior while ignoring the obvious contradictions.

His publicity mill had been so successful that Milosevic was attracting upwards of a million people to his rallies. Given this amount of reinforcement, it was not hyperbole for him to declare at one of these rallies: "Serbia will be whole, or it will not be anything at all—fulfill my wishes or I will destroy everything" (Stevanovic 2004, 42.)

Thus, the personality cult surrounding Milosevic was slowly evolving and intentionally filling the vacuum created by the death of Marshal Tito. By 1990, the photograph of the grim-looking Milosevic was found virtually everywhere—on buses, trains, schools, and billboards, as well as in homes. Many of the Russian Orthodox faithful kept his portrait next to the candles and icons of the saints. Such was the myth of Slobodan Milosevic.

On one famous occasion, Milosevic literally came down from the heavens to redeem the Serbs. At a 600th anniversary celebration of Serbia's defeat of Kosovo, the crowd looked up to see what looked like a little dot coming down upon them. It turned out to be a helicopter that was landing among the crowd. Debarking from the helicopter was Milosevic, who then proceeded to deliver such an inspirational speech that it had the crowd singing, "Tsar Laza, you were not lucky enough to have Slobo by your side" (Stevanovic 2005, 44).

Milosevic even had the audacity to place his name in the hat for the Nobel Peace Prize in the midst of the Yugoslavian war, which he initiated. The Serbian ambassador in Stockholm declared: "If Mr. Arafat, a world-renowned terrorist, was worthy of such an honor, why not Milosevic?" (Stevanocic 2004, 112).

The Political Frame

Leaders operating out of the political frame clarify what they want and what they can get. Political leaders are realist above all. They never let what they want cloud their judgment about what is possible. They assess the distribution of power and interests. As with his counterparts, the political frame was perhaps Milosevic's strongest. Milosevic used political frame leadership behavior early on when he consciously made certain by maintaining a low profile, especially outside party circles, that his Communist colleagues did not perceive him as a rival. He never aired his disagreements in public and was never a Marxist ideologue. He was more interested in the business of politics.

Thus, Milosevic owed his rise to power not to chance but to his astute application of political frame leadership behavior. He used his brother's party influence and connection with the KGB. The symbiotic relationship with the secret police was one where they knew that they needed Milosevic to stay in power, and he needed them to gain access to even more power within the Communist Party inner circle in his quest to become a member of the political elite.

Once he gained power Milosevic made still more use of political frame behavior when he used Serbian nationalism as a smokescreen to achieve his real goal—the privatization of state property with himself as its sole owner. By gaining power in Serbia, Montenegro, Vojvodina, and Kosovo, he was in a position to ensure a majority on any issue in which the eight republics of Yugoslavia had to vote.

Milosevic used his political frame acuity in dealing with the majority Albanians in Kosovo. He never overtly expressed his personal hatred of them, employing instead more subtle means to eradicate them. He exploited the inherent dislike that the Serbians had for the Albanians, who tolerated and even encouraged his series of brutal acts toward them.

As we have seen, Milosevic utilized symbolic leadership behavior to establish himself as the reformer, democrat, religious man, and Serbian hero. In reality, however, he was a devious and cunning politician. For example, he ostensibly began the process of democratization by postponing the Serbian election to the end, knowing that he would win that election in a landside, so that the results of all the other republics' elections would already be known. He knew from his experience within the Communist Party that the final speaker was almost always the one who influenced and formulated national policy.

Milosevic further manipulated the process of democratization by creating as many parties as he could so that his opposition would be diluted and he could gain power with a plurality rather than a majority. He was very astute at utilizing the divide-and-conquer approach to gain power initially and then consolidate that power to the point where he became a virtual dictator.

Since his political status was secure in Serbia, there was no need for a formal dictatorship. An ostensive democracy would serve him better than a one-party system in that foreign opinion was much more supportive of a democracy than a dictatorship. By the time the world discovered the real truth, it was almost too late.

Among the groups with which his political frame behavior was most effective was the Russian Orthodox Church. There was much to gain from being seen as an ally of the Church. The Orthodox clergy was present in every nook and cranny of the country, sermonizing on both their religious and political views. So Milosevic ingratiated himself to the Church, giving the impression that he was a true believer. The reality, however, was that his communist heart despised the Church.

Milosevic was an expert at playing both ends against the middle. For example, when Serbia was at war with some of the other Yugoslav republics, but at the same time denying it, there was a need for someone to act simultaneously as a combatant and a pacifist—enter Milosevic. He managed to be both a frontline commander and an innocent bystander who was only interested in a peaceful resolution. His propaganda mill effectively set the stage for him to serve both roles.

After losing Russian and European support for his regime and in the midst of a war that he initiated, Milosevic displayed still more political frame leadership behavior by capitalizing on the Clinton administration's desire to resolve the Yugoslav question before the presidential election. Always willing to accommodate when it was to his advantage, Milosevic took on the role of peacemaker in his dealing with the United States. "All the world's diplomats know that, regarding the war in the former Yugoslavia I always supported a peaceful solution to conflict between warring parties," he proclaimed (Stevanovic 2004, 108).

Ultimately, the Dayton Peace Agreement was negotiated to settle the Yugoslavian conflict. Again utilizing political frame behavior, Milosevic manipulated the media and had the world convinced that he had been the impetus behind the agreement. Ever the political animal, however, he used passive aggressive behavior, feigning compliance with the peace terms while violating them at every opportunity. It seemed that the only way to ensure that he adhered to the treaty was to threaten him with air strikes. But when this happened, Milosevic would retreat briefly and apologize, only to advance again at the next opportunity (Stevanovic 2004).

The Moral Frame

The moral frame is my own contribution to situational leadership theory. In my view, the moral frame completes situational leadership theory. Without it, leaders could just as easily use their leadership skills for promoting evil as for promoting good. Leaders operating out of the moral frame are concerned about their obligations and responsibilities to their followers. Moral frame leaders use some type of moral compass to direct their behavior. They practice what has been described as servant leadership and are concerned with those individuals and groups that are marginalized in their organizations and in society. In short, they are concerned about equality, fairness, and social justice.

Considering the number of wars that he instigated and the brutality that was associated with his regime, it is quite obvious that the moral frame was not one of Milosevic's strongest. Being obsessed with the acquisition of power and having been nurtured in the belief that the end justifies the means, Milosevic never really developed a moral code through which he could filter his leadership behavior. As a result, he could accurately be described as being amoral.

In the areas in which Milosevic had most control, Serbia and Montenegro, the crime rates soared. Much of the increase was attributed to the tolerance that Milosevic had for criminal organizations. It was claimed that he not only turned a deaf ear toward them, but also extracted a "tax" from them. Such was the relativity of his moral code (Stevanovic 2004).

Situational Leadership Analysis

Situational leadership models differ from earlier trait and behavioral models in asserting that no single way of leading works in all situations. Rather, appropriate behavior depends on the circumstance at a given time. Effective managers diagnose the situation, identify the leadership style or behavior that will be most effective, and then determine whether they can implement the required style. Since we have seen that Milosevic was at least minimally active in all five frames, he could be legitimately categorized as a leader in the situational leadership tradition. However, his use of some of the frames was quite flawed. The way Milosevic dealt with the Serbian intelligentsia demonstrated his facility with using situational leadership theory. They did not perceive him as an adversary because he was able to gain their confidence through structural behavior in the form of strategic planning, symbolic behavior in the form of propaganda, and political behavior in the form of manipulation.

In addition to being a devotee of situational ethics, behaving in a situational way in other areas became a time-honored tradition for Milosevic. When the question of the crimes perpetrated in Kosovo was referred to the United Nations for resolution, it presented Milosevic with a new opportunity to engage in situational leadership behavior. Whereas he had operated out of the structural frame in instigating the atrocities in Kosovo, he now operated out of the symbolic and political frames in casting himself as a peacemaker and pillar of justice (Stevanovic 2004).

Leadership Implications and Conclusion

Slobodan Milosevic is yet another example of a successful leader who was not a good and heroic one. This characterization is due to the fact that although he was appropriately active in three of the five leadership frames, he almost completely ignored the other two, namely, the human resource and moral frames.

Milosevic effectively utilized situational leadership in being recognized as the savior of the Serbs and the preserver of Yugoslavia as an extended Serbia. He used his leadership behavior to appeal to the right, the left, and the moderates. He presented himself as the only viable representative of the differing political factions in Yugoslavia. He made friends with both atheists and believers, but inwardly despised both. He had no real moral code and considered ethics to be relative. He provoked needless conflict, but paradoxically, was considered by many to be the great peacemaker worthy of Nobel Prize consideration. Through the astute use of situational leadership theory, he was able to work his way past these apparent contradictions. Nevertheless, because of his lack of a moral code, his leadership behavior would certainly not be something today's educational leaders and potential leaders would want to emulate.

Chapter Eleven

Carter v. Hussein

I. JIMMY CARTER

The sad duty of politics is to establish justice in a sinful world.

—Jimmy Carter

Background

Jimmy Carter was born in 1924 and was the thirty-ninth president of the United States. A down-to-earth personality, great intelligence, and strong moral conviction propelled Jimmy Carter to the nation's highest office. During much of his Plains, Georgia, childhood he lived without electricity or indoor plumbing, and he was the first member of his devout Baptist family to finish high school. He won an appointment to the U.S. Naval Academy at Annapolis and afterward became a senior officer in Admiral Rickover's nuclear submarine program.

When his father died in 1953, Carter returned to Georgia to work in the family's failing peanut business, eventually making it prosper. All the while, he remained an outspoken critic of segregation. In a fiercely contested election in 1962, he gained a seat in the state senate, where he pushed for strict budgeting, efficient bureaucracy, and aid for the needy. Upon reaching the governor's mansion in 1971 he was very inclusive, extending his arms to everyone, mandating integration and appointing a significant number of blacks to government positions.

As the Democratic Party campaign chairman in1974, Carter caught the attention of national and international leaders alike. He now had enough support to make a run for the presidency. During the primaries his populist focus on honesty in government caught on. He won the nomination and went on to defeat Gerald Ford in the presidential election.

To maintain his image as the people's president, Carter did away with many of the amenities ritually enjoyed by his predecessors. He largely dispensed with limousines, sold off the presidential yacht, and on occasion even carried his own bags. The president granted pardons to conscientious objectors who had resisted the Vietnam draft. Confronted with an energy crisis, he launched a two-tiered program that would simultaneously stimulate domestic production of oil and natural gas and decrease U.S. dependency on OPEC. He made several televised energy addresses, styled as "fireside chats," in which, cardigan-clad, he appealed to his fellow Americans to be energy efficient.

Carter spoke out with uncommon eloquence against human rights transgressions, though he did lift travel bans on offending countries—Cuba and North Korea among them—and extended full diplomatic recognition to China despite its treatment of Tibet. In November 1979 the American embassy in Tehran was seized by followers of the Ayatollah Khomeini and sixty-three Americans were taken hostage. Carter would prove unequal to the crisis. As a result, his approval rating plummeted to the lowest of any modern president, and he suffered a humiliating defeat in the 1980 presidential election to Ronald Reagan.

For Jimmy Carter, there has been life, and some vindication, after the presidency. Indeed, he has become perhaps the most productive of our living presidents, being an indispensible elder statesman consulted on foreign affairs by virtually every chief executive who followed him. He had also been supremely active in humanitarian causes, Habitat for Humanity being but one of his many such activities. In 2002, Carter received the Nobel Peace Prize for his work in finding peaceful solutions to international conflicts and the advancement of human rights (Aronson 1997; Felzenberg 2008; Morris 1996; Taranto and Leo 2004).

The Structural Frame

Structural frame leaders seek to develop a new model of the relationship of structure, strategy, and environment for their organizations. Strategic planning, extensive preparation and effecting change are priorities for them. Although he was not always recognized and given credit for being a structural leader, we will find that Jimmy Carter was very active in this frame.

Although Jimmy Carter was criticized by some for having no ideological vision, he did use other forms of structural frame behavior. For example, Norman Mailer once said of him: "If he could make a government come alive, it would be only because he worked over the problem like a piece of broken machinery not because he was guided by any overarching political philosophy" (Morris 1996, 55). In his 1980 reelection campaign, Carter's pollster put it bluntly: "You suffer because you are held to have no vision, no grand plan" (Morris 1996, 56).

In preparing for admission to the Naval Academy, Carter showed his structural frame tendencies. He memorized most of his dog-eared copy of the academy's admissions catalog and made sure he did what was required for acceptance. He studied hard, made good grades, and worked to develop the kind of character one had to have in order to gain acceptance into the academy.

In a sometimes annoying use of structural frame behavior, Carter had a penchant for pointing out faults in others by correcting their writing and grammar like some rigid schoolmarm. His attention to detail was legendary and sometimes counterproductive. Having vowed to read every bill in its entirety before voting on it, he did just that. But this picayune attention to detail was one of his most annoying traits. Reg Murphy, an Atlanta newspaper writer, wrote that "Jimmy Carter will never be human enough to overlook the faults of anybody else" (Morris 1996, 141).

During his service in the Georgia senate and then later, Carter engaged in a positive use of structural behavior and became intensely interested in the process of planning. He helped found and later headed his regional planning commission, secured both state and matching federal funding for the agency, and maintained an image of himself as an effective planner throughout his presidential campaign.

Similarly, Carter's capacity for work during his peak years was enormous. As governor of Georgia, he would take a stack of papers, sometimes over a foot thick, home and go over it until one o'clock in the morning. In his "spare time," he planned his presidential campaign and wrote his autobiography, *Why Not the Best?*

During his journey to the White House, Carter displayed many of the structural traits that would characterize his presidency; a meticulous attention to detail, extraordinary self-discipline, and an understanding of the power of symbolism (Felzenberg 2008).

Using a combination of structural and political frame behavior, Carter turned his penchant for detail to mastering the recently adopted Democratic Party rules that significantly changed the way delegates would be selected. He learned that one could win the nomination by placing first in a number of carefully selected states and picking up spare delegates in smaller states where he finished second or worse.

Once again, in true structural frame fashion, by 1970 Carter's master file was organized by zip codes, and booklets were prepared for each zip code grouping, listing supporters by name, occupation, and political philosophy. And, based upon a careful assessment and mathematical weighting of the many variables believed to be politically significant on different areas of a particular state, the Carter campaign ingeniously used a computerized procedure known as linear progression to calculate the amount of time he should allot to each area.

As we shall see, the personal touch was in fact the essence of the Carter presidential campaign. In a combination of human resource and structural frame behavior, he pushed his body to the limit when virtually every weekday morning for two years was spent shaking hands with factory workers at the plant gate at 6 AM. His greeting, "Hello, I'm Jimmy Carter and I'm running for president," thereafter entered America's lexicon.

As soon as he was elected president, Carter immediately engaged in structural leadership behavior and began a series of comprehensive legislative initiatives in such intractable and controversial areas as welfare reform, tax code revisions, national health care, and an energy policy. Even activist Senator Edward Kennedy remarked that Carter's "reforms are already lined up bumper to bumper" (Morris 1996, 242).

In his second year in office, Carter achieved two major achievements in international affairs through the use of structural behavior. He transferred control of the Panama Canal to Panama and brokered the Camp David Peace Accords between Egypt and Israel. However, he ultimately paid the price for concentrating too exclusively on these matters to the detriment of other pressing domestic problems.

The Human Resource Frame

Human resource leaders believe in people and communicate that belief. They are passionate about productivity through people. Along with the moral frame, the human resource frame of leadership behavior may be Jimmy Carter's strongest. Carter's concern for humanity, which fostered his extensive use of the human resource frame goes back to his childhood. His high school valedictorian speech was entitled, "The Building of a Community," and his greatest achievements would be to build bridges of reconciliation between the adversarial communities of black and white America, Arab and Jew in the Middle East, and China and the United States.

Later in life when he was in the navy, Carter gave a not-so-surprising explanation for his enjoyment of submarine duty. "The crew and the officers lived in intimate contact. There was a closeness among the men, which I liked" (Morris 1996, 106).

Because of his concern for human rights, Carter reassessed America's diplomacy policy of overlooking, or not publically criticizing, the human rights violations of its political allies. Always one to put his money where his mouth was, when the Soviet Union responded to Carter's strong human rights stance with renewed adventurism, which included invading Afghanistan, Carter cancelled American participation in the Moscow Olympics.

However, despite his many efforts in promoting human rights, it ended up making him look weak, and he ended his presidency being remembered mostly for a thirteen-month stalemate with Iran over sixty-three American diplomatic personnel who had been taken hostage on trumped-up charges. A failed rescue attempt in which eight military service personnel were killed dramatically punctuated Carter's apparent ineffectiveness.

Nevertheless, after leaving office Carter's reputation, especially in the areas of human rights and diplomacy, has improved. In 1982, he established The Carter Center in Atlanta to advance human rights and alleviate unnecessary human suffering. He further engaged in human resource leadership behavior through his work with Habitat for Humanity and in speaking out against the death penalty both in the United States and abroad. His prolific use of human resource leadership behavior was publically recognized in 2002 when he received the Nobel Peace Prize.

The Symbolic Frame

In the symbolic frame, the organization is seen as a stage, a theater in which every actor plays certain roles and the symbolic leader attempts to communicate the right impressions to the right audiences. Jimmy Carter frequently operated out of the symbolic leadership frame, but not always to his political advantage. One such instance was his so-called "malaise speech." Carter's aim in this speech was to address the crisis of confidence that he perceived in the American people and to engender hope for the future. The energy crisis that resulted in cars being lined up around the block waiting for gasoline was only the symptom of a "moral and spiritual crisis" in America, he declared. Too many were "worshiping self-indulgence and consumption." Never was there such a collapse of the "national will" or a "crisis of the American spirit," he continued. But this effort at using symbolic leadership behavior backfired when it was depicted in the media that he was blaming the energy crisis on the American people rather than on his administration's policies (Morris 1996, 5).

Carter began engaging in symbolic leadership behavior early in life. He gravitated more toward his mother's values, especially when opposed to his father's. For example, in an overt display of symbolic behavior, he joined his mother in attending black peoples' funerals that his father refused to attend.

Carter often used what he called "The Parable of the Cookies" to get his points across. Carter's mother had baked some cookies. "Honey, would you like some cookies?" she asked. Carter had collected some pebbles in his hands for his slingshot and hesitated over whether to refuse the cookies and keep the pebbles or vice versa. The cookies, Carter said in relaying this story, stood for the goals of racial integration and social justice, while the pebbles represent segregation and injustice. He considered himself foolish for wanting to hold on to the pebbles instead of dropping them and accepting the cookies (Morris 1996, 79).

Perhaps his most enduring instance of utilizing symbolic behavior began in the first grade in Plains, Georgia, when Carter began thrusting his right hand for a handshake and said to his future classmates and new friends, "Hello, I'm Jimmy Carter." Even today, this remains the most remembered utterance of Jimmy Carter. Fittingly, he opened his acceptance speech at the 1976 Democratic convention with this greeting to the good-natured laughter of the delegates.

The notion of Carter hailing from Plains, Georgia, was a purposely created myth. In one of the first presidential campaigns to appeal to "values," Carter campaign strategists decided to use some symbolic behavior to celebrate the value of community. Nominally headquartered in Plains, the campaign was actually run out of its Atlanta office. And Carter was actually born in an even smaller town.

Carter used symbolic leadership behavior in highlighting his lifelong penchant for physical exercise and fitness. A television interviewer once described Carter as "one of the healthiest looking 65-year-olds I've seen" (Morris 1996, 94). Much earlier, his dedication to physical fitness resulted in his easily passing the Naval Academy physical examination.

Carter considered his interview with one of his heroes and the father of the nuclear submarine, Admiral Hyman Rickover, his most memorable moments and used symbolic behavior to perpetuate it. He not only survived the infamous interviewer but was offered a position, which Carter rapidly accepted. Rickover ended up influencing Carter more than anyone other than his parents. He named his first book after Rickover's famous last interview question and challenge, *Why Not the Best?*

When Carter was a peanut farmer, the White Citizens Council tried to coerce him into joining. They even offered to pay the $5 membership fee. In typical symbolic leadership style, Carter took a $5 bill from his cash register and told the Council members that he would rather flush the bill down the toilet than give it to a vigilante organization. He also supported public school consolidation to hasten integration. The morning after the consolidation vote, he found a sign on the front door of his warehouse which read, "Coons and Carters Go Together" (Morris 1996, 119).

As a result of his effective use of symbolic frame behavior, a 1976 Gallop poll found that 68 percent of the American public believed Carter was "a man of high moral character," while 72 percent deemed him "bright and intelligent," adjectives that suggested competence. Of course, the "competence" part of this image changed drastically by 1980 (Morris 1996, 202).

Carter constantly pounded away symbolically at his two pet themes; first was that the federal government had lost its basic integrity after the Nixon years, and second, that the government was incompetent. Convincing the American public of these two claims got him elected president, but ironically, the majority of the American public came to view him as incompetent by the end of his first and only term and elected Ronald Reagan as president.

Carter symbolically projected a populist flair during his inauguration ceremonies when he defied both tradition and his own Secret Service agents to walk rather than ride the mile and a half down Pennsylvania Avenue to his swearing-in ceremony. Instructing the Marine Corps band to discontinue playing "Hail to the Chief," ordering White House staff to use their own cars instead of limousines, and selling the presidential yacht, not to mention insisting on being called "Jimmy," all symbolically and intentionally suggested he was a man of the people (Felzenberg 2008, 164).

Perhaps Carter's greatest measure of symbolic leadership behavior came when he attempted to reinforce his position on human rights in a confrontation with the Soviet Union. As mentioned earlier, when the Soviet Union ignored Carter's appeal for respecting human rights and declared war on Afghanistan, Carter withdrew U.S. participation in the Moscow Olympics. Instead of supporting him in his decision, however, most Americans considered it a case of cutting off one's nose to spite one's face.

Carter continued to utilize symbolic leadership behavior to an even greater extent after his presidency. His reputation was rehabilitated by his work with Habitat for Humanity, the establishment of the Carter-Menil Human Rights Prize and Global 2000. In China, Carter helped initiate a program to provide artificial limbs for amputees.

The Political Frame

Leaders operating out of the political frame clarify what they want and what they can get. Political leaders are realists above all. They never let what they want cloud their judgment about what is possible. They assess the distribution of power and interests. As with all politicians, Jimmy Carter had to be active in the political frame in order to succeed in his profession. The question we pose in Carter's case and in that of the other presidents profiled, is whether he used the correct quality and quantity of political frame leadership behavior and if he did so in the appropriate situations.

According to some of his biographers, Carter's political strategy some-times included reducing his opponents to "bad guy" caricatures. This began with his success in defeating Joe Hurst in a senate Democratic primary by portraying him as a criminal. Since he was later jailed for election fraud, it was probably an apt depiction. Carter also parlayed his status as a party "outsider" from a potential liability to an advantage. He would become the quintessential maverick, whose selfless devotion to the community is dis-played in his efforts to reform a corrupt and inept government.

However, Carter was accused of misusing political frame behavior when he campaigned for governor of Georgia. His campaign platform of states' rights gave one the distinct impression that he was ambivalent toward civil rights. But after winning the election and delivering his inaugural address in favor of civil rights, it was obvious where he really stood. Then when he announced that his major gubernatorial objective would be the reorganization of state government, a pledge he had not bothered to mention during the campaign, his sincerity was further questioned. Lester Maddox expressed his view of Carter after the election in his usual colorful way, saying, "When I put my pennies into a peanut machine, I don't expect to get bubble gum" (Morris 1996, 189).

In typical political leadership fashion, when Carter received an endorse-ment from a newspaper, he used it as evidence of his popularity. But when, as was more often the case, a newspaper opposed him, Carter used it as evidence that his candidacy was opposed by the Georgia or Washington political establishment. As we have seen, Carter presented himself as a man of the people and a Washington outsider.

During the era in which he ran for president there was a national mistrust of liberals dating back to the turbulent sixties. Had he allowed himself to be defined as a liberal, his electability to state and national office would be in serious jeopardy. Thus, he employed political frame leadership behavior and symbolic behavior to have himself defined as a populist, which had far fewer negative connotations.

Carter took political advantage of the perceived incompetence and the numerous scandals in the federal government at that time. He declared: "This may be the first year in our history when it is better to run for President as a peanut farmer from Plains, Georgia, than as a United States Senator from Washington, D.C." (Morris 1996, 203).

Carter was careful during his presidential campaign to avoid singling out Richard Nixon for personal criticism, lest he be accused of being mean-spirited. At the same time, he wanted his opponent, Gerald Ford, to be identified with Nixon. So he spoke generally about people being "excluded" from government and "lied to" by public officials (Morris 1996, 214).

After he became president, Carter used some political frame behavior with the judicious appointment of experienced and respected Washington figures for his cabinet to reassure those who were concerned about him as a Washington outsider. But this turned out to be the extent of his effective use of political frame behavior.

Carter took office believing he owed nothing to the political establishment that he had defeated on the way to the presidency. That belief, however, was mutual, and the intransigence of both parties in Congress led to his ultimate demise (Felzenberg 2008, 167).

In what turned out to be a misuse or lack of the use of political leadership behavior, Carter seemed to intentionally snub Tip O'Neill, the House Speaker. The division between the two became apparent when O'Neill's family received seats near the kitchen at the inaugural gala. This incident started a pattern of such instances to the point where the single most consistent criticism of the Carter presidency was that he was inept in his dealings with Congress.

Carter seemed to ignore congressional folkways or operating methods and made very little attempt to establish personal relationships with many representatives or senators. Time spent with Carter was strictly business.

In a further misuse of political frame behavior, Carter became perceived by the majority of the American public as ineffective in foreign affairs as he was in domestic affairs. When the Shah of Iran was deposed, Carter reluctantly granted him political asylum in the United States. Iranian terrorists took revenge by taking sixty-three Americans hostages, most of whom remained in captivity for the duration of Carter's presidency. During their captivity, the Islamic revolutionaries paraded in the streets and burned effigies of Carter and set American flags aflame before the many television cameras present. When a hostage rescue attempt was gravely mishandled, Carter's reputation for competency reached its nadir (Morris 1996).

The Moral Frame

The moral frame is my own contribution to situational leadership theory. In my view, the moral frame completes situational leadership theory. Without it, leaders could just as easily use their leadership skills for promoting evil as for promoting good. Leaders operating out of the morel frame are concerned about their obligations and responsibilities to their followers. Moral frame leaders use some type of moral compass to direct their behavior. They practice what has been described as servant leadership and are concerned with those individuals and groups that are marginalized in their organizations and in society. In short, they are concerned about equality, fairness and social justice.

Perhaps more than any other president in American history, Jimmy Carter consistently operated out of the moral frame. The product of Southern populism and the civil rights movement, as well as being a born-again Christian, Carter was totally immersed in the philosophy that morality should be integrated into public life. He asserted that America's greatness rested primarily on its morals and ideals, not its policies or its economic structure.

Although many questioned Carter's lack of a clearly defined vision, there was almost universal agreement that he had very clear ideas about morality and the part it played in politics, especially in the area of human rights.

In running for governor of Georgia, he said:

> There is a mandatory relationship between the powerful and influential and the socially prominent and the wealthy on the one hand, and the weak, the insecure, and the poor on the other hand. In a free society we do see very clearly that one cannot accept great blessings bestowed on him by God without feeling an inner urge and drive to share those blessings with others of our neighbors who are not quite so fortunate as we (Morris 1996, 152).

Situational Leadership Analysis

Situational models of leadership differ from earlier trait and behavioral models in asserting that no single way of leading works in all situations. Rather, appropriate behavior depends on the circumstances at a given time. Effective managers diagnose the situation, identify the leadership style or behavior that will be most effective, and then determine whether they can implement the required style.

There is no question but that Jimmy Carter was a leader in the situational mold. Unlike his Georgia gubernatorial campaign, which was said to lack an ideological theme, Carter immediately used situational leadership behavior and identified the dual themes of morality and competence for the presidential campaign. In *Why Not the Best?*, Carter asked two basic questions: "Can our government be honest, decent, open, fair and compassionate?" And, "Can our government be competent?" (Morris 1996, 195).

We saw how in the governor's race in 1970, Carter used political frame leadership behavior in portraying himself as a populist candidate of the people who was opposed by the state's entrenched political and financial interests.

Carter innately understood the need to operate out of multiple leadership frames. When reporters asked him if he was a liberal, conservative or moderate, he replied, "I believe I'm more complicated than that," implying that he spanned the ideological continuum depending on the *situation*. He also noted that "as important as honesty and openness are [moral frame behavior], they are not enough. There must also be substance and logical direction in government [structural frame behavior]" (Morris 1996, 223).

Leadership Implications and Conclusion

There is much to learn about leadership from the complex leadership behavior of Jimmy Carter. Although he was appropriately active *among* the five leadership frames described here, one could question whether Carter was always effective *within* the various frames. Some of his critics would argue that he was perhaps too extreme in his use of the moral frame, for example. As a result, he sometimes came across as being somewhat self-righteous.

His alleged misuse of the structural frame resulted in his administration being faulted by its critics for trying too much too quickly and thereby losing focus. Misuse of the symbolic frame projected the impression that his administration did not speak with one voice and left the American public confused and made his administration appear to be adrift and incompetent.

Just two years into his administration the public agreed with the political pundits by a margin of 67 to 17 percent that the administration initiated too many new programs without appropriate follow through (Morris 1996, 55). Thus, along with flaws in his political frame behavior, one can point out perceived excesses in the use of virtually every one of the five leadership frames.

A somewhat harsh depiction of Jimmy Carter's image was recently described by Steven R. Weisman, in his review of Carter's new book *White House Diary* in the September 27, 2010, issue of the *New York Times*, observing that "the writings here reflect the Mr. Carter we know: boastful and painfully confessional, sanctimonious and callous, insightful and un-self-aware. These are the thoughts of a secular preacher and calculating politician, surrounded by friends and yet often alone." This stands as an unfortunate outcome for a man whose heart is definitely in the right place. Fortunately, Jimmy Carter's leadership legacy also includes the outstanding leadership behavior that he exhibited in his post-presidential years. He is certainly a leader worth emulating.

II. SADDAM HUSSEIN

Don't provoke a snake before you make up your mind and muster up the ability to cut its head. It will be of no use to say that you have not started the attack if it attacks you by surprise. Make the necessary preparations required in each individual case and trust in God.

—Saddam Hussein

Background

Saddam Hussein was president of Iraq from 1979 until 2003 when he was deposed after the Iraqi conflict with the United States and a coalition of its allies. He was born in Al-Awja to a family of shepherds. His name in Arabic means "one who confronts." Hussein left his family when he was only ten years old and went to Baghdad to live with his uncle Kharaillah Tulfah, who was a devout Sunni Muslim and a member of the revolutionary Baath Party. Tulfah had a great influence on the young Hussein.

Hussein became active in the Baath Party and rose to the position of general in the Iraqi army. As his friend and cousin Ahmed Hassan al-Bakr became increasingly ill, Hussein assumed many of al-Bakr's duties, especially in foreign affairs. When al-Bakr began discussing a treaty with Syria, also under Baathist leadership, Hussein saw the distinct possibility that his power would diminish, so he forced the ailing al-Bakr to resign. Hussein became president of Iraq in 1979 and immediately engaged in a "cleansing" process with his political enemies. Almost one hundred were arrested and over twenty were executed for treason.

Hussein oversaw a mainly secular government that was very liberal by traditional Iraqi standards. He irritated Islamic conservatives by granting many freedoms to women and established a Western European style of legal system. He tried to modernize the country but was thwarted in his efforts by the Islamic fundamentalists who made up the vast majority of the population. Since Hussein and his fellow Sunni Muslims made up only about twenty percent of the population, he believed that he had to rule the country with an iron hand. Thus, in addition to the regular armed forces, he established what he called the People's Army to seek out his political enemies so he could retain his power.

In addition to the use of force, Hussein maintained his power by promoting his own personality cult. His face appeared virtually everywhere: on posters, murals, statues, and billboards throughout Iraq. He also signed a pact with the Soviet Union in 1972 whereby the Soviets provided him with arms and military advice.

In the 1980s, Hussein sought to build nuclear capability with the aid of France. It was about that time that the Ayatollah Khomeini became the ruler of Iran, Iraq's historical enemy. The enmity between the two countries escalated into the Iran-Iraq War. With the support of the United States, the Soviet Union, and most of the Arab states, Hussein took on the mantle of defender of the Arab world against Islamic extremists.

Iran and Iraq quickly found themselves in a protracted and destructive war of attrition. During the war, Iraq used illegal chemical weapons against not only the Iranians, but also against the Kurds, who were Iraqi citizens.

When the bloody eight-year war ended in a stalemate, the economically devastated Iraq sought a remedy by invading neighboring Kuwait, aiming to take possession of their lucrative oil fields.

When Hussein invaded Kuwait in 1990, the United States and its allies declared war on Iraq. Desert Storm, as the operation was called, forcibly removed Hussein from Kuwait, but not before he vengefully set Kuwait's oil wells aflame. As part of the cease-fire agreement, Iraq was to abandon its efforts to pursue nuclear capability and to dispose of its chemical weapons.

In the intervening years, Hussein constantly taunted the United States and refused to allow U.N. inspectors to enter Iraq to search for any nuclear weapons that he might have. Despite United Nations–backed economic sanctions against Iraq, Hussein continued to violate the terms of the Gulf War cease-fire agreement. Finally, in 2003, the United States and its coalition partners invaded Iraq on the grounds that Hussein was developing weapons of mass destruction.

Iraq's military forces collapsed within three weeks of the invasion, but Hussein was nowhere to be found. However, about nine months after the ground war ended, Hussein was found hiding in an underground shelter at a farmhouse in the small town of ad-Dawr. Upon his capture, Hussein was tried by the Iraqis, found guilty of murdering at least 148 people, and sentenced to death. He was hanged on December 30, 2006 (Anderson 2004; Kaplan and Kristol 2003).

The Structural Frame

Structural frame leaders seek to develop a new model of the relationship of structure, strategy, and environment for their organizations. Strategic planning, extensive preparation and effecting chance are priorities for them. The structural frame was not one of Saddam Hussein's strongest. As we shall see, the lack of forethought and poor preparation, both structural frame deficiencies, were often observed in his leadership behavior.

If Hussein practiced structural leadership at all, it was done to the extreme. Brutality toward both his friends and enemies was his modus operandi. He often proudly compared himself to Joseph Stalin when it came to ruthlessness. He retained his political power by denouncing and sometimes even indiscriminately murdering anyone who stood in his path or might in anyway challenge his rule.

In addition, Hussein used the same structural frame behavior in the form of terrorism with his closest aides as he did with the general population of Iraq. Whether requiring his staff to attend mandatory weapons demonstrations at his staff picnics or monitoring their foreign language typewriters to identify possible traitors, or simply executing them and their families to set an example, radical structural frame behavior became the rule.

On the other hand, when Hussein should have used structural frame leadership behavior, he oftentimes did not. As a result, instead of planning things out before he acted, he became a notorious risk taker. For example, he attacked Iran under the foolish and unfounded belief that its regime would immediately collapse. Eight years later, the war was still not settled. During that same war, he attacked Israel under the false assumption that the Arab world would abandon its support of the United States in the war effort. And, he attacked Kuwait and challenged the United States, never thinking that they would respond in kind. He continually overestimated his own capabilities and underestimated those of his enemies, mostly because he did not operate out of the structural frame and "do his homework."

The Human Resource Frame

Human resource leaders believe in people and communicate that belief. They are passionate about productivity through people. There is little to no evidence that Hussein sincerely operated out the human resource frame. To the contrary, his enduring image was that of a strong-armed bully.

The Symbolic Frame

In the symbolic frame, the organization is seen as a stage, a theater in which every actor plays certain roles and the symbolic leader attempts to communicate the right impressions to the right audiences. The symbolic leadership frame was Hussein's forte. Hussein's image as a strong-armed bully was something that he began cultivating in his early life. His classmates remember him as being very bellicose to the point of actually carrying a gun to school. Having been raised by his uncle Tulfah only exacerbated the situation, in that he was a Baath Party revolutionary who plotted a number of their coups. Uncle Tulfah tutored young Hussein in socialism, fascism, and nationalism, and his book, *Three Whom God Should Not Have Created: Persians, Jews and Flies*, could have been the manifesto of both men (Kaplan and Kristol 2003, 4).

Hussein propagated his macho image with a several real or imagined stories about his alleged courage and bravery. One that he was fond of telling was about his failed attempt to assassinate the prime minister of Iraq. Wounded in the incident, he often bragged about having extracted the bullet from his leg with a pocketknife.

Further cultivating his image of brutality, Hussein joined the Baath Party security force, a group reminiscent of Hitler's Brownshirts and gloried in slaughtering Baath opponents and their families and dumping their bodies in the streets for all to see. Hussein even engaged in symbolic frame behavior with his own family. His sons often related the story of being taken by their father to the local prison to witness torture and execution as part of their "toughening up" process.

Once he became president of Iraq, one of his first acts was to execute fourteen Jews who he claimed were part of a Zionist spy ring. They were hanged in a public square in Baghdad after which he rationalized, "We hanged spies, but the Jews crucified Christ" (Kaplan and Kristol 2003, 5).

Hussein engaged in symbolic leadership behavior when he deposed his cousin, Ahmed Hassan al-Bakr and immediately abandoned the democratic ideals of the Baath Party in favor of his own personality cult that he preceded in establishing. In time, it would rival those surrounding Lenin, Stalin, and Mao. Portraits of Hussein were seen everywhere, especially at the entrances of cities, villages, schools, and public buildings. Virtually every household had his picture hanging in one room or another. The "Great Uncle" as he liked to be called, made certain that his image was everywhere.

Hussein built an image of invincibility with the Iraqis, and even when holes in that image appeared, he rationalized it away to the Iraqi public. For example, even though the Iran-Iraq War was a failure by any objective judgment, he portrayed it to the populace as a great victory and a proving ground for the Iraqi army. As a result, less than two years later, he felt confident in launching his military forces against Kuwait, knowing that the United States would most likely intervene. And, true to his delusionary symbolic frame form, he declared victory in the Desert Storm conflict even though he was fortunate to get out of it with his life intact.

Hussein continued his flamboyant use of symbolic behavior until the very end. Americans everywhere were exposed to the stage-managed dramas taking place in Iraq leading up to the recent war with the United States. The mass media was a willing party in cooperating with Hussein's image-building as a revered and fearless leader. Meanwhile, those in Iraq were simply much too afraid to indicate otherwise.

Knowing that he may soon die as a martyr for the cause, the ever-symbolic Hussein had the following quote placed in gold lettering on the wall of the Triumphant Leader Museum:

> The clock chimes away for time to keep record of men and women, some leaving behind the mark of great and lofty souls, while others leave naught but the remains of worm-eaten bones. . . . As for martyrs, they are alive in the Heavens, ever immortal in the presence of God. No heritage is worthier or more sublime than theirs" (Anderson 2004, 11).

Hussein had his countrymen so brainwashed by his effective use of symbolic frame behavior that their knee-jerk reaction was to defend him even under that most incriminating of circumstances. For example, one of his followers in defending his brutality declared: "Iraq needs a strong ruler. This country is like a wild horse, and it needs a tough trainer. Even if he makes mistakes, it's better to have someone strong like Saddam than someone who is weak" (Anderson 2004, 17).

The Political Frame

Leaders operating out of the political frame clarify what they want and what they can get. Political leaders are realists above all. The never let what they want cloud their judgment about what is possible. They assess the distribution of power and interests. In addition to the symbolic frame, Hussein was equally prolific operating out of the political frame.

Using his security forces as his foundation, Hussein engaged in political frame behavior in removing his predecessor and cousin from the presidency of Iraq. He made certain that all of his opponents for the presidency were eliminated so that there was really no choice. His fellow candidates were tortured and forced to confess to being enemies of the state. In case others may have missed his point, Hussein had the confessions and executions videotaped for viewing by Iraqi citizens throughout the country. "We are now in our Stalinist era," Hussein announced loudly in 1989. "We shall strike with an iron fist against the slightest deviation or backsliding" (Kaplan and Kristol 2003, 7).

Hussein frequently used political frame leadership behavior in keeping the majority Shiites under control. For example, Hussein ostensibly drained swamps to create a central waterway to irrigate land in the area, ordering the diversion of the Tigris and Euphrates rivers away from the marshes. As a result the marshland, which was where the Shiites lived, became a desert. As soon as the Shiites left the area, his army units moved in and claimed the land for the government.

As we have seen, Hussein often used political frame behavior in the form of instigating conflicts to achieve his ends. For example, in an effort to regain the Shatt al Arab waterway that Iraq surrendered to Iran in 1975, and to depose the Ayatollah, he declared war on Iran. Unfortunately for Hussein, this attempt at political frame behavior was not productive in that despite the killing and maiming of three million people, neither objective was realized.

Hussein tried this strategy once again in invading Kuwait. He did so to force OPEC to raise oil prices so that Iraq could eliminate its $2 billion debt to Kuwait. He also wanted to regain the Kuwaiti oil fields on the border of Iraq that he claimed were historically the possession of Iraq. Despite diplomatic progress being made along these fronts, instead of continuing to apply political frame behavior, Hussein chose the more radical approach and invaded neighboring Kuwait. And, as had been the case in the Iraq-Iran war, he accomplished nothing.

In another misuse of political frame behavior, Hussein turned down a chance to save face in the Kuwait debacle by refusing the United Nations' offer to mediate the situation. Instead, as was his modus operandi, he chose war over political diplomacy.

In one of his more demonic uses of political frame behavior, Hussein routinely subsidized the families of Palestinian suicide bombers by offering them several thousands of dollars if their offspring were killed in an attack on the Israelis. When presented with a choice between the political frame behavior in the form of diplomacy or the use of force, Hussein consistently chose force (Anderson 2004).

The Moral Frame

The moral frame is my own contribution to situational leadership theory. In my view, the moral frame completes situational leadership theory. Without it, leaders could just as easily use their leadership skills for promoting evil as for promoting good. Leaders operating out of the moral frame are concerned about their obligations and responsibilities to their followers. Moral frame leaders use some type of moral compass to direct their behavior. They practice what has been described as servant leadership and are concerned with those individuals and groups that are marginalized in their organizations and in society. In short, they are concerned about equality, fairness, and social justice.

Being a devout Muslim, there is no doubt that Saddam Hussein had a moral compass upon which to base his leadership behavior. The question, however, is how evenly and consistently he applied his moral code to his behavior.

The more one learns about Hussein, the more obvious it becomes that he had an aversion to applying a moral code to his behavior, and when he did, it was oftentimes pure rationalization. He was a man who imposed a violent dictatorship on the people of his homeland. He was responsible for imprisoning, torturing and killing thousands of his opponents and gassing thousands of his own subjects in his war against the Kurds. One is left to ponder how he could have done these terrible things while consistently filtering them through a moral frame lens. The only logical conclusion one could draw is that he never bothered to do so or did so in a warped way.

Instances of citizens disappearing were an everyday occurrence in Iraq under Hussein's leadership. Human Rights Watch reported that Iraq had more instances of "disappearances" than any other country in the world. And, according to Amnesty International, atrocities such as female enemies of the state being hung upside down during menstruation while their children were forced to watch were commonplace in Hussein's Iraq.

Hussein's treatment of his own countrymen, especially the Kurds and the Shiites was virtually genocidal. The German holocaust and the ethnic and religious cleansing that Hussein practiced had much in common. Tens of thousands of Iraqis were deported, imprisoned, tortured, or murdered simply because of their ethnic and religious heritage.

Hussein saved his most brutal treatment for the Kurds. Despite being full-fledged citizens of Iraq, the Kurds were not Arabs and dwelled in a number of mostly Middle East countries. Since they did not share the ethic kinship that the Shiites did, Hussein treated them particularly cruelly. Forty thousand Kurds were deported in the first year of Hussein's rule alone. He was so obsessed in his hatred of the Kurds that, during a war with Israel, he reserved the bulk of his army to battle the Kurds instead.

Hussein once again demonstrated the absence of a moral code in a military policy that he called "War of the Cities," whereby he justified the waging of war on the opposing country's civilian population. For example, during the Iraq-Iran War, he launched missile attacks indiscriminately on Iranian schools and mosques. He followed the same pattern in the Gulf War against Kuwait, proceeding to execute Kuwaiti civilians in the streets and use them and other foreigners as human shields. Such despicable conduct could not have taken place if one had a moral compass to guide one's leadership behavior (Anderson 2004).

Situational Leadership Analysis

There are signs aplenty of Saddam Hussein being a situational leader. He was active in all five of the leadership frames, albeit spending an inordinate amount of time in the symbolic and political frames while spending way too little time in the structural, human resource, and moral frames.

He never seemed interested in developing a strategic plan to guide the pursuit of his goals, which a structural frame leader would have done. He more or less seemed to act spontaneously and sporadically. Any successes he had seemed to be serendipitous. The same could be said of his use of human resource frame behavior. Being as self-centered as he was, he never seemed interested on how his actions affected others. And his use of moral frame behavior was almost completely nonexistent or badly flawed when it did exist.

Nonetheless, he was very proficient in the use of symbolic and political frame behavior. We saw how he was able to establish a personality cult in Iraq with his portrait becoming virtually ubiquitous. Displaying the traits of a consummate political frame leader, he seemed to view the world as a jungle he had to traverse, using any means to reach his ends (Kaplan and Kristol 2003).

Leadership Implications and Conclusion

We can logically conclude that Hussein was indeed a leader in the situational mold, but not one that any contemporary leader would want to emulate. Saddam Hussein is yet another instance of an otherwise outstanding leader having gone astray because of the lack of a moral compass to guide his leadership behavior. In addition to his moral frame flaws, Hussein was deficient in the effective use of the structural and human resource frames. He did not spend nearly enough time planning his strategies and preparing for their implementation. And the only time he used human resource frame leadership behavior was to further his own interests. In other words, he very seldom seemed to employ human recourse frame behavior sincerely.

If it were not for his ability to operationalize his might-makes-right philosophy through his acts of brutality, Hussein would have never achieved the leadership status that he ultimately did. Fortunately for him if not his country, he found himself in a situation where such tactics could be effective, and he became a notable world leader. However, his leadership style cannot be generalized for use in other situations. In fact, outside of the unique situation in which he found himself, it would almost certainly not be effective. What leaders and potential leaders can take away from the study of Hussein's leadership behavior is that in order to be effective as a leader in a variety of circumstances, a more consistent use of all five leadership frames needs to be employed.

Hussein's leadership behavior is not unlike the superintendent of schools who alters standardized test results to make him or herself and the school district look good and/or qualify for special services or additional funding. In this case, both of these leaders failed to filter their leadership behavior through a creditable moral lens and neither one's behavior is worth emulating.

Chapter Twelve

Buffett v. Madoff

I. WARREN BUFFETT

I think that when it is finally over junk bonds will live up to their name.

—Warren Buffett

Background

Warren Buffett was born in Omaha, Nebraska, in 1930. He is one of the most successful investors in the world and is the chairman and CEO of Berkshire Hathaway. Referred to as the Oracle of Omaha, he is consistently ranked as one of the wealthiest people in the world according to *Forbes* magazine. He is also a noted philanthropist, having donated and pledged a large share of his wealth to the Gates Foundation and other charitable organizations.

Buffett's father, Howard, was a four-term U.S. congressman and moved his family to Washington, D.C., where Warren attended elementary and high school. He attended the Wharton School of the University of Pennsylvania for a short time and graduated from the University of Nebraska, class of 1950. He then acquired his master's degree in economics at Columbia University.

Buffett had an interest in finances at an early age and visited the New York Stock Exchange for the first time when he was only ten years old. After graduating from college, he accepted a position at his mentor, Benjamin Graham's company. When Graham retired in 1956, Buffett used his own personal savings to start his own investment company. After acquiring control over a number of businesses, he merged them all under one umbrella company called Berkshire Hathaway. At that time, Berkshire stock was trading at about $15 per share.

In 1973, Buffett began the process of acquiring the Washington Post Company, which was followed by the purchase of Capital Cities/ABC. In effect, he controlled significant portions of the communications and publication industries. As a result, by 1979, the value of the Berkshire stock rose to almost $800 per share, making Buffett a multimillionaire.

Buffett continued acquiring companies through the 1990s and by the turn of the millennium Buffett's fortune reached the $50 billion mark. In 2008, *Forbes* magazine listed him as the world's richest person. Two years previous, Buffett had announced that he would gradually give 85 percent of his profits in Berkshire to charitable foundations, most of which would go to the Bill and Melinda Gates Foundation. Having survived the Great Recession reasonably well, Buffett's wealth continues to grow.

The Structural Frame

Structural frame leaders seek to develop a new model of the relationship of structure, strategy, and environment for their organizations. Strategic planning, extensive preparation and effecting change are priorities for them. One does not achieve the level of success of a Warren Buffett without being very active in the structural frame. In typical structural frame fashion, Buffett would have his disciples and associates troop off to Omaha like salmon swimming north to hear Buffett wax eloquent on the nuances of investing, business, and finance. In investment circles, his annual meetings became like a Woodstock of economics and finance.

Like many structural frame leaders before him, Buffett could be a workaholic. He would often go to his California waterfront vacation home and end up mulling over financial reports and statements while never stepping foot on the beach or sticking his toes in the ocean.

From an early age, Buffett had a fascination with numbers. One of his first and most valuable possessions was a nickel-coated moneychanger that he had strapped to his belt every waking moment of the day. At an age when most boys were following the most recent accomplishments of their favorite sports teams and figures, Buffett was getting rolls of ticker tape from his stockbroker father and analyzing which companies had the best price-to-earnings ratio.

Buffett even made his paper route into a thriving business. The centerpiece of his paper route was an eight-story apartment building near Washington, D.C. He quickly used his ingenuity to maximize the efficiency with which he could deliver his newspapers. Taking a page out of Henry Ford's assembly-line approach, he would drop off half the papers on the eighth floor of each building in the complex and the other half on the fourth floor. Then he would run down each corridor leaving a paper at each of his customer's doors. On collection day, he left the bills at the front desk so that he would not have to go door-to-door to collect.

Like many structural frame leaders, Buffett was notoriously frugal, living in the same modest house that he purchased as a young family man even after he became a billionaire. But the story about his parsimoniousness that stands out among the others is the often-told one of when he and his wife had their first child and he made a bed for her in a dresser drawer.

Once again operating out of the structural frame, Buffett was well known for an almost fetish-like dependency on research. Searching for investment ideas, he would read the telephone-book-sized Moody's manuals page for page with the enthusiasm of a boy reading a Harry Potter novel.

One of Buffett's most important steps in ensuring his later success was not so much his excellent preparation and education that he received at Columbia University, but his initiative in taking a Dale Carnegie public speaking course. And he continued to hone his public speaking and presentation skills by teaching a course at the University of Omaha.

Buffett wasted no time in utilizing structural frame leadership behavior in his very first job on Wall Street in 1954. He took Rockwood and Company, a Brooklyn chocolate maker, up on its offer to trade its excess cocoa beans in order to buy back some of its stock. Buffett redeemed his stock for the beans and then sold them on the commodities market and made a huge profit. This practice is now known as arbitrage and has become a common practice for investors on Wall Street.

Like many structural frame leaders, Buffett had a steel trap for a brain. He committed the financial details of hundreds of companies to memory so that he could act on the information at a moment's notice. But he was also known to be extremely patient when the situation called for it. Once he purchased a company or a stock, he tended to keep it for years giving up short-term gains in favor of the generally more lucrative long-term and more moderately taxed long-term gains.

In 1962, Buffett made the seminal purchase of his career when he bought Berkshire Hathaway, Inc., a clothing manufacturer, and it would became the holding company for his other investments. His structural frame behavior continued when he purchased American Express. Buffett's meta-analysis had shown that American Express was a company that was well placed in the marketplace and poised to make even greater profits in the credit card and investment advising businesses. But by 1964, the share price plunged, so most everyone, except Buffett, sold. Buffett, in fact, bought even more American Express stock, continuing his investment approach of buying low and selling high. Three years later, American Express was selling at six times higher.

As any effective structural frame leaders would do, Buffett set goals for himself. His overall investment strategy was to beat the Dow by an average of ten points a year. In his view, the Dow, an unmanaged group of thirty stocks, should be easily outdistanced by any intelligent portfolio manager. Why, he wondered, was it that "the high priests of Wall Street, with their brains, training, and high pay, could not top a portfolio managed by no brains at all?" In his first ten years in business he beat the Dow by 100 to 1, and as a result, by age thirty-five he was already a multimillionaire (Lowenstein 1995, 85).

Once Buffett purchased a business, he identified the best person he could find to run it and stepped out of the way. For example, he bought Hochschild and Associated, another clothing manufacturer in 1967, and installed the former owner as the CEO. Upon retirement twenty years later, the former owner told Buffett: "I'll tell you why it worked. You forgot you bought this business, and I forgot I sold it" (Lowenstein 1995, 101).

In another structural frame move, with a little symbolic behavior mixed in, Buffett took the brazen step of closing the partnership to new accounts in 1966. He did not want the quality of his work to diminish because of overexpansion. During this time of a bull market, he prophetically stated: I am not attuned to this market environment, and I don't want to spoil a decent record by trying to play a game I don't understand just so I can go out a hero" (Lowenstein 1995, 85).

By 1972, however, Buffett got back into the investment business. Typically, he got back into the market at a low point after the bull market of the late 1960s waned. True to his strategy of buying low, Berkshire purchased twenty companies in that year alone. One of them was the *Washington Post* newspaper conglomerate. When an inexperienced Katherine Graham inherited the *Post* after her husband died, Buffett saw his chance to own a nationally prominent newspaper. Using a little political frame behavior, he worked his way onto the *Post*'s board of directors and eventually became the majority stockholder in the company. By the time he left the board ten years later, Berkshire's $10 million investment had turned into a $200 million one.

Ever the structural leader, Buffett was loath to rest on his laurels. Shortly after he joined the *Post*'s board he became enamored with another business, GEICO. GEICO had grown dramatically in recent years by insuring more at-risk drivers. But the chickens came home to roost when its insurance claims increased drastically and the car insurance company suffered a staggering loss—enter Buffett. He bought low, got rid of all the at-risk clients, and lo and behold, GEICO was making huge profits once again.

Buffett's next conquest was the acquisition of the *Buffalo Evening News*. At the time, the *News* did not publish a weekend edition, conceding that to the *Courier Express*. Buffett strategized that if the *News* started publishing the weekend news, its circulation would rise from its current 80 percent to a virtual monopoly and Buffalo would become a one-newspaper town. Despite a restraint of trade lawsuit and protestation from the local AFL-CIO, Buffett finally got his newspaper monopoly and the millions that came with it.

Buffett's next venture was at once both structural and symbolic of the way he did business. For a long time he had his eye on a furniture store in his home town of Omaha. The Nebraska Furniture Mart met all the criteria that Buffett required in his takeovers—it was profitable and well managed. One day, as he made his way through the sprawling store, he encountered the store's diminutive owner, Rose Blumben, affectionately known throughout the Omaha environs as Mrs. B.

Mrs. B. was patrolling the store in her golf cart when Buffett approached her inquiring whether she would like to sell The Nebraska Furniture Mart to Berkshire Hathaway. When she agreed to do so for $60 million, it became Berkshire's largest purchase to date. Upon receiving the check for the purchase of the largest furniture store in the nation, Mrs. B. declared: "Mr. Buffett, we're going to put our competitors through the meat grinder." This of course, was music to Buffett's ears and was why he retained Mrs. B. as his new company's CEO (Lowenstein 1995, 247).

Buffett then one-upped himself in purchasing 18 percent of Cap Cities, the media conglomerate. This deal was worth over $500 million, by far his company's biggest purchase. Following the purchase, the ABC network came into its own among its primary competitors, NBC and CBS.

Next, Buffett became the first to recognize the enormous potential of the already successful Coca-Cola Company. In 1989, Buffett purchased almost $4 billion in Coca-Cola stock. Three years later, mostly through its international initiatives and the popularity of Cherry Coke, his stock rose in value 64 percent. Buffett's astute use of structural leadership behavior had made him the richest man in the world.

The Human Resource Frame

Human resource leaders believe in people and communicate that belief. They are passionate about productivity through people. Over the years, Buffett has utilized the human resource frame often enough for him to be perceived almost universally as a very wealthy, but "regular guy." Unlike many of his business counterparts, Buffett was always as concerned with the people in his many companies as he was with the companies' profitability. For example, when he had to lay off a hundred employees of his Dempster Mill Company and was criticized for doing so, he replied: "If we'd kept them, the company would have gone bankrupt. I've kept close tabs and most of them are better off." But this incident had such an effect on him that he never again laid people off. He would place them in other positions or give them a job in one of his other companies.

In another indication of the importance he attached to human resource frame behavior, Buffett was always very sympathetic to the plight of the substantial black population in Omaha. Unlike his father, who was an active member of the extreme right-wing John Birch Society, Buffett was a progressive with regard to race relations. For example, he resigned from the Omaha Rotary Club because he objected to its racist and elitist policies.

In what was both a human resource and symbolic gesture, Buffett established the Buffett Foundation, a private philanthropic trust in 1971. The first beneficiaries of the trust were fifty black students, who received college scholarships. Very recently, Buffett joined forces with Bill Gates in convincing some thirty billionaires to commit to leaving 75 percent of their wealth to charity upon their deaths.

Perhaps the best example of Buffett's inclination toward human resource frame behavior is how he reacted to his friend Mrs. B's plight with The Nebraska Furniture Mart. Now ninety-five years of age, Mrs. B. was stripped of her power in the furniture company by her grandsons, who were now running the company. Although it was his policy not to interfere in the management of any of his companies, Buffett felt so bad that he personally delivered two dozen pink roses to Mrs. B. on her birthday to try to ameliorate her differences with her family. A few years later, at age ninety-nine she returned to the company and all was well again. On her 100th birthday, Buffett shunned the traditional birthday gift and presented Mrs. B with a million-dollar check made out to the Rose Blumkin Performance Arts Center that she was renovating to house a children's theater (Lowenstein 1995).

The Symbolic Frame

In the symbolic frame, the organization is seen as a stage, a theater in which every actor plays certain roles and the symbolic leader attempts to communicate the right impressions to the right audiences. Consciously or unconsciously, Warren Buffett frequently operated out of the symbolic frame. On Wall Street, Buffett's use of symbolic leadership behavior made him cult figure of major proportions. His homespun manner endeared him to the public, and he had the ability to explain complex financial concepts in very simple terms that would be understandable to the lay person. He never forgot that at the source of all stocks and bonds was a very tangible business. It has been said that what most people expect of a Wall Street tycoon is J. P. Morgan and what they got from Buffett was Will Rogers (Lowenstein 1995, xiv).

As an investor Buffett was famous for ignoring the esoteric strategies like leverage, hedging, and trading in futures, and concentrated on the business in which he was investing. He restricted his investors to a relatively few business that he had thoroughly researched. He often ridiculed his Wall Street counterparts, quipping that it was the bankers "who should be wearing the ski masks," or that he would no more ask an investment banker's opinion on a deal than he would ask a barber whether he needed a haircut (Lowenstein 1995, xv).

Buffett went out of his way to project the image of a homespun regular guy. He never flaunted his enormous wealth, having no fancy art collection or luxury automobile. He famously dined on hamburgers and Cokes and still lives in a modest home in Omaha that he purchased when he was first married.

It was well-known that Buffett's financial guru was his Columbia University professor and mentor, Benjamin Graham. After he read his books *Security Analysis* and *The Intelligent Investor*, he became a fan for life. Graham was the first to make investing a science rather than an art. No longer would Buffett need to do his investing by the roll of the dice. Now, using Graham's approach, he did so on a much more methodical and rational basis.

Buffett also made good use of symbolic frame behavior as an adjunct professor at the University of Omaha. He would mockingly close the doors of the classroom and then counsel his students in a hushed voice that the way to get rich on Wall Street was that "you try to be greedy when others are fearful and you try to be very fearful when others are greedy." Over time he became famous for these homespun aphorisms (Lowenstein 1995, 50).

Buffett used symbolic frame behavior to project his image as a spend-thrift. As stated earlier, he was never one to spend his wealth on material comforts. To him, that was not the purpose of having money. His attitude is that the purpose of money is to make more money. Why spend a nickel today, when it will be worth more tomorrow? He never even bought life insurance, believing that he could compound the premiums just like the insurance company did—maybe even better.

Buffett rather dramatically displayed his attitude toward money when he and his family were touring California one summer and took a tour of the William Randolph Hearst mansion. The guide was giving the usual details about how much Hearst had paid to build and furnish the mansion when an impatient Buffett blurted out: "Don't tell us how he spent it. Tell us how he made it!" (Lowenstein 1995, 88).

So by the time he was thirty-five Buffett had become a multimillionaire and had established an image whereby his followers almost worshiped the ground on which he walked. Buffett encouraged such faithfulness by the conscious use of symbolic frame behavior. He showed confidence, but also modesty. His penchant for using self-effacing quips at just the right moment served to confirm his colleagues' god-like view of him.

As a self-styled maverick in the way he conceptualized investing, Buffett reinforced his point by telling the story of an oil prospector who arrived at the pearly gates only to learn that the places reserved for oilmen had been filled. Given his disappointment with the news, St. Peter allowed him to say some last words. He yelled, "Oil discovered in hell," whereupon every oil-man left for hell. When St. Peter offered him one of the empty spaces, the oilman thought twice and decided: "No, I think I'll go along with the rest of the boys, there might be some truth to that rumor" (Lowenstein 1995, 104).

Another one of his stories that he often used to make a point about asking the right questions and not taking anything for granted involved a stranger who was visiting a small town. The stranger went to the town square, figuring that he would run into someone who could tell him a little more about the town. There he uncounted an old man and a dangerous looking German shepherd. He looked at the dog and said, "Does your dog bite?" The old-timer said, "Nope." So the visitor reached down to pet the dog and it bit him on the arm. The startled stranger turned to the man and side, "I thought you said your dog doesn't bite." The old man said: "My dog don't bite, but this here ain't my dog" (Lowenstein 1995, 281).

Despite his liberal leanings, Buffett had a lifelong skepticism about liberals' impulse to tax and spend. It turns out that Buffett was very friendly with George McGovern and initially endorsed his candidacy for president. That was until he announced that as president he would give every person a yearly stipend of $1,000, whereupon Buffett engaged in some symbolic frame behavior and summarily dropped his endorsement of McGovern and placed his support behind Richard Nixon.

The Political Frame

Leaders operating out of the political frame clarify what they want and what they can get. Political leaders are realists above all. They never let what they want cloud their judgment about what is possible. They assess the distribution of power and interests. Buffett only rarely utilized political frame behavior, but did so when it was appropriate. During World War II in Washington, D.C., Buffett's paper route customers would often move and not pay him. Engaging in an early display of political frame behavior, Buffett made a deal with the elevator operators at the apartment complex where he had most of his customers. They received free papers from him if they agreed to let him know when someone was planning to move.

Later in life, Buffett used political frame behavior more frequently. For instance, Buffett had an interest in newspaper companies dating back to his youth. When Boston was on the verge of becoming a one-newspaper town, the time was ripe for him to get into the business because the *Boston Globe* would now have a monopoly on the newspaper business in Boston. However, to bring the selling price down, he faked indifference. Once the purchase price declined sufficiently, he jumped in with both feet and Berkshire became the largest share holder in the *Boston Globe*.

With GEICO insurance's stocks at an all-time low, Buffett once again used political frame behavior in getting integrally involved with the purchase of the foundering insurance business. He believed that if he could effectively address the management problems, the company would become profitable once again. However, in typical political frame style, he had someone else prepare the way.

Washington Post owner, Katherine Graham introduced him to GEICO's CEO, but Buffett was snubbed. So Graham got GEICO's elder statesman, Lorimer Davidson, to intervene, and as planned, Buffett was granted an audience with the CEO. Buffett convinced management to return to insuring only low-risk loans, and as a result, Buffett's $4 million investment increased in value to a staggering $16 million in only six months.

The takeover barrage of the 1980s gave Buffett another opportunity to engage in political frame leadership behavior. Upon hearing from many of his CEO friends that they were besieged by hostile takeover threats, it occurred to Buffett that Berkshire with its reputation of not micromanaging, could act as a friendly babysitter until the movement blew over. Berkshire was offered as a safe haven for companies trying to avoid the less attractive alternatives of succumbing to a stock raid or going into bankruptcy. As a result of these kinds of transactions, Berkshire's stock was now selling at more than $3,000 per share, and by 1986 Buffett was on the *Forbes* list of billionaires, trailing only Sam Walton, Ross Perot, and Harry Helmsley (Lowenstein 1995).

The Moral Frame

The moral frame is my own contribution to situational leadership theory. In my view, the moral frame completes situational leadership theory. Without it, leaders could just as easily use their leadership skills for promoting evil as for promoting good. Leaders operating out of the moral frame are concerned about their obligations and responsibilities to their followers. Moral frame leaders use some type of moral compass to direct their behavior. They practice what has been described as servant leadership and are concerned with those individuals and groups that are marginalized in their organizations and in society. In short, they are concerned about equality, fairness, and social justice.

Wall Street's brokers were getting rich by exploiting the public's interest in making a fast buck. Their essential tack was to show their investors a quick gain and then to sell them out at the first opportunity, ultimately leading to the Great Recession. But Buffett shunned that approach and the other Wall Street excesses. Rather, he practiced a kind of pure capitalism which was sometimes cold-blooded, but eminently fair.

Buffett inherited his father's ethics and concern for society and social justice. Buffett would find the corporate theft of the public's money as repugnant as his politician father found the government's misuse of taxpayers' money. As a result of this developing moral code, he became repelled by the Republicans' indifference to civil rights, and decided to break from his father's party and become a Democrat.

As his father was to him, Buffett prided himself on being a moral exemplar to his own children. It was enormously important to Buffett that his children saw him as trustworthy and having personal integrity, so he put more than 90 percent of his personal money in with his partners at Berkshire Hathaway.

Once when Buffett received advanced information that Home Insurance Company was about to be bought by City Investing Company at a large premium, he instructed his brokers to stop buying either company's stock because even though it would be legal, it would not be ethical. As a result of operating out of the moral frame in this way he effactually bypassed a $50,000 payday.

In another display of moral frame behavior, with a little political behavior thrown in, Buffett observed that his golf club, the Omaha Club, would not accept Jews. So he applied for membership at the all-Jewish Highland Club. He then returned to the Omaha Club flashing his new membership card and intimidated them into accepting Jewish members (Lowenstein 1995).

Buffett's moral frame sense was such that he felt compelled to expose the fiscal malfeasance of one of Omaha's most famous institutions, Father Flanagan's Boys Town. Buffett discovered that despite having an endowment of over $162 million, higher than that of most colleges, they were conducting a mail fund-raising campaign feigning poverty. Buffett leaked the story to the local newspaper with a title from scripture reading: "Give an account of thy stewardship" (Lowenstein 1995, 146).

Situational Leadership Analysis

Situational models of leadership differ from earlier trait and behavioral models in asserting that no single way of leading works in all situations. Rather, appropriate behavior depends of the circumstances at a given time. Effective manages diagnose the situation, identify the leadership style or behavior that will be most effective, and then determine whether they can implement the required style.

Having seen evidence of being active in all five leadership frames, it is obvious that Warren Buffett is a leader in the situational leadership mold. Although he has been pretty much a hard-nosed structural frame leader in his business practices and has used a very deliberate approach to his investing, he has moved out of the structural frame on occasion to make some more visceral decisions. "The really sensational ideas I have had over the years," he declared, "have been heavily weighted toward the qualitative side." He was most likely thinking of the Walt Disney and American Express purchases (Lowenstein 1995, 108).

We saw, too, that he operated out of the human resource frame in being sincerely concerned with the plight of humankind and the poor in particular. His public image was cultivated by the liberal use of symbolic frame behavior and his use of political behavior, although somewhat sparse as compared to the others, was appropriate. Finally, it is obvious that Buffett filters his leadership behavior through a moral/ethical lens.

Leadership Implications and Conclusion

Perhaps this one story sums up Warren Buffett's almost universal appeal. Typical of Buffett, he even worked when he was on vacation. It seems that one summer while vacationing in Southern California, the Buffett's made a stop at Disneyland. While the children were on the various amusement rides, Buffett delved into the financial side of the park, analyzing ride by ride the profit margin that would be forthcoming. Subsequently, he scheduled a visit with Walt Disney himself and was impressed with the childlike enthusiasm that he had for his work—much like his own (Lowenstein 1995).

Warren Buffett's huge success as a businessman and as a human being is no accident. His astute use of situational leadership theory and the five frames of leadership behavior are exemplary. Leaders and aspiring leaders can learn much by modeling their leadership behavior after that of the Oracle of Omaha.

II. BERNARD MADOFF

> It is the destiny of man to learn that evil treads closely on the footsteps of good.
>
> —James Buchanan

Background

Bernard Madoff was born in Queens, New York, in 1938 and graduated from Hofstra College in 1960. He attended Brooklyn Law School, but did not graduate. At the age of twenty-two Madoff founded his own Wall Street firm.

Madoff started his stock trading firm with $5,000 that he had saved doing odd jobs and with the assistance of his accountant father-in-law, Saul Alpern. In order to compete with his more financially resourced competitors, Madoff developed an innovative and sophisticated computer information system that was the state of the art at the time. His system eventually morphed into what is now called NASDAQ.

In the 1990s, Madoff Securities was the largest firm at the NASDAQ and by 2008 was the sixth-largest on all of Wall Street. In addition to the stock trading branch, the firm also had an investment management and advisory division. It was this division that Madoff used to conduct an illegal Ponzi scheme.

Madoff was very active in the National Association of Securities Dealers, (NADS) which ironically was an agency that self-regulated the security industry. In fact, he had served as both the chairman of its board of directors and a member of its board of governors. Many experts have speculated that it was because of his connections with NSDS and NASDAQ that Madoff's illegal activities went undetected by the SEC for so long.

Major concerns about the integrity of Madoff's business began to surface in 1999. At that time, an investigative reporter who specialized in financial matters, Harry Markopolos, informed the SEC that he believed that the gains that Madoff was reporting were a mathematical impossibility. However, his concerns were virtually ignored. His book, *No One Would Listen*, details the ten frustrating years he spent trying to convince various regulators that Madoff's operation was a sham.

Finally, in December of 2008, one of Madoff's sons went to the FBI and reported that his father had told him that he was struggling to make good on about $7 billion in redemptions that were due to his clients. Madoff allegedly told his son that he was engaged in a giant Ponzi scheme and his investment fund was a fraud.

Madoff was arrested and charged with securities fraud, and on March 12, 2009, pleaded guilty to defrauding his clients of $65 billion, making it the largest Ponzi scheme in American history. Three months later, a federal judge sentenced Madoff to 150 years in prison (Arvedlund 2009).

The Structural Frame

Structural frame leaders seek to develop a new model of the relationship of structure, strategy, and environment for their organizations. Strategic planning, extensive preparation and effecting change are priorities for them. Like most successful businessmen, we shall see that Bernie Madoff engaged in his fair share of structural frame leadership behavior. In fact, although deviously applied, one could argue that the structural frame was his most dominant.

In the 1990s Madoff was one of the most recognized names on Wall Street. He had built from the ground up one of the most successful brokerage houses in New York. He utilized structural frame behavior in doing so, creating what is known as a "third market," which traded outside the two established markets, the New York Stock Exchange and the American Stock Exchange. By trading faster and less expensively than the big two, he was able to execute trades on over a million shares a day.

He engaged in structural frame leadership behavior in recognizing early on the benefits of computerized trading. Using his unique system, he was able to quickly build his firm into one of the top six traders on Wall Street. Eventually, his computerized information system was adopted by NASDAQ.

Utilizing his structural frame skills still further, Madoff realized that in order to have credibility on Wall Street he needed a big-name client. So he went out and secured one, namely, Carl Shapiro. Shapiro was a well-known quantity on Wall Street, having made a fortune in the garment industry as the founder and CEO of Kay Windsor, Inc. Madoff lured Shapiro to his stable of clients by promising to clear his trades in three days, which was well below the industry standard. As anticipated, Shapiro drew other clients Madoff's way, and the rest is history.

By 1971, NASDAQ, a computerized communications web that Madoff helped develop and establish had come to challenge the New York and American stock exchanges for dominance in the market. Between his Shapiro-led client base and his strong connections with NASDAQ, Madoff quickly became a major player on the Wall Street scene.

Again using structural frame behavior, Madoff played a major role in the creation of the Intermarket Trading System (ITS). This system connected the smaller stock exchanges to the two major ones and increased Madoff's influence on Wall Street even more. Engaging in a little political frame behavior at the same time, his revolutionary system of trading stocks and other securities enabled him look good to the regulators, since it increased competition. His popularity and trust among the regulators enabled him to operate his Ponzi scheme for more than ten years without being detected.

Madoff's innovative computer system not only lowered his costs, but also allowed his traders to hedge or offset any risks by being able to buy and sell so quickly, a distinct advantage over those who traded from the floor of the stock exchanges. Over time, more companies had their share prices quoted in NASDAQ than the other two major exchanges put together.

Another instance of an astute use of structural frame behavior was when Madoff and his wife perfected the strategy of pairing off two competing stocks with one another and betting that one stock would rise and the other would fall, a practice now known as arbitrage. The Madoffs took this statistical strategy to a new level and at one point their arbitrages were yielding a phenomenal 20 percent per year.

However, Madoff eventually utilized his structural frame genius for unethical purposes. All the time Madoff was making a name for himself by revolutionizing the way equities were bought and sold, he was also building his illegitimate stock advising business. It was on this side of the business that he engaged in the rob-Peter-to-pay-Paul Ponzi scheme for which he became infamous.

Madoff's fraudulent advisory business was his elaborate way of borrowing money from the public rather than the traditional method of borrowing from a bank. He used the money from his Ponzi scam to invest in the legitimate side of his business, and in doing so, avoided the prying eyes of the bankers. As long as he maintained his integrity with his clients and they left their principle in the funds, Madoff was fine. It was when they began demanding redemptions that the scheme collapsed (Arvedlund 2009).

The Human Resource Frame

Human resource leaders believe in people and communicate that belief. They are passionate about productivity through people. Although one is left to wonder if he was sincere, there is evidence that Bernie Madoff engaged in human resource frame behavior. One instance of Madoff's use of human resource behavior was his insistence in not implicating anyone else in his wrongdoing. After orchestrating and being found guilty of a $65 billion Ponzi scheme that was the largest such fraud in American history, Madoff decided to forgo a public trial and not implicate anyone else in a plea bargaining attempt. Given the scope of the fraud, there were almost certainly others who might be vulnerable, but he refused to take advantage of that to reduce his sentence.

Madoff was known to have utilized human resource frame behavior in his day-to-day interactions. He was described by his employees as being even tempered and pleasant. There was one incident where one of his assistants had made a mistake in a telephone quote to a client that resulted in the Madoff firm losing some money in the trading process. The fearful assistant was heartened when the next day Madoff made light of the situation. He jokingly instructed the assistant "to buy MHP. That stands for Madoff has a prick!" (Arvedlund 2009, 52).

The Symbolic Frame

In the symbolic frame, the organizations is seen as a stage, a theater in which every actor plays certain roles and the symbolic leader attempts to communicate the right impressions to the right audiences. Although not overly dramatic, Madoff did have a certain flare for engaging in symbolic leadership behavior.

In the beginning, Madoff used his father-in-law, Saul Alpern, to carry the torch for his image building. Alpern bragged to his many friends and associates about how savvy an investor his young son-in-law was. As a result, many of Alpern's connections began giving him money for Madoff to invest.

This indirect use of symbolic behavior became Madoff's template for future fund-raising. He guaranteed his friends and relatives a 20 percent annual return on their investment, making them so grateful that they became his public relations force and proceeded to encourage their friends and acquaintances to invest with him. What better way to acquire new clients than to do so through satisfied ones.

Through the astute application of symbolic leadership behavior, Madoff became recognized as a statesman and peacemaker in the securities industry. He actively sought the chairmanship of the Securities Industry Association so that he could serve these roles. And after the terrorist attacks of 9/11 left the Twin Towers offices of the SIA in ruins, Madoff offered them space in his Manhattan offices.

So successfully did Madoff and his firm project a positive public image, a business associate of his was prompted to intone: "They were smart—they always seemed to be a step ahead, and they rarely got in trouble with regulators. They were very buttoned up as well. I never saw Madoff without at tie on, and their suits were better than anyone else's I knew" (Arvedlund 2009, 53).

To that end, Madoff was almost obsessed with the outward appearance of his offices and employees. He was often seen shuffling around the office making certain that the blinds were all drawn to the same level and ensuring that his employees were all writing with black ink pens and that there was no stray paper on their desks.

So solid was Madoff's reputation that, unlike many of his counterparts in the securities industry, he had no trouble staying open and continuing to do business during the crash of 1987. He even received a letter from the Securities and Exchange Commission thanking him for doing so.

Madoff used symbolic frame behavior in attracting the "rich and famous" to his investment scheme. He lured such entertainment, sports, and political figures as Kevin Bacon, Steven Spielberg, Philadelphia Eagles owner Norman Braman, and Senator Frank Lautenberg to his Ponzi scheme. The obvious method behind the madness being that other, noncelebrity, investors would be attracted to him because of his affiliation with these so-called big names (Arvedlund 2009).

The Political Frame

Leaders operating out of the political frame clarify what they want and what they can get. Political leaders are realists above all. They never let what they want cloud their judgment about what is possible. They assess the distribution of power and interests. Bernie Madoff would never have been able to pull off his Ponzi scheme without the frequent application of political frame behavior. Using political frame leadership behavior, it was not long before

Madoff had made a name for himself in the seat of political power, Washington, D.C. He was a generous donor to both the Democratic and Republican parties and was an active lobbyist for stock market restructuring. And as the chair of the industry-funded Securities Industry Association, he was well-known to the Wall Street regulators and became an advisor to the Securities and Exchange Commission.

Knowing that the SEC did not like the monopoly that existed on Wall Street in trading only New York Stock Exchange–listed stocks, Madoff used political frame behavior to insert himself into the process of restructuring the rules that dictated how brokers and exchanges worked together. Much to the SEC's satisfaction, Madoff was able to introduce more competition through his establishment of NASDAQ. His friendly relationship with the SEC enabled Madoff's Ponzi scheme to prosper and avoid detection for almost twenty years.

Madoff operated out of the political frame in appointing so many of his trusted family members to important positions in his firm. Keeping the policy-making decisions within the family was another factor that allowed his scheme to go undetected for such a long period of time.

In addition, Madoff made certain that his family and the others who were bringing in huge amounts of business were very well compensated for their efforts. In this way, he guaranteed that they would not be too quick to question his tactics for fear of endangering this lucrative source of income.

In one particular instance, Madoff used both political and symbolic frame behavior to enhance his self-interests. Walter M. Noel, the Vanderbilt- and Harvard-educated founder of the Fairfield Greenwich Group was a very well respected commodity in the financial securities business. Madoff knew that a partnership with Fairfield Greenwich would bode well for his financial well-being, so he ingratiated himself to Noel, and Fairfield Greenwich became Madoff's biggest partner, raising funds and funneling them to him for investing.

Madoff cemented the relationship with Fairfield Greenwich by not charging them any fees. As a result, FGG could charge their investors the 20 percent per trade that Madoff would have charged and an additional 10 percent that their competitors were charging. In the process, FGG earned over $100 million per year and Madoff had over $300 million per year to "invest" (Arvedlund 2009).

The Moral Frame

The moral frame is my own contribution to situational leadership theory. In my view, the moral frame completes situational leadership theory. Without it, leaders could just as easily use their leadership skills for promoting evil as for promoting good. Leaders operating out of the moral frame are concerned about their obligations and responsibilities to their followers. Moral frame leaders use some type of moral compass to direct their behavior. They practice what has been described as servant leadership and are concerned with those individuals and groups that are marginalized in their organizations and in society. In short, they are concerned about equality, fairness, and social justice.

To say the least, the moral frame was not one of Madoff's strongest. The irony of this matter is that Madoff did not need to be dishonest. He had the financial skills to make a very good living on Wall Street. But he decided instead upon a life of crime in which he defrauded hundreds of people many billions of dollars. Both the scope of the crime and the person responsible for it shocked Wall Street. The conventional wisdom was that Madoff could have easily earned a similar fortune legally. So why did he not do so? The answer is that he never developed a strong enough moral code to guide his behavior.

Upon investigation, Madoff's Ponzi scheme most likely began in reaction to the enormous losses that he experienced on the legitimate side of his business during the crash of 1987. In order to be able to report a gain to his legitimate clients, he used the funds raised from his illegitimate operations until he was in so deep that there was no honest way out. At any rate, his moral conscience was weakened to such a point that he gave in to the temptation of criminal behavior (Arvedlund 2009).

Situational Leadership Analysis

Situational models of leadership differ from earlier trait and behavioral models in asserting that no single way of leading works in all situations. Rather, appropriate behavior depends on the circumstances at a given time. Effective managers diagnose the situation, identify the leadership style or behavior that will be most effective, and then determine whether they can implement the required style.

As we have seen, Bernie Madoff was a leader in the situational mold, having engaged in every leadership frame with the possible exception of the moral frame. The fact is that Madoff's fraudulent scheme might have endured if it were not for the global financial crisis of 2006. But with the crashing of the stock market, his investors were demanding to redeem their principal, which of course, was no longer available. Such was the predicament of an otherwise successful leader who had failed to develop a moral compass to guide his leadership behavior.

Leadership Implications and Conclusion

Obviously, fraudulent activities such as those engaged in by Bernie Madoff are not exclusive to the securities industry. Such activities happen all too often in every field, including education. I feel certain that we have all been witness to the recent front-page newspaper articles exposing various financial embezzlement schemes in both our public and nonpublic schools. These problems seem especially to be present among today's charter schools, possibly because of comparatively looser state supervision.

When we analyze this sort of criminal activity through the lens of situational leadership theory, we find that in most cases the recalcitrant leaders are deficient in their use of the human resource and moral frames of leadership behavior. They may otherwise be among our most effective educational leaders, but because they do not consistently filter their leadership behavior through a moral lens, they do not become truly heroic leaders. Instead of leading with a conscience, they are leading without one, and as a result, do immense harm to themselves and their followers. Rather than their behavior being something for developing leaders to emulate, it is something that they should avoid. Once again, a word to the wise should be sufficient.

Chapter Thirteen

Leadership Lessons Learned

> The greatest discovery of my generation is that man can alter his life simply by altering his attitude of mind.
>
> —William James

What do we learn about leadership from the twenty leaders profiled in this study? First, we learn that situational leadership theory makes eminent sense. Virtually all of these leaders were effective as leaders because they were able to adapt their leadership behavior to changing situations. None of them was "stuck" in one paradigm. Some might be criticized for using one or another leadership frame too exclusively, but the reality is that, by and large, they were successful because, to a person, they were able to balance their use of the four leadership frames enunciated by Lee Bolman and Terrence Deal very effectively.

More specifically, we have learned that there are four requisites for effective leadership:

1. A *knowledge* of, and *passion* for, one's field (competency).
2. An ability to engender mutual *trust and respect* with one's followers (moral frame behavior).
3. A knowledge of the organizational *culture* (readiness level) of one's followers.
4. An ability to apply *situational leadership theory* to one's practice.

THE IMPORTANCE OF THEORY

We cannot underestimate the value and importance of theory in the field of leadership, or in any other field for that matter. As indicated in the fourth point above, without theory we have no valid way of diagnosing, analyzing, and correcting failed practice. Without a theoretical base, we oftentimes lead by trial and error, or by the proverbial "seat of your pants (or pantyhose)."

Theory is to leadership as the fundamentals are to sport. For example, if a basketball player is suddenly shooting a lower percentage of baskets than his or her career average, something is obviously wrong. He or she has experienced "failed practice." What to do? Most athletes in this situation are coached to "go back to the basics or the fundamentals." The basketball player will review the fundamentals of shooting, like squaring oneself to the basket, keeping the shooting elbow in, keeping the guide hand off the ball upon release, snapping the wrist, and exaggerating one's follow-through. It is likely that one of these fundamentals is being violated and causing the shooting percentage to decline and when corrected, the percentage will rise again to its most recent average.

If the athlete does not know the fundamentals of shooting, *shooting theory*, if you will, he or she can only correct the problem through the very inefficient means of trial and error. The same goes for leaders who are losing their impact on their followers. If they have not adopted a leadership theory to guide their behavior, they can only correct the leadership decline by trial and error.

However, if the leader has adopted a leadership theory, the leader can review the tenets or principles of the theory and most likely diagnose the deficiency and correct it rather quickly. For example, the leader might find that his or her followers are no longer responding to the leader's friendly persuasion and active support (human resource leadership behavior). In analyzing the *situation*, the leader might conclude that he or she is using human resource behavior with the followers when structural leadership behavior may be more appropriate. As a result of this analysis, the leader may decide to utilize a more structural approach and "lay down the law" to his recalcitrant followers. This rather simple example demonstrates the importance and value of theory in providing leaders with the knowledge and skills they need to be able to diagnose and correct failed practice in an efficient and effective way.

LEADING WITH MIND

Knowledge of one's field is a sine qua non for effective leadership. This quality usually manifests itself in one's structural frame leadership behavior. In sports terms, the leader must have a good command of the fundamentals of the game. In business terms, the effective leader must have a thorough knowledge of the technical aspects of how a business operates and a sense of how to develop a viable business plan. In education, the leader needs to know how schools and school systems operate and what the best practices in the field are in curriculum and instruction. In a family situation, the leader (parent or guardian) needs to have at least a modicum of knowledge regarding the principles of child psychology. In short, leaders in any field need to know that field and be able to apply that knowledge through the theory and practice of organizational development, which would include the following:

1. Organizational Structure: how an institution is organized.
2. Organizational Culture: the values and beliefs of an institution.
3. Motivation: the system of rewards and incentives provided.
4. Communication: the clarity and accuracy of the communication process.
5. Decision Making: how and by whom decisions are made.
6. Conflict Management: how dysfunctional conflict is handled.
7. Power Distribution: how the power in an institution is distributed.
8. Strategic Planning: how the mission, vision and strategic plan are developed.
9. Change: how change is effectively implemented in an institution.

I will not go into detail about these processes here. If the reader is interested in a comprehensive look at these processes, I would recommend an earlier publication of mine, *Educational Administration: Leading with Mind and Heart*, third edition. However, included in the appendix is a pair of diagnostic tools entitled "The Heart Smart Survey" and "The Heart Smart Organizational Diagnosis Questionnaire," which I developed to help leaders assess the organizational health of their institutions and to identify which factors are in need of improvement in leading with heart.

LEADING WITH HEART

To recap, then, the effective leader needs to be *technically* competent. However, being technically competent is not enough. To be truly effective and heroic, leaders need to master the *art* of leadership and learn to lead with *heart*. In effect, leaders need to operate out of both the structural and political frames (science) and the human resources, symbolic, and moral frames (art) to maximize their effectiveness. This means that they must be concerned about the person (cura personalis). They must abide by the Golden Rule and treat others as they wish to be treated. As noted in chapter 2, truly effective leaders treat their employees like volunteers and empower them to actualize their true potential, thus engendering mutual trust and respect among virtually all of their colleagues.

In their book entitled *Leading with Kindness* (2008), William Baker and Michael O'Malley reiterate my views. They explore how one of the most unheralded features of leadership, basic human kindness, drives successful organizations. And while most scholars generally recognize that a leader's emotional intelligence factors into that person's leadership behavior, most are reticent to consider it be as important as analytical ability, decision-making skills, or implementation skills. Such emotions as compassion, empathy, and kindness are often dismissed as unquantifiable, and are often seen as weaknesses. Yet, research in neuroscience and the social sciences clearly reveals that one's physiological and emotional states have measurable effects on both individual and group performance.

In the jargon of the day, individuals who lead with heart or kindness are said to have a high degree of emotional intelligence. Most of us are familiar with the current notion of multiple intelligences; that is, individuals have a number of intelligences in addition to cognitive intelligence. Among these intelligences is emotional intelligence. Several theories within the emotional intelligence paradigm seek to understand how individuals perceive, understand, utilize, and manage emotions in an effort to predict and foster personal effectiveness.

Most of these models define emotional intelligence as an array of traits and abilities related to emotional and social knowledge that influence our overall ability to effectively cope with environmental demands; as such, it can be viewed as a model of psychological well-being and adaptation. This includes the ability to be aware of, to understand, and to relate to others; the ability to deal with strong emotions and to control one's impulses; and the ability to adapt to change and to solve problems of a personal and social nature. The five main domains of these models are intrapersonal skills, interpersonal skills, adaptability, stress management, and general mood. If the reader sees a similarity between emotional intelligence and what I term *leading with heart* and what Baker and O'Malley call *leading with kindness*, it is not coincidental.

LEADING WITH MIND AND HEART

So, the truly heroic leaders lead with *both* mind (science) and heart (art)—with cognitive intelligence and emotional intelligence. One or the other will not suffice. Only by mastering both will the leader succeed. For example, former president Bill Clinton was rendered ineffective as a leader because of the Monica Lewinsky affair and was nearly removed from office. Why? Because he suddenly lost the *knowledge* of how government works (science)? No! He lost his ability to lead because he lost the *trust and respect* of much of the American public (art). He could still lead with his mind, but he had lost the ability to lead with his heart. It is only recently, several years later, that he is reestablishing his integrity with the American public.

On the contrary, one could argue that former president Jimmy Carter lost his ability to lead because of a perceived lack of competency. Rightly or wrongly, the majority of the voting public did not believe that he had the knowledge necessary to manage government operations and effectively lead with mind. However, virtually no one questioned his concern for people, his integrity, and his ability to lead with heart. Absent the perceived ability to do *both*, however, he lost the 1980 election to Ronald Reagan.

I conclude, then, that effective leaders are situational; that is, they are capable of adapting their leadership behavior to the situation. They utilize structural, human resource, symbolic, political, and moral leadership behavior, when appropriate. They lead with both mind (structural and political behavior) and with heart (human resource, symbolic, and moral behavior). They master both the science (mind) and art (heart) of leadership, and in doing so, they are transformational, leading their organizations to new heights. As Chris Lowney (2003) writes in, *Heroic Leadership*, such leaders are, in a word, truly "heroic."

ORGANIZATIONAL CULTURE

Effectively balancing the use of the five frames of leadership behavior assumes that the leader has a thorough knowledge and understanding of the leader's organizational culture. In the words of Harold Hill in *The Music Man*, the leader needs "to know the territory." Knowing the territory, or knowing the organizational culture, means that the leader must know the beliefs, expectations, and shared values of the organization, as well as the personality of the individuals and the organization as a whole. Without such knowledge, the leader cannot appropriately apply the correct leadership frame to the situation.

As mentioned in chapter 1, Paul Hersey and Ken Blanchard contribute to our understanding of what it means to know the culture of the organization with their concept of *readiness level*. They define readiness level as the follower's ability and willingness to accomplish a specific task; this is the major contingency that influences what leadership frame behavior should be applied. Follower readiness incorporates the follower's level of achievement motivation, ability, and willingness to assume responsibility for his or her own behavior in accomplishing specific tasks, as well as his or her education and experience relevant to the task. So, a person with a low readiness level should be dealt with by using structural frame behavior (telling behavior), while a person with a very high readiness level should be dealt with using human resource and symbolic frame behavior (delegating behavior).

At this point, the reader may be thinking that using leadership theory to determine one's leadership behavior is an exercise in futility. How can one be realistically expected to assess accurately and immediately the individual's or group's readiness level before acting. It seems like an utterly complex and overwhelming task. When confronted with this reaction, I relate using leadership theory to determine one's leadership behavior to riding a bike. When we first learn to ride a bike, we have to concern ourselves with keeping our balance, steering, pedaling, and being ready to brake at a moment's notice. However, once we learn and have had experience riding the bike, we seldom think of those details. We have learned to ride the bike by instinct or habit.

Having used situational leadership theory to determine my own leadership behavior, I can attest to the fact that its use becomes as instinctive as riding a bike after awhile. At this point, I can almost always instantly assess the readiness level of an individual or group and apply the appropriate leadership frame behavior—and believe me when I tell you that if I can do it, so can you.

TRANSFORMATIONAL LEADERSHIP

We all aspire to be transformational leaders—leaders who inspire positive change in their followers. As we saw in chapter 1, charismatic or transformational leaders use charisma to inspire their followers. They talk to the followers about how essential their performance is and how they expect the group's performance to exceed expectations. Such leaders use dominance, self-confidence, a need for influence, and conviction of moral righteousness to increase their charisma and consequently their leadership effectiveness. A transformational leader changes an organization by recognizing an opportunity and developing a vision, communicating that vision to organizational members, building trust in the vision, and achieving the vision by motivating organizational members.

Virtually all of the leaders profiled in this book could be considered transformational leaders at some level. In the case of the ten heroic ones, they moved their organizations from being ineffective to being extremely effective. Most of them inherited inferior situations only to *transform* them into supremely effective ones. They achieved this success by displaying the characteristics of a transformational leader. They all had a vision and had the personal charisma and ability to convince others to join them in achieving that vision.

Nevertheless, they achieved their visions in different ways by applying the appropriate leadership behavior to their differing situations. They were able to gauge the *readiness level* of their followers accurately and apply the appropriate leadership behavior, whether it be structural, human resource, symbolic, political, or moral frame behavior, or some combination thereof. Although this is easier said than done, studying these leaders' leadership behavior as depicted in this book should be helpful to anyone aspiring to become a transformational leader.

LEADERSHIP AS A MORAL SCIENCE

Left on its own, situational leadership theory is secular and amoral. As such, it is just as likely to produce a leader like Adolf Hitler or, in the modern era, Bernie Madoff, as it is to produce a leader in the Abraham Lincoln or the Joe Paterno mold. Throughout this book we have seen examples of immoral and unethical leadership behavior. In education we have all witnessed instances of this kind of behavior—examples ranging from the trivial, like stealing a box of paper clips, to the more serious, like fabricating standardized test scores, engaging in multimillion-dollar embezzlements, and stealing to support alcohol and gambling additions. So, to ensure that leaders lead with heart as well as mind, I have suggested the use of the Ignatian vision as a moral lens through which one views his or her leadership behavior.

As recommended in chapter 2, asking ourselves whether our leadership behavior conforms to Ignatius's principles of the magis, cura personalis, discernment, service to others, and social justice will bring to completion our understanding and use of situational leadership theory and transform leadership into a moral science. In my view, using the Ignatian vision, or a similar model, as a moral compass to direct our leadership behavior will help ensure that history will witness more leaders like Abraham Lincoln and fewer like Adolf Hitler.

CONCLUSION

Recently, a plethora of research studies have been conducted on leadership and leadership styles. The overwhelming evidence indicates that there is not one singular leadership style that is most effective in all situations. Rather, it has been found that a leader's leadership behavior should be adapted to the situation so that at various times structural, human resource, symbolic, political, or moral frame leadership behavior may be most effective.

The emergence of transformational leadership has seen leadership theory come full circle. Transformational leadership theory combines aspects of early trait theory with the more current situational models. The personal charisma of the leader, along with his or her ability to formulate an organizational vision and communicate it to others while embodying the virtues of trust and respect determines the transformational leader's effectiveness.

Since the effective leader is expected to adapt his or her leadership style to an ever-changing environment, leadership becomes an even more complex and challenging task. However, thorough knowledge of one's organizational culture and of leadership theory can make some sense out of the apparent chaos that a leader faces on a daily basis. It is my hope that this text will shed some light on the *situation*—pun intended.

Appendix: Diagnostics

Just as there are vital signs in measuring individual health, it is believed that there are vital signs for measuring the health of educational institutions. This survey will help to identify those vital signs in your school or school system. It, along with The Heart Smart Organizational Diagnosis Questionnaire, will indicate further whether the institution's leaders are leading with both mind and heart.

The Heart Smart Survey I

Please think of your *present work environment* and indicate the degree to which you agree or disagree with each of the following statements. A "1" is *Disagree Strongly* and a "7" is *Agree Strongly*.

Agree Strongly	Agree	Agree Slightly	Neither Agree nor Disagree	Disagree Slightly	Disagree	Disagree Strongly
1	2	3	4	5	6	7

1. The manner in which the tasks in this institution are divided is a logical one.
2. The relationships among co-workers are harmonious.
3. This institution's leadership efforts result in it fulfillment of its purposes.

4. My work at this institution offers me an opportunity to grow as a person.
5. I can always talk to someone at work, if I have a work-related problem.
6. The faculty actively participates in decisions.
7. There is little evidence of unresolved conflict in this institution.
8. There is a strong fit between this institution's mission and my own values.
9. The faculty and staff are represented on most committees and task forces.
10. Staff development routinely accompanies any significant changes that occur in this institution.
11. The manner in which the tasks in this institution are distributed is a fair one.
12. Older faculty's opinions are valued.
13. The administrators display the behaviors required for effective leadership.
14. The rewards and incentives here are both internal and external.
15. There is open and direct communication among all levels of this institution.
16. Participative decision making is fostered at this institution.
17. What little conflict that exists at this institution is not dysfunctional.
18. Representatives of all segments of the school community participate in the strategic planning process.
19. The faculty and staff have an appropriate voice in the operation of this institution.
20. This institution is not resistant to constructive change.
21. The division of labor in this organization helps its efforts to reach its goals.
22. I feel valued by this institution.
23. The administration encourages an appropriate amount of participation in decision making.
24. Faculty and staff members are often recognized for special achievements.
25. There are no significant barriers to effective communication at this institution.
26. When the *acceptance* of a decision is important, a group decision making model is used.
27. There are mechanisms at this institution to effectively manage conflict and stress.
28. Most of the employees understand the mission and goals of this institution.

29. The faculty and staff feel empowered to make their own decisions regarding their daily work.
30. Tolerance toward change is modeled by the administration of this institution.
31. The various grade level teachers and departments work well together.
32. Differences among people are accepted.
33. The leadership is able to generate continuous improvement in the institution.
34. My ideas are encouraged, recognized and used.
35. Communication is carried out in a non-aggressive style.
36. In general, the decision making process is an effective one.
37. Conflicts are usually resolved before they become dysfunctional.
38. For the most part, the employees of this institution feel an "ownership" of its goals.
39. The faculty and staff are encouraged to be creative in their work.
40. When changes are made they do so within a rational process.
41. This institution's organizational design responds well to changes in the internal and external environment
42. The teaching and the non-teaching staffs get along with one another.
43. The leadership of this institution espouses a clear educational vision.
44. The goals and objectives for the year are mutually developed by the faculty and the administration.
45. I believe that my opinions and ideas are listened to.
46. Usually, a collaborative style of decision making is utilized at this institution.
47. A collaborative approach to conflict resolution is ordinarily used.
48. This institution has a clear educational vision.
49. The faculty and staff can express their opinions without fear of retribution.
50. I feel confident that I will have an opportunity for input if a significant change were to take place in this institution.
51. This institution is "people-oriented."
52. Administrators and faculty have mutual respect for one another.
53. Administrators give people the freedom to do their job.
54. The rewards and incentives in this institution are designed to satisfy a variety of individual needs.
55. The opportunity for feedback is always available in the communications process.
56. Group decision making techniques, like brainstorming and group surveys are sometimes used in the decision making process.
57. Conflicts are oftentimes prevented by early intervention.
58. This institution has a strategic plan for the future.

59. Most administrators here use the power of persuasion rather than the power of coercion.
60. This institution is committed to continually improving through the process of change.
61. This institution does not adhere to a strict chain of command.
62. This institution exhibits grace, style and civility.
63. The administrators model desired behavior.
64. At this institution, employees are not normally coerced into doing things.
65. I have the information that I need to do a good job.
66. I can constructively challenge the decisions in this institution.
67. A process to resolve work-related grievances is available.
68. There is an ongoing planning process at this institution.
69. The faculty and staff have input into the operation of this institution through a collective bargaining unit or through a faculty governance body.
70. The policies, procedures and programs of this institution are periodically reviewed.

The Heart Smart Survey II

Please think of your *present work environment* and indicate the degree to which you agree or disagree with each of the following statements. A "1" is *Disagree Strongly* and a "7" is *Agree Strongly*.

Agree Strongly	Agree	Agree Slightly	Neither Agree nor Disagree	Disagree Slightly	Disagree	Disagree Strongly
1	2	3	4	5	6	7

1. There is not much evidence of faculty and staff holding and espousing ethical values.
2. There is not much evidence of mutual respect and understanding among the faculty and staff.
3. There is not much of a sense of voluntarism and dedication among the teachers and staff.
4. There is not much indication that teachers and staff have committed themselves to the modeling of moral and ethical values.
5. There is not much trust and respect shared among faculty, staff, and administration.
6. There is little evidence that teachers encourage students to be concerned for the underserved in their communities.

7. There is not much evidence that the teachers are supportive of a moral or ethical code to guide one's behavior.

8. There are not many occasions when the faculty and staff get to interact with one another.

9. There are not many opportunities presented to students to develop an appreciation of and respect for cultures other than their own.

10. Teachers do not often bear witness to their values and beliefs through their daily behavior.

11. The faculty and staff do not seem to support one another in various events and activities.

12. There are not many occasions when faculty members accompany their students on community service activities.

13. There are no occasions when faculty and students discuss their values and beliefs.

14. There is not much in the way of promotion of justice and fairness among students.

15. There is not a culture that fosters service to the community at this institution.

16. The faculty does not seem to go out of its way to model their belief system to the students.

17. There is not much evidence of the promotion of justice and fairness among teachers.

18. There are not many occasions when teachers engage in community service by donating space, time, resources, and personal help.

19. There are not many times when the faculty and staff articulate or speak out on their values and beliefs.

20. There is not much evidence of the promotion of justice and fairness between teachers and administrators.

21. There are not many instances of faculty evidencing compassion and giving service to the needy, the disadvantaged, and troubled students and coworkers.

22. There are not many occasions when the faculty discusses teaching values and ethics.

23. There are significant barriers to effective communication at this institution.

24. The overall morale of the school is not very good.

25. The faculty and staff do not show much concern for world problems, like hunger, poverty, war, pollution, and social justice.

26. The faculty does not openly express its support of ethical and moral values.

27. The conflicts that arise among individuals and groups are not resolved very well.

28. The teachers do not encourage a sense of service and social justice in their students very much.
29. The faculty do not avail themselves of professional development opportunities to develop their skills in teaching values education.
30. The sense of trust and respect at this institution is not very high.
31. There is a tendency to merely "go through the motions" at this school.
32. There is a tendency for the superficial to be more important than the substantial at this school.
33. There is a dark tension that exists among key individuals at this school.
34. It seems that the attainment of short-term goals is preferred to the achievement of long-term goals.
35. There seems to be a loss of grace, style, and civility at this institution.
36. There is a tendency to do the minimal and not "go the extra yard" at this school.
37. The administration seems to use coercion to motivate employees here.
38. We do not ever seem to be able to find the time to celebrate accomplishments here.
39. The teachers and staff seem to treat students like customers or impositions here.
40. The employees feel manipulated and exploited here.
41. There don't seem to be many stories and storytellers to carry on the tradition at this school.
42. The leaders here seem to want to be served rather than to serve.
43. There seems to be a certain arrogance among the leaders at this school.
44. There seems to be a sense of competition here whereby one person or group's gain always has to be at another's expense.
45. Teachers here won't pick up a piece of paper because "that's the janitor's job."
46. When something goes wrong here, there is a tendency to want to cast blame.
47. Diversity and individual charisma are not respected here.
48. Teachers here seem to use up all their sick days even if they are not sick.
49. The administration seems to accumulate power rather than sharing it at this institution.
50. The climate in this school seems to encourage competition rather than collaboration.
51. Teachers seem to work solely for a paycheck here.
52. Teachers are asked to teach to the test to improve test scores at this school.

53. There is a tendency for the faculty rooms to be sources of malicious gossip and rumors.
54. There is a union mentality here whereby teachers do not want to do anything extra unless they are paid.
55. Administrators here seem to dwell on people's weaknesses rather than their strengths.
56. Individual turf is protected to the detriment of institutional goals at this school.
57. There is definitely a caste system here among the administration, the faculty, and the clerical and custodian staffs.

THE HEART SMART ORGANIZATIONAL DIAGNOSIS QUESTIONNAIRE

Just as there are vital signs in measuring individual health, we believe that there are vital signs in measuring the good health of organizations. This survey will help us to identify those vital signs in your school or school system. The purpose of the Heart Smart Organizational Diagnosis Questionnaire, therefore, is to provide feedback data for intensive diagnostic efforts. Use of the questionnaire, either by itself or in conjunction with other information-collecting techniques such as systematic observation or interviewing, will provide the data needed for identifying strengths and weaknesses in the functioning of an educational institution, and, along with The Heart Smart Survey, help determine whether the leaders are leading with both mind and heart.

A meaningful diagnostic effort must be based on a theory or model of organizational development. This makes action research possible as it facilitates problem identification, which is essential to determining the proper functioning of an organization. The model suggested here establishes a systematic approach for analyzing relationships among the variables that influence how an organization is managed. The Heart Smart Survey II provides for assessment of three areas of formal and informal activity: moral integrity, a sense of community, and a dedication to service and social justice. The Heart Smart Survey I provides for assessment in ten areas of formal and informal activity (see diagram below). The outer circle in the following table represents an organizational boundary for diagnosis. This boundary demarcates the functioning of the internal and external environments. Since the underlying organizational theory upon which this survey is based is an open-systems model, it is essential that influences from both the internal and external environment be considered for the analysis to be complete.

The Heart Smart Wheel

Structure

How is this institution organized?

Conflict Resolution

Is this institution functional or dysfunctional?

Culture

What values and beliefs are important here?

Goal Setting and Planning

Are the goals clear, accepted, and operationalized?

Leadership

How effectively are the boxes kept in balance?

INTERNAL

ENVIRONMENT

Power Distribution

Are the faculty and staff empowered?

Motivation

Are the rewards and incentives effective?

Attitude

Is this institution continually improving?

Communication

Is the message being transmitted clearly?

Decision Making

How and by whom are decisions being made?

EXTERNAL ENVIRONMENT   **EXTERNAL ENVIRONMENT**

HEART SMART SCORING SHEET I

Instructions: Transfer the numbers you circled on the questionnaire to the blanks below. Add each column and divide each sum by seven. This will give you comparable scores for each of the ten areas.

Structure	*Culture*	*Leadership*	*Motivation*
1_____	2_____	3_____	4_____
11_____	12_____	13_____	14_____
21_____	22_____	23_____	24_____
31_____	32_____	33_____	34_____
41_____	42_____	43_____	44_____
51_____	52_____	53_____	54_____
61_____	62_____	63_____	64_____

Total

_____   _____   _____   _____

Average

_____   _____   _____   _____

Communication	*Decision Making*	*Conflict Resolution*	*Goal Setting/ Planning*
5_____	6_____	7_____	8_____
15_____	16_____	17_____	18_____
25_____	26_____	27_____	28_____
35_____	36_____	37_____	38_____
45_____	46_____	47_____	48_____
55_____	56_____	57_____	58_____
65_____	66_____	67_____	68_____

Total

_____   _____   _____   _____

Average

_____   _____   _____   _____

Power Distribution	*Attitude toward Change*
9_____	10_____
19_____	20_____
29_____	30_____
39_____	40_____
49_____	50_____
59_____	60_____
69_____	70_____

Total

_____   _____

Average

_____   _____

Interpretation Sheet

Instructions: Transfer your average scores from the Scoring Sheet to the appropriate boxes in the figure below. Then study the background information and interpretation suggestions that follow.

Background

The Heart Smart Organizational Diagnosis Questionnaire is a survey-feedback instrument designed to collect data on organizational functioning. It measures the perceptions of persons in an organization to determine areas of activity that would benefit from an organizational development effort. It can be used as the sole data-collection technique or in conjunction with other techniques (interview, observation, etc). The instrument and the model reflect a systematic approach for analyzing relationships among variables that influence how an organization is managed. Using the Heart Smart Organizational Diagnosis Questionnaire is the first step in determining appropriate interventions for organizational change efforts.

Interpretation and Diagnosis

A crucial consideration is the diagnosis based upon data interpretation. The simplest diagnosis would be to assess the amount of variance for each of the ten variables in relation to a score of 4, which is the neutral point. Scores *below* 4 would indicate a *problem* with organizational functioning. The closer the score is to 1, the more severe the problem would be. Scores *above* 4 indicate the *lack of a problem*, with a score of 7 indicating optimum functioning.

Another diagnostic approach follows the same guidelines of assessment in relation to the neutral point (score) of 4. The score of each of the seventy items on the questionnaire can be reviewed to produce more exacting information on problematic areas. Thus, diagnosis would be more precise. For example let us suppose that the average score on item number 8 is 1.4. This would indicate not only a problem in organizational purpose or goal setting, but also a more specific problem in that there is a gap between organizational and individual goals. This more precise diagnostic effort is likely to lead to a more appropriate intervention in the organization than the generalized diagnostic approach described in the preceding paragraph.

Appropriate diagnosis must address the relationships between the boxes to determine the interconnectedness of problems. For example, if there is a problem with *communication,* could it be that the organizational *structure* does not foster effective communication. This might be the case of the average score on item 25 was well below 4 (2.5 or lower) and all the items on organizational *structure* (1, 11, 21, 31, 41, 51, 61) averaged above 5.5.

HEART SMART SCORING SHEET II

Instructions: Transfer the numbers you circled on the questionnaire to the blanks below. Add each column and divide each sum by 19. This will give you comparable scores for each of the three areas.

Moral Integrity	*Community*	*Service/Social Justice*
1_____	2_____	3_____
4_____	5_____	6_____
7_____	8_____	9_____
10_____	11_____	12_____
13_____	14_____	15_____
16_____	17_____	18_____
19_____	20_____	21_____
22_____	23_____	24_____
25_____	26_____	27_____
28_____	29_____	30_____
31_____	32_____	33_____
34_____	35_____	36_____
37_____	38_____	39_____
40_____	41_____	42_____
43_____	44_____	45_____
46_____	47_____	48_____
49_____	50_____	51_____
52_____	53_____	54_____
55_____	56_____	57_____

Total

_____   _____   _____

Average (Divide by 19)

_____   _____   _____

Average (Divide by 3)

_____

Interpretation Sheet

Instructions: Study the background information and interpretation suggestions that follow.

Background

The Heart Smart Organizational Diagnosis Questionnaires are survey-feedback instruments designed to collect data on organizational functioning. They measure the perceptions of persons in an organization to determine areas of activity that would benefit from an organizational development effort. It can be used as the sole data-collection technique or in conjunction with other techniques (interview, observation, and so forth). The instrument and the model reflect a systematic approach for analyzing relationships among variables that influence how an organization is managed. Using the Heart Smart Organizational Diagnosis Questionnaires is the first step in determining appropriate interventions for organizational change efforts.

Interpretation and Diagnosis

A crucial consideration is the diagnosis based upon data interpretation. The simplest diagnosis would be to assess the amount of variance for each of the three variables in relation to a score of 4, which is the neutral point. Scores above 4 would indicate a problem with organizational functioning. The closer the score is to 7, the more severe the problem would be. Scores below 4 indicate the lack of a problem, with a score of 1 indicating optimum functioning.

Another diagnostic approach follows the same guidelines of assessment in relation to the neutral point (score) of 4. The score of each of the fifty-seven items on the questionnaire can be reviewed to produce more exacting information on problematic areas. Thus, diagnosis would be more precise. For example let us suppose that the average score on item number 8 is 6.4. This would indicate not only a problem in the sense of community in the institution, but also a more specific problem in that there are not enough occasions provided for the teachers to interact with one another. This more precise diagnostic effort is likely to lead to a more appropriate intervention in the organization than the generalized diagnostic approach described in the preceding paragraph.

References

Anderson, J. L. 2004. *The Fall of Baghdad*. New York: Penguin Press.

Aronson, M. L. 1997. *Fandex Family Field Guides*. New York: Workman Publishing.

Arvedlund, E. 2009. *Too Good to Be True: The Rise and Fall of Bernie Madoff*. New York: Penguin Press.

Auchincloss, L. 2001. *Theodore Roosevelt*. New York: Henry Holt & Company.

Baker, W., and O'Malley, M. 2008. *Leading with Kindness*. New York: AMACOM.

Baldwin, N. 1995. *Edison Inventing the Century*. New York: Hyperion.

Biggart, N. W., and Hamilton, G. G. 1987. "An Institutional Theory of Leadership." *Journal of Applied Behavioral Sciences* 23(4).

Bolman, L. G., and Deal, T. E. 1991. *Reframing Organizations: Artistry, Choice, and Leadership*. San Francisco: Jossey-Bass.

Bullock, A. 1952. *The Hitler of History*. New York: Knopf.

Chang, J., and Halliday, J. 2005. *Mao: The Unknown Story*. New York: Knopf.

Chapple, C. 1993. *The Jesuit Tradition in Education and Missions*. Scranton: University of Scranton Press.

Cogner, A., and Kanungo, R. N. 1987. "Toward a Behavioral Theory of Charismatic Leadership in Organizational Settings." *Academy of Management Review* 12(4).

Davis, A. F. 1973. *American Heroine: The Life and Legend of Jane Addams*. New York: Oxford University Press.

De Pree, M. 1989. *Leadership Is an Art*. New York: Dell Publishing.

Diliberto, G. 1999. *A Useful Woman: The Early Life of Jane Addams*. New York: Scribner.

Erickson, F. 1984. "School Literacy, Reasoning and Civility: An Anthropologist's Perspective." *Review of Educational Research* 54.

Ericson, D. P., and Ellett, F. S. 2002. "The Question of the Student in Educational Reform." *Education Policy Analysis Archives* 10(31).

Felzenberg, A. S. 2008. *The Leaders We Deserved*. New York: Perseus Books.

Fiedler, F. E., and Chemers, M. M. 1984. *Improving Leadership Effectiveness: The Leader Match Concept*. 2nd ed. New York: Wiley.

Fiedler, F. E., and Garcia, J. E. 1987. *New Approaches to Effective Leadership*. New York: Wiley.

Field, R. H. G. 1982. "A Test of the Vroom Yetton Normative Model of Leadership." *Journal of Applied Psychology* 67(5).

Fleishman, E., and Harris, E. F. 1998. "Patterns of Leadership Behavior Related to Employee Grievances and Turnover." *Personnel Psychology* 15(1).

Fleishman, E., Harris, E. F., and Buret, R. D. 1955. *Leadership and Supervision in Industry*. Columbus: Ohio State University Press.

Foster, W. 1986. *Paradigms and Promises*. New York: Prometheus Books.

Glasser, W. 1984. *Control Theory, a New Explanation of How We Control Our Lives*. New York: Harper & Row.

Griffiths, D., and Ribbins, P. 1995. "Leadership Matters in Education: Regarding Secondary Headship." Inaugural lecture, University of Birmingham, Edgbaston.

Hall, J. P. 1987. *Gone from the Promised Land*. New Brunswick, NJ: Transaction Books.

Halliday, J. 2005. *The Unknown Mao*. New York: Knopf.

Hersey, P., and Blanchard, K. H. 1988. *Management of Organizational Behavior*. 5th ed. Englewood Cliffs, NJ: Prentice Hall.

House, R. J. 1971. "A Path Goal Theory of Leader Effectiveness." *Administrative Science Quarterly* 16(3).

House, R. J. 1977. "A 1976 Theory of Charismatic Leadership." In J. G. Hunt and Larson, eds., *Leadership: The Cutting Edge*. Carbondale, IL: Southern Illinois University Press.

House, R. J., and Mitchell, T. R. 1974. "Path Goal Theory of Leadership." *Journal of Contemporary Business* Autumn.

Institute of Jesuit Sources. 1995. *Documents of the 34th General Congregation of the Society of Jesus*. St. Louis: The Institute of Jesuit Sources.

Kaplan, L. F., and Kristol, W. 2003. *The War Over Iraq*. San Francisco: Encounter Books.

Kirkpatrick, S. A., and Locke, E. A. 1991. "Leadership: Do Traits Matter?" *Academy of Management Executive* 5(2).

Kobler, J. 1971. *Capone: The Life and World of Al Capone*. New York: G.P. Putnam & Sons.

Lowenstein, R. 1995. *Buffett: The Making of an American Capitalist*. New York: Random House.

Lowney, C. 2003. *Heroic Leadership*. Chicago: Loyola Press.

Lubienski, R. 1999. *Montessori for the New Millennium*. Mahwah, NJ: Lawrence Erlbaum Publishers.

Lukacs, J. 1997. *The Duel: The Eighty-Day Struggle between Churchill and Hitler*. New Haven, CT: Yale University Press.

Machtan, L. 2001. *The Hidden Hitler*. New York: Basic.

McGovern, G. 2009. *Abraham Lincoln*. New York: Henry Holt & Company.

McGregor, D. 1961. *The Human Side of Enterprise*. New York: McGraw Hill.

Menand, L. 2001. *The Metaphysical Club*. New York: Farrar, Straus & Giroux.

Mintzberg, H. 1979. *The Nature of Managerial Work*. 2nd ed. Englewood Cliffs, NJ: Prentice Hall.

Morris, K. E. 1996. *Jimmy Carter: American Moralist*. Athens: University of Georgia Press.

Paterno, J., and Asbell, B. 1989. *Paterno: By the Book*. New York: Berkeley Publications.

Ravier, A., SJ. 1987. *Ignatius of Loyola and the Founding of the Society of Jesus*. San Francisco: Ignatius Press.

Redlich, F. 1998. *Hitler: Diagnosis of a Destructive Prophet*. Oxford: Oxford University Press.

Ribbins, P. 1995, May 9. "Leadership Matters in Education: Regarding Secondary Headship." Paper prepared for Inaugural Lecture, School of Education, University of Birmingham.

Roberts, P. 2000. *Education, Literacy, and Humanization*. Westport, CT: Bergen & Garvey.

Schein, E. H. 1974. *The Hawthorne Studies Revisited: A Defense of Theory Y*. Sloan School of Management Working Paper #756 74. Cambridge: Massachusetts Institute of Technology.

Senge, P. M. 1990. *The Fifth Dimension: The Art of Practice of the Learning Organization*. New York: Doubleday.

Service, R. 2000. *Lenin*. Cambridge, MA: Harvard University Press.

Solzhenitsyn, A. 1978. *A World Split Apart*. New York: Harper & Row.

Stevanovic, V. 2004. *Milosevic: The People's Tyrant*. London: I.B. Tauris.

Stogdill, R. M., and Coons, A. E., eds. 1957. *Leader Behavior: Its Description and Measurement*. Columbus: Ohio State University Bureau of Business Research.

Taranto, J., and Leo, L. 2004. *Presidential Leadership*. New York: Wall Street Journal Books.

Toner, J. J., SJ. 1991. *Discerning God's Will: Ignatius of Loyola's Teaching on Christian Decision Making*. St. Louis: The Institute of Jesuit Sources.

Tripole, M. R., SJ. 1994. *Faith Beyond Justice*. St. Louis: The Institute of Jesuit Sources.

Volkoganov, D. 1991. *Stalin: Triumph and Tragedy*. New York: Grove Weidenfeld.

Vroom, V. H., and Jago, A. G. 1988. *The New Leadership: Managing Participation in Organizations.* Englewood Cliffs, NJ: Prentice Hall.

Vroom, V. H., and Yetton, P. W. 1973. *Leadership and Decision Making.* Pittsburg: University of Pittsburg Press.

Willner, A. R. 1984. *The Spellbinders: Charismatic Political Leadership.* New Haven, CT: Yale University Press.

Zuckoff, M. 2005. *Ponzi's Scheme.* New York: Random House.

About the Author

Robert Palestini is graduate dean emeritus and professor of educational leadership at Saint Joseph's University in Philadelphia. In over forty-five years in education, he has served as a teacher, principal and superintendent of one of the largest school systems in the United States. He has written more than ten books on various aspects of educational leadership.